THE COMPLETE
AMATEUR PHOTOGRAPHER

THE COMPLETE
AMATEUR
PHOTOGRAPHER

An introduction to the art and technique of photography
for amateurs and those studying photography as a profession

DICK BOER

DIRECTOR, INTERNATIONAL FOCUS SALON, AMSTERDAM

Edited by A. L. M. SOWERBY, B.A., M.SC., F.R.P.S.

EDITOR, 'AMATEUR PHOTOGRAPHER'

LONDON : ILIFFE & SONS, LTD.

Translated from the original Dutch by Joyce Loman.

FIRST PUBLISHED 1948
SECOND EDITION 1954
THIRD EDITION © Iliffe & Sons, Ltd. 1959

Published for 'Amateur Photographer' by Iliffe & Sons, Ltd., Dorset House,
Stamford Street, London, S.E.1

Made and printed in England at The Chapel River Press, Andover, Hants
Offset lithography and photogravure printed in Holland

BKS 3342

Contents

Introduction

THE mysterious charm of photography attracts thousands of people, but many who take it up as a hobby quickly lose interest, discouraged by their lack of success. My aim in this book is to encourage all beginners in the art and to help them so that in a short time they will be able to take good photographs. The book is meant also for the young professional photographer and the photographic dealer, both of whom must understand and love their work if they are to do well at it. Amateur and professional have a great deal in common nowadays so far as equipment and methods are concerned, and it is hoped that the book will serve both classes equally well.

Care and thought, rather than any special talent, are needed to make a good photographer. In these pages, I do not attempt to teach *all* there is to know about photography, but I have set out to give the beginner, in a simple and interesting way, the basic knowledge he needs before he can take satisfactory pictures. After this, if he wishes, he will be able to progress to a more advanced study of photographic technique.

DICK BOER

PART ONE *The Technique of Photography*

1 FIRST PRINCIPLES

ALL cameras are basically alike, and so it does not matter very much what your particular type of camera is. Every camera has a lens in front, and a light-sensitive layer at the back. The lens throws a picture of the outside world on to the sensitive material, and produces there a picture of the subject the camera was aimed at. The choice of a *good* subject is up to the photographer.

We shall start by discussing the working of cameras and what are suitable subjects. Later on we shall talk about the pros and cons of different types of camera, but we shall have to begin with the fundamentals of photography.

In this first chapter, therefore, we shall follow the making of a picture from beginning to end. Remember that each step in this process remains basically the same in all forms of photography, no matter what camera may be used. If you come to see the process as a whole, you will appreciate the scope and limitations of the camera.

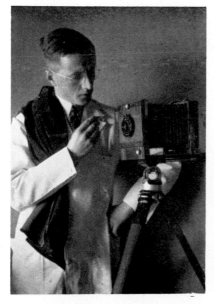 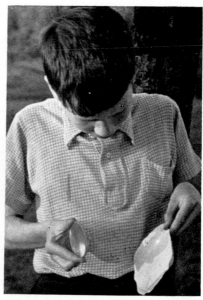

Fig. 2—The simple stand camera in use— just a dark box, the lens at the front, the sensitive layer at the back

Fig. 3—John focuses his magnifying glass on the " burning point", which is really a small picture of the sun

Fig. 4—Our first picture, taken at Penhurst in Kent.   The sun is in just the right place

2

Fig. 5—On the ground glass of the stand camera, the house is upside down

Our First Picture

Fig. 4 is our first photograph—though perhaps a good deal better than most first attempts! In this case the sun is just right for a picture of the cottage.

What are the essentials for a photographic picture?

(a) A camera, which gives a picture of the cottage.

(b) A sensitive plate or film which will record that picture permanently.

The camera is a little box which is quite dark inside. Centuries ago it was called a " camera obscura " and used for making drawings from nature. It has widely varied forms nowadays—a Leica looks quite different from a Rolleiflex— but inside it is still just a dark box. Fig. 2 shows a " bellows " camera, with

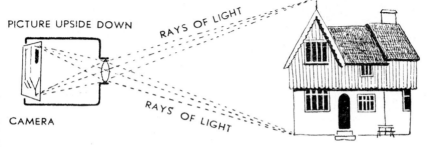

Fig. 6—Rays of light travel in straight lines. Can you imagine them not doing so?

3

Fig. 7—The house is sharp and the girl very blurred, because the camera was focused on the house.   Short distance between lens and ground glass

Fig. 8—Here, the girl is sharp and the house very blurred, because the camera was focused on the girl.   Longer distance between lens and ground glass

4

only the most essential fittings. In front is the lens, picturing the outside world; the ground glass on which the picture is shown is at the back.

In a lens you will recognize the magnifying glass of your schooldays. The little bright spot it produced for you was nothing but a picture of the sun which, if focused sharply, was very small and hot. Just as a lens can give a picture of the sun, so it can picture anything. However, in the pictures the scene is shown upside down (Fig. 5). This is because light always travels in straight lines, so that the ray which comes downward on to the lens from the roof of the house will continue its downward path to the bottom of your focusing screen. A ray from the ground goes similarly to the top of the screen.

Focusing

You move your magnifying glass to *and* fro to get the image of the sun at its sharpest and hottest. Why? Because every object at a different distance has its *own* spot where it is seen sharpest. This focusing must be done most accurately: we want our pictures very sharp! For example, the girl in Fig. 7 is quite blurred, but the house is excellent, while in Fig. 8 the girl is beautifully clear, but the house is blurred.

When you have *focused* you have made sure that the principal object is the sharpest on your focusing screen. The background may sometimes be blurred. You now close the lens with a shutter, an arrangement with which the lens can be opened for a longer or shorter period. Next, you replace the ground glass by a metal or wooden holder containing a plate that is sensitive to light.

Many materials are sensitive to light: curtains fade, the human skin darkens. This plate grows darker too, but to an extent far too small to be visible. Under the microscope you would discover very tiny silver grains on it; in that very short moment of exposure, the light separates these grains from the emulsion, as the sensitive layer of silver bromide and gelatine on the surface of the plate

Fig. 9—A shutter: the front part of the lens has been removed to show the leaves

Fig. 10—A plate and its dark slide. The slide must be dusted out before inserting the plate

5

CLOSED   ¹/25 OPEN —   CLOSED
                AT THE RIGHT MOMENT PLEASE

Fig. 11—The leaves of the shutter open for only a fraction of a second

is called. When the picture you saw on the ground glass falls on the plate, it is recorded there in the form of those tiny specks of silver. These grains are the beginning of our photographic picture.

The plate is so tremendously sensitive to light that only an extremely short time is necessary for exposure. The shutter opens for 1/25th part of a second, then closes. But even this is long enough to imprint on the plate an exact picture of the house. In that fraction of a second nature's paint brush has produced a picture so precise, and of such fine detail and perfect drawing, that no painter could better it.

But this picture is still invisible. It must now come to life, and for this we need that wonderful chemical, the developer. In a room lit only with a dark red light (because our plate is sensitive to light of any other kind) the plate is put into the developing liquid. This developer strengthens the picture of very fine silver grains, invisible at first, so considerably that it is clear and strong after development. The time required for this is some four minutes.

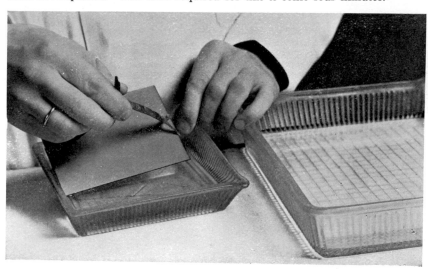

Fig. 12—The sensitive plate goes into the developer. Never use your fingers, use plate forceps. On the right is the fixing bath, in which the unused part of the sensitive layer is dissolved, leaving the black picture standing out against a clear and transparent background

Among the grains forming the newly developed picture, there is still a good deal of light-sensitive emulsion, corresponding to the points which were not affected by light. These light-sensitive materials must be removed, otherwise they will turn black when you switch on the light.

This removing of light-sensitive chemicals is done in the fixing bath, where the cream-coloured emulsion (the silver bromide) is dissolved. The plate now becomes clear and transparent where it was not affected by light, while the parts that received a little light, turn grey; and in those that received much light it is black. You will see that the sky is black on the plate and the dark roof transparent, which is exactly the opposite of reality. That is why this plate, with its reversal of light and dark, is called a *negative*. A negative and its positive are shown in Figs. 13 and 14.

Fig. 13—A negative, with shadows, lights and half-tones   Fig. 14—The positive. " Home again after the concert " (Leica picture with self-timer)

Don't think it a pity that you don't get a positive right away; in that case you could only get one copy of your picture. Daguerre's system produced positives without negatives, and although results were very beautiful (and very expensive) there could be only one copy of each photograph. A negative, however, is the starting point for small pictures (contact prints), big pictures (enlargements), and lantern slides (Figs. 15, 16, 17, 18), for I can print my negative as often as I please on either paper or glass. The negative is only a means to an end and must be printed; the print is the finished picture.

To make the print I again use the light-sensitivity of certain silver salts. I take a dry negative and put it into a printing frame, with the glass side underneath and the picture on top. On the picture side, in safe yellow light, I lay a piece of light-sensitive paper, and tightly close the back of the frame. Then I turn the frame over and expose the paper for a few seconds to electric light. Light from the bulb passes through the negative on to the sensitive paper. Where the negative is very thin, at the transparent places, a lot of light will reach the paper, and at these points the paper will turn dark when placed in the developer. Where the negative is very opaque—for example at the part representing the sky—very little light can reach the paper, and here it remains white when developed. Thus the sky is shown light while the shadows are dark, which is just as in nature. After this the paper, which is now a positive, must be fixed, washed and dried.

You see, it is a good thing to have a negative! After that first print I can make hundreds more. I can also, with an enlarger, make large pictures instead

7

A. NEGATIVE

B. PRINT ON PAPER

C. PRINT ON GLASS
LANTERNSLIDE

Three kinds of positive

1. **Contact print on paper**
2. **Lantern slide on glass**
3. **Enlargement**

For many purposes the contact print is too small; an enlargement shows the full beauty of the picture. By projecting a lantern slide in a darkened room we can show a picture to a number of people at once

Figs. 15, 16, 17 and

D. ENLARGEMENT

9

of small prints. And finally I can do my printing on glass instead of on paper, so producing a lantern slide which can be projected on to a screen where many people can see its picture.

It is important to realize that the printing paper is light-sensitive in exactly the same way as a plate or film. Like a film, it is affected by light, and so turns black in the developer where light has fallen on it. There is nothing to stop my using paper instead of film in the camera, except that the paper does not react quickly enough. Nevertheless, printing paper becomes quite black if exposed to sufficient light.

When I print from my negative, a good deal of light passes through the dark roof (which is transparent in the negative), so that in the print the roof is dark, as it should be. Little light passes through the sky of the plate, because the negative is so dense there. Thus I get a positive picture on my printing paper: light sky, grey walls, dark roof.

Please remember all this, and do not think that you must necessarily get a positive on paper just because it *is* paper. If you could expose it long enough in the camera, the printing paper would give you a negative picture exactly as does the plate. The following is an instructive experiment. Put a pair of scissors on a piece of printing paper. Just for an instant, turn on a bulb which shines on the paper. Then develop; you will have white scissors on a black background. Really beautiful prints are possible this way: for example, of leaves, peacock's feathers, and many other subjects.

Fig. 19—It is easy to print on gaslight paper in your own sitting room

2 WHAT TO PHOTOGRAPH

MANY people carry a camera but fail to see subjects that would make good photographs. The following pages are intended to help them by giving examples of what to photograph and what to leave alone. Besides both good and bad subjects, these pages show the value of concentration, and finally they demonstrate how part of a poor photograph may sometimes be made into a good picture.

You will see from these examples that a good picture is essentially a simple picture. A single subject in a good light against a quiet background: that is the first rule to follow.

Lighting

The choice of lighting is important. Most beginners, following an old-established instruction for the box-camera user, use light coming from behind the camera. This is excellent—but only for colour photography. For normal black-and-white pictures it is very much better to have the lighting from the side, for then the photograph will include shadows as well as sunlit parts.

This side-lighting is obtained by working round the subject until you find a position such that, when the camera is pointed in the desired direction, one of your shoulders is turned to the sun. This gives a much better lighting of the scene, with people or animals standing out clearly from the background.

Good lighting is especially easy to find in the early morning or late evening when the sun is low, giving a strong side lighting with long shadows.

Background and Colour

In ordinary surroundings it is not always easy to find a suitable background. The rule is that the background must be subsidiary to the main subject and must not draw attention to itself. Its tone should be as even as possible: black and white patches are especially to be avoided, and a wall makes a particularly intrusive background. In the open it is often useful to lower the camera so that the subject is seen against the sky, which makes an excellent background, especially when there are clouds.

If your photograph will be in plain black and white, try to imagine what it will look like with the natural colour gone before taking the picture. Are subject and background of the same brightness? If so, they will merge in the photograph, no matter how sharply the colour of the subject makes it stand out in reality.

Criticism

It is a good plan to have one's pictures criticized by someone with knowledge. Get him to give a frank opinion about your photographs, and take to heart what he says. Study the reproductions in a pictorial annual such as " Photograms of the Year " (published for *Amateur Photographer*), and, as a first step towards achieving comparable results, study the rules given in the following pages.

SUBJECTS NEED SEEING

Fig. 20—A PICTURE WHICH HAS
NOTHING TO SAY

There is no centre of interest here to
attract one's attention. Instead, we have
an empty foreground, which is too light,
and many patches of sky between the
trees, giving a restless effect. In all
respects a bad photograph

(Right) Fig. 21—HERE IS SOMETHIN
WORTH WHILE

The windmill is a centre, and the thr
trees fill up the foreground. There
good reproduction of the slightly mi
atmosphere. The dark trees emphas
the distance between the first and seco
" planes ". This shows you need not w
for fine weather in order to take a go
photograph

CHAOS OR ORDER?

Fig. 22—CHAOS

With no special point of interest to catch the eye, this is a bad subject—it is not restful. However, technically the picture is good

(Right) Fig. 23—ORDER

Rest is suggested by the simple lin There is rhythm in the repetition of groups of steps. An even backgrou gives simplicity and clarity. (Leica pictu

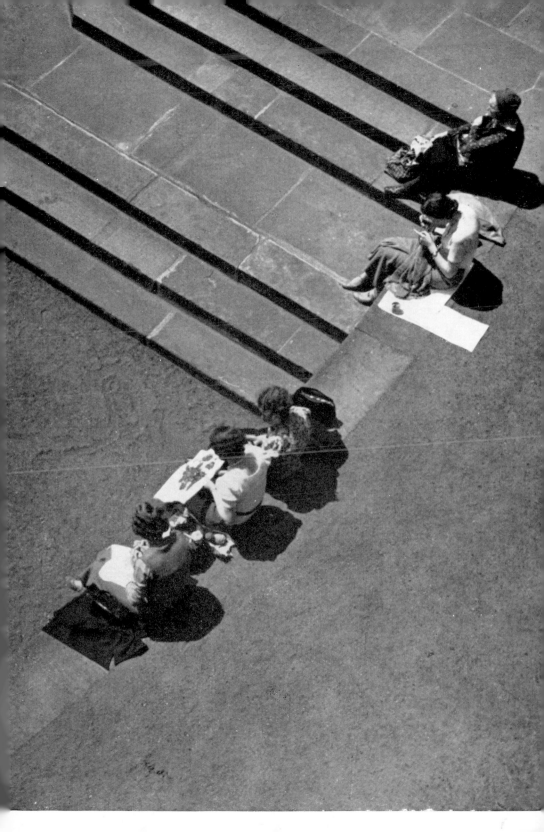

CONCENTRATION OF INTEREST

Fig. 24—THERE REALLY WAS SOME-
THING HERE. BUT THE LENS TOOK
IN FAR TOO MUCH

No concentration of light, with spotty
light and shade, make the subject a poor
one.   Light attracts the eye, so only the
important parts should be brightly lit,
while here four corners are light.   The
centre part outlined tempted the maker
to take the photograph, but he included
far too much

Fig. 25—THIS SIMPLE SCENE IS VIVID
AND INTERESTING

Here the brightly-lit subject is shown in
a frame of darker surroundings. The
light glancing along the wall gives the
picture life and brilliance. (Contax.
coated lens)

MOVEMENT AND REST

Fig. 26—Unrestful and confused, this was a movie-type picture taken in the middle of action

(Right) Fig. 27—" MORNING IN T
CITY "

This is also a snap, but movement shown in one direction, and is support by the restful lines of big office buildi

THE ART OF LEAVING OUT

Fig. 28—This picture has the good quality of brightness, and was taken at the right instant, but it is spoilt by distracting detail. The edges of the tub are disturbing: the main subject alone would be much better. The art of leaving out is most important when you arrange your subject; it is demonstrated in the next illustration

(Right) Fig. 29—" DID YOU CALL, MUMMY ? "

(Contax, coated lens)

Fig. 30—A typical amateur snap. It is nice and sharp and is well exposed, but it is not really a success because what the photographer had in his mind was the big photograph on the opposite page. In this the intrusive doors in the background have disappeared, leaving only the essentials of the picture. The pictures were taken, almost simultaneously, of the same model. The background used for that on the right was the dark entrance to the shed

(Right) Fig. 31—" THE REFEREE "

(Rolleiflex Automat f/5·6, yellow filter panchromatic film, 28° Sch., 1/50 sec)

PLACING THE
HORIZON

Fig. 32—We can decide how high the horizon should be in our picture. If we point the camera downwards, it makes the horizon high, which is very suitable for sea or river pictures, as seen here. (Contax, coated lens)

(Right) Fig. 33—"IN DOCK"

Here, the horizon is low, because the camera was pointed up. The result is a good impression of the size of the ship. If you want to reproduce something large, a close range, with the camera held low and the lens pointing upwards, is suitable for children's portraits, photos of people; but it is dangerous for buildings (see page 216). (Leica picture, taken while passing in motor launch, 1/200 sec)

24

Fig. 34—" LEICESTER SQUARE, PENSHURST "

Such a scene is only worth while because of the lighting. Without sunlight this picture would be very dull and uninteresting. The good foreground gives distance to the second part of the picture, which is brightly lit. The exposure was rather long in order to obtain the necessary shadow details. Always bear in mind that photography is " painting with light ", and look for the best lighting of your subjects.

(Rollei picture)

The Next Steps

Now we know the outline of the photographic process, and have seen examples of what to photograph and what to leave out. But this is only a beginning. We are now going through everything again in fuller detail, so that you may *really* understand the technique of the photographer. In the following chapters:

We choose a camera.

We enquire into the mysteries of the lens.

We learn to know the properties of films.

We look for good subjects.

We learn to expose correctly.

We find out how to develop films by modern methods.

We learn about fine grain.

We learn to make good prints for our friends.

We see how our best negatives can be enlarged for the album.

Finally, we see how to finish a picture as a professional would.

When you have learnt the technique we shall look for subjects; after all, these are the most important of all. Four of the most important kinds of subjects are seen in the pictures below (Figs. 35 to 38). They are a landscape, a good portrait, an interior, and a clever still-life.

PICTURES WORTH HAVING

LEFT TO RIGHT BELOW:

Fig. 35—Mountain and river
Fig. 36—Tiny in the evening sun
Fig. 37—At the Zoo
Fig. 38—Glass

3

3 CAMERAS AND ACCESSORIES

A DUFFER can do nothing whatever with an expensive camera, but give a cheap box camera to an artist and he will make a fine picture with it. The man behind the camera, in fact, counts more than the instrument itself!

When you buy this book, you are likely to have a camera already. Are you satisfied with it? Probably not. All amateurs long for a better camera. If you have one already, learn to use it well. But if you still want to buy a camera, then read the following pages carefully, for they will help you.

Be careful how you buy a secondhand camera; there may be something wrong with it. Get your camera from an established dealer, for it is to his interest to help you purchase a good one with which you can make first-rate pictures. You will go back to him later on to buy a more expensive camera, as well as for your films and papers. The amateur and the dealer need each other. Remain good friends with your dealer and do not worry him with complaints and grumbles. Nearly always poor results are *your* fault, not his. So instead of complaining to him, ask his advice.

If you can get the advice of an experienced amateur when purchasing your camera, do so. A good dealer will be pleased to sell you a good camera. Tell him how much you wish to spend on it. You need not buy an expensive one at first; indeed, it is usually better for the beginner to start with quite a simple one. Expensive cameras and lenses are complicated. If you buy a simple one first, you will have the thrill of a new camera all over again when you buy something more elaborate later on.

What Size of Negative?

Since the first little black box there have been cameras of all kinds and of all shapes and sizes. According to many advertisements, the miniature camera is usually considered the best, but we shall see later on how far this is true. These various cameras produce negatives which may be large or small. The usual negative sizes are:

24×36 mm (miniature) ($1 \times 1\frac{1}{2}$ in)	6×6 cm ($2\frac{1}{4} \times 2\frac{1}{4}$ in)	6×9 cm ($3\frac{1}{4} \times 2\frac{1}{4}$ in)	$\frac{1}{4}$ plate ($3\frac{1}{4} \times 4\frac{1}{4}$ in)

In the last century, during the early days of photography, professionals took their pictures on glass plates at least $8\frac{1}{2} \times 6\frac{1}{2}$ in, or whole-plate size. Even amateurs once used to drag about the country the large cameras which were needed. By about 1910 amateurs mostly used $3\frac{1}{4} \times 4\frac{1}{4}$ in plates (quarter-plate). The roll film pioneered by Eastman, the founder of the Kodak factories, brought the $3\frac{1}{4} \times 2\frac{1}{4}$ in size into fashion, but now even this is considered a " large " size, and is hardly used except for a few quite inexpensive cameras. Nearly all amateur roll film cameras now make $2\frac{1}{4}$ in sq. negatives.

In 1925 Oscar Barnack's Leica was marketed; this was the first modern miniature camera. It employed 35 mm cinema film, using the perforations along each edge for moving the film through the camera. The size of the picture was 24×36 mm, and this is now the most usual miniature size.

Let us say at once that working with miniature film requires considerable experience, and therefore it is sensible to start with a larger camera. When

THE MINIATURE CAMERA

Fig. 39—A well-known miniature: the Leica with coupled rangefinder. $5\frac{1}{4}$ in long, $1\frac{3}{16}$ in thick, $2\frac{11}{16}$ in high, weight $20\frac{1}{2}$ oz

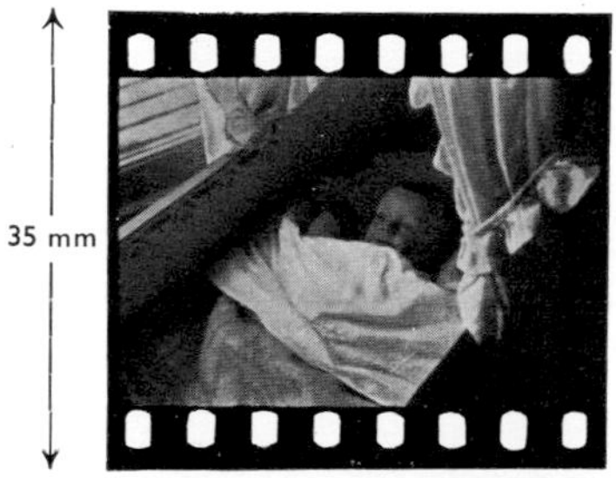

35 mm

Fig. 40—A miniature picture, actual size, which must be enlarged. Note the film perforations at top and bottom

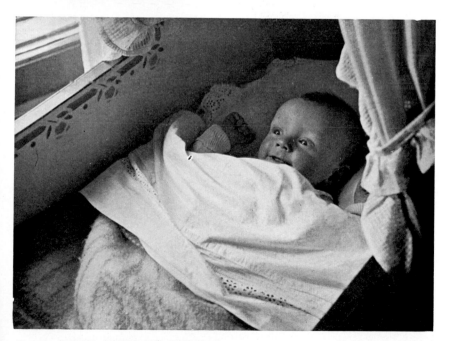

Fig. 41—" HERE COMES MY SUPPER!"   (Contax, coated lens)

An enlargement of the picture in Fig. 40. This is to three and a half times only. Ten times would be even better; the picture would then be 12 in wide

29

Fig. 43—Contact print from 6 × 6 cm negative. Very useful for the album

Fig. 42—A 6 × 6 cm twin-lens reflex such as this Rolleiflex, with its clear picture on the focusing screen, is a tremendous help in choosing the subject. Its parts are numbered as follows:

1 Lock for back
2 Counter window
3 Setting dial for shutter speeds
4 Film winding crank
5 Shutter release, with thread for wire release
6 Synchronizing contacts
7 Lever for X or M synchronization
8 Setting dial for stops
9 Focusing knob
10 Delayed-action release
11 Exposure setting window

Fig. 44—Kodak Sterling II camera, giving negatives $2\frac{1}{4} \times 3\frac{1}{4}$ in. Very few roll film cameras, and these mostly of the inexpensive type, are now made for negatives larger than $2\frac{1}{4}$ in sq.

Fig. 45—Contact print from $3\frac{1}{4} \times 2\frac{1}{4}$ in negative

Fig. 46—" CHIDDINGSTONE "

A Rollei picture, enlarged from a 6 × 6 cm negative (see Fig. 43). Though only two and a half times as large as the original print, it shows much more. It would easily make a fine print of 12 × 15 in size

Fig. 47—(Left) Stand camera, 5 in × 4 in or larger, for studio work or where maximum sharpness is needed. (Right) Metal folding technical camera (Linhof) with all the movements of a stand camera

Fig. 48—" GOING OUT "

This still-life subject is just the kind of thing best done by careful composition on the focusing screen of a large camera

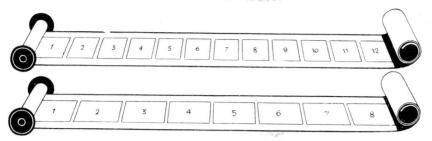

Fig. 49—A spool of ordinary $2\frac{1}{4} \times 3\frac{1}{4}$ in roll film (120 or 620 size; also known as BII) gives 12 pictures 6×6 cm ($2\frac{1}{4} \times 2\frac{1}{4}$ in), or 8 pictures $3\frac{1}{4} \times 2\frac{1}{4}$ in, or 16 pictures $4\frac{1}{2} \times 6$ cm, according to the camera used

you have learnt to work successfully with this, you should have little difficulty with a miniature.

Now there are two things you can do: one is to buy a modern camera for pictures 6×6 cm, using the normal 120 or 620 roll film. From that you will get 12 pictures per spool. Or you can obtain a $3\frac{1}{2} \times 2\frac{1}{2}$ in or $4\frac{1}{4} \times 3\frac{1}{4}$ in plate camera, and this, for the sake of learning, I strongly advise you to do. When you have learnt to handle it well by the help of this book, you will attain the goal you have in mind; that is, to become a good photographer.

We are now going to discuss briefly the various cameras your dealer stocks.

The Box Camera

This is our little dark box in its simplest form. It is the kind of camera which is suitable for young beginners, and also those who have little feeling for technique. Because its small lens is slow, that is, passes but little light, it is only suitable for use in bright weather.

Fig. 50—The Brownie is a popular example of the simple box camera. This one can be fitted with attachments, as shown, for flashlight photography

33

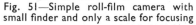

Fig. 51—Simple roll-film camera with small finder and only a scale for focusing

Fig. 52—A more advanced roll-film camera, with a big viewfinder and coupled rangefinder. This model also has a built-in electric exposure meter

The box camera has one shutter speed only of about 1/35th second. As its focusing cannot be adjusted, near objects cannot be sharply photographed with it unless special supplementary lenses (portrait attachments) are used.

Unfortunately the box camera, as a rule, is not only simple but of inferior quality, so that photographs taken with it are seldom sharp enough to enlarge well. Nevertheless a man who understands photography will do excellent work with it, though the range of subjects it can take is limited.

As this type of camera is clumsy, square, and awkward to carry, the manufacturers' next step was to produce

The Folding Roll-film Camera

This camera is the most popular of all, but notwithstanding that I do not think it is the best type for a beginner, because you never know exactly what you are photographing with it nor do you know for certain whether your picture will be sharp—not, that is, unless you have had much experience—because the miserably small finder fitted to so many of these cameras does not permit a really good choice of subject, while a normally-equipped one offers no real control of the sharpness of the picture: you have to guess the distance and set a scale to suit. Hence we cannot recommend this camera as an ideal one for serious work, and it is particularly difficult for the beginner.

However, we must say at once that there are exceptions: a few of the more expensive cameras of this class are equipped with an excellent rangefinder and a large and accurate viewfinder, and naturally our comments do not apply to these.

The Stand Camera

This can be considered ideal for serious work (see Fig. 2, page 7). The advantages of the tripod camera are as follows.

First, there is a ground glass on which the whole picture can be focused. As a result, the choice of subject, arrangement of composition, and exact focusing are very much easier. Work can be carefully done, and every picture can be dealt with separately, which is a tremendous advantage for serious work, and an immense help to the beginner who really wants to learn. Such a camera, in my opinion, should be in the hands of every amateur who wants to progress.

The ground-glass camera is perfected in what is called the reflex.

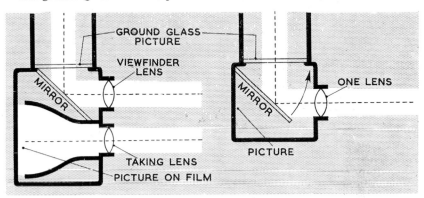

Fig. 53—Cross-section of a twin-lens reflex camera   Fig. 54—Cross-section of a single-lens reflex camera

Fig. 55—Inside a twin-lens reflex (Rolleiflex). a-b is the depth of focus of the upper (viewfinder) lens. This is rather slight, making it easy to focus exactly. c-d, the depth of focus of the taking lens, is greater. The picture is upside down on the film, but the picture from the viewing lens, going via the mirror, is the right way up on the ground glass, though reversed from left to right

Fig. 56—Single-lens reflex (Agiflex). The picture is diverted by the mirror to the ground glass. When the release is pressed the mirror hinges up, and light then falls on the film at the back of the camera. The picture on the ground glass instantaneously disappears, but that does not matter: it is recorded on the film

35

Fig. 57—The famous Rolleiflex, a twin-lens reflex, with finder picture always visible. Planar f/2·8 lens, Compur shutter up to 1/500 sec, built-in exposure meter

Fig. 58—The Microcord, a British-made twin-lens reflex with f/3·5 Ross Xpres lens in a fully speeded and synchronized shutter

The Reflex

What is a reflex? It is the modern version of the old " camera obscura ". In the centre of our basic model, the square box, there is a sloping mirror that throws the light up on to the ground glass, which, instead of being at the back, is now conveniently located on top. On it we see a picture which shows us all the possibilities of the subject.

This picture is upright, so that full control of composition and sharpness is possible. It is true that it is reversed from left to right, like yourself in a mirror, but one soon gets used to that. The great popularity of the small reflex camera for roll films is due to that marvellous ground-glass picture.

Ask an experienced amateur what he would prefer: the single-lens or the twin-lens reflex. You will find that, whichever he recommends, he will be enthusiastic. The reflex is undoubtedly the best modern camera for the average amateur. Either type has the outstanding advantage that the picture can be carefully focused and composed on the screen.

The ground-glass screen of the reflex has helped thousands of amateurs to find and compose their subjects and to become successful photographers.

36

These amateurs will, later, get along much better with their miniatures because, with the aid of the ground-glass screen, they will have learnt to *see a good subject*. In other words, they will have learnt how to choose from the enormous variety of possible subjects and to recognize which will make good pictures. This is most essential, and it is for this reason that we advise everyone to begin with a reflex.

Besides the Rolleiflex $2\frac{1}{4} \times 2\frac{1}{4}$ in (Fig. 57) there is now the new Rolleiflex 4×4 in, which takes the 127 or A8 film. This film is also available as colour film and gives 12 pictures 4×4 cm, which can be put into miniature size mounts, to be projected in normal miniature projectors. The projection lenses must be of good quality to ensure that pictures are sufficiently sharp up to the edges of the screen.

The Reflex in Use

To load a reflex is easy, but this must be done exactly according to the instruction book. After doing it once or twice, you will remember the correct procedure. Always do it in the shade, or better still indoors, remembering how sensitive modern films are, and how readily fogged at the edges by light creeping between film and paper.

Now to use the camera—to photograph, perhaps, a house. First, look at the house itself, decide whether the lighting pleases you and whether it seems a good subject. Then look at the ground glass to see how it will appear in a photograph. Give thought to the composition; should the picture be upright or horizontal? Square pictures are not often artistically pleasing. Choose the largest stop that will give the necessary depth of field, and adjust the exposure-time accordingly. If the shutter speed is to be slower than 1/50th second, use a tripod to avoid camera-shake, which will show as a slight lack of sharpness, especially in a big enlargement. It is claimed of certain gadgets that with their aid exposures as long as a tenth of a second can be given with perfect sharpness, the camera being held only in the hand. These claims, however, cannot be relied upon.

A reflex can be used in several positions, each giving a different viewpoint. The usual position is on the chest, with the hood just below the eyes, but it is possible to kneel on one knee and rest the camera on the other, or the camera can be put on the ground and pointed up a little. If you are in a crowd and want to take the Queen's State Coach as it passes by, hold the camera upside down over your head (Fig. 58a). It must previously have been focused on the right distance, and as it cannot be held very steadily in this position, speed the shutter up to 1/100th second or faster. If you prefer to use your camera at eye-level, there is the sportsfinder, or perhaps a mirror in the hood for eye-level focusing.

It makes quite a difference whether the camera is held high or low. Try taking two photographs of a friend, one with the camera at eye-level, one with it on the ground, and notice the differences, especially in the relationship of figure and background. For standing persons a low viewpoint is often effective, but on the other hand an extra-high viewpoint—a first-floor window, perhaps—is also worth trying, for by giving the ground as a background the picture is often simplified.

37

Fig. 58a—For photographing in crowds, it is a good idea to hold the camera above the head, so that the view is not obstructed by the people in front. The same trick is useful when a high viewpoint is wanted

Fig. 58b—How to photograph people: hold the camera steady and look over it direct at the sitter instead of relying on the focusing screen

Here is a most useful tip for photographing people. First focus the camera, and set stop and shutter; the next step is to wait for the right expression or pose. This can be done by watching the ground glass, but it is much better to look over the camera directly at the person you wish to photograph, with the camera held ready for the exposure, and with a finger on the trigger. In this way you are in closer contact with the subject and can see expressions much better, so that it is far easier to expose at the right moment. Fig. 58b shows how this is done.

THE MINIATURE CAMERA

With the Leica, the first of the miniatures, a new picture size was born, namely 24 × 36 mm; simultaneously there came a new branch of photography: miniature photography. Though originally thought a toy because of its small size, the Leica, and with it the other miniatures it brought in its train, is now fully accepted as a serious camera. The question " big or small ? " no longer causes arguments. The accepted attitude now is: big *and* small. Both these methods of photography are soundly established. They are not competitors; each is a very welcome complement of the other. Both these methods have limits which we ought to recognize.

38

Both methods also have their advantages, and we should appreciate these more clearly still. The miniature has made itself extremely popular because of its many advantages. For that reason this book is to a considerable extent a miniature manual. We deal with small negatives, but large pictures.

The negative material used is the standard perforated film of 35 mm width used for professional ciné work. Barnack constructed his first Leica when he was the camera-man for a film company. He wanted a convenient camera with which he could make trial pictures on the same film that he was using in his movie camera. That first Leica has branched out into a complete system of photography. The ciné picture had a size of 18 × 24 mm. That was too small: Barnack chose double that size, or 24 × 36 mm.

Though the term " miniature " is used from time to time for several different sizes of negative, when used without qualification in this book it means this double-frame picture on ciné film. But it is fair also to apply it to smaller negatives (24 × 24 mm, 18 × 24 mm) on ciné film, and the very slightly larger roll-film sizes 28 × 40 mm (Bantam size) and 3 × 4 cm, and perhaps even to the 4 × 4 cm negatives from which one seldom enlarges an area greater than 3 × 4 cm. In inches, this last, the largest, is $1\frac{9}{16} \times 1\frac{9}{16}$ in, but we shall adhere to the accepted custom of referring to these sizes in millimetres or centimetres, which give convenient figures instead of awkward ones.

Just as the small picture on the film is enormously enlarged on the screen at the cinema, the miniature negative can give a print enlarged up to any size desired. This, then, is the system: to make small negatives and enlarge them in printing.

This is, in all circumstances, the most convenient way of working, but it is not always the best. One would not deliberately *choose* a miniature for land-scape work; the job could be better done with a large stand camera. In the first place, the subject can be arranged and composed far more perfectly on the big focusing screen than it ever could in the small finder of a miniature, and in the second place, the larger negative will naturally record more fine detail. Not much more, perhaps, for the gap in this respect between the miniature and larger cameras has narrowed greatly of recent years (as a result of improved

The latest Leica—and the earliest

Fig. 59—Leica M3, with coated lens, the most advanced model at the time of writing

Fig. 60—Oskar Barnack's hand-made Leica of 1913 (now in the Leitz Museum)

lenses and high-resolution films) but the difference is still there. Your miniature camera is meant for such purposes as catching the expression of your little daughter when, for the first time, she hears your watch ticking. The miniature is not meant for a quiet architectural picture. A number of rapid sports pictures is much more in its line, and it can do this sort of thing much better than any large-sized camera.

A clear distinction must be made between the two different fields: the one, a restful, well thought-out photo—say, the reproduction of light and line, of the delicate texture of surfaces, of silk and glass in a still-life, of architecture; the other, such places as the swimming pool, with its innumerable subjects. These represent two different facets of life, but both are equally worth recording with the camera. Do the one, after careful study, with the big camera. Do the other, working fast and concentrating hard, with your miniature.

The special field of the miniature has not yet been sufficiently exploited. Frequently the miniature is used for work which could be done equally well or better with a big camera. A half-plate Leica enlargement need not be as perfect technically as a half-plate print made direct from a glass negative, so long as the *spirit* of the miniature picture is different. For a still-life, in which we require the most perfect sharpness, with delicate rendering of the finest details, the big camera should be chosen. On the other hand, facial expressions, fleeting episodes of our daily life, precious moments from the lives of our children, are subjects for the miniature. It is a valuable instrument for other subjects too. The miniature has won itself a place in science, in exploration, and indeed in almost every department of life. We shall see how later.

How the Miniature Works

The square shape of our little dark box, the old camera obscura, has been abandoned entirely in the miniature. The apparatus has been built round the use of film rolled up on a spool.

If you hold the camera in front of you, ready to make the picture, you will see on the left the space for the cassette of film, from which the film runs along the picture opening to the take-up spool. The inverted picture made by the lens falls within the picture opening, which measures 24×36 mm, or about $1 \times 1\frac{1}{2}$ in.

Just in front of the film is the shutter. In miniature cameras two kinds of shutter are used; some models have a blind just in front of the film, while others have a shutter in the lens. After the film has been exposed, the winding knob at the top of the right-hand side is turned, causing the film to move on one picture further, simultaneously winding up the spring of the shutter ready for the next picture. When the release button is pressed, the focal-plane shutter, which consists of a fabric blind with a narrow slit running across it, passes over the film to make the exposure. Then the winding knob, which has been locked until the exposure was made, can be turned again to prepare for the next exposure. This can be repeated 36 times for each black-and-white film and with some colour films, but the latter are mostly used in 20-exposure lengths.

Such a rapid winding of the film, and the large number of exposures which can be made, are advantages, but they may become dangers too. Self-control

Fig. 61—" TICK-TOCK "
This happy picture was taken close to a window. A white screen, as a reflector, was on the left. (Contax, coated lens, f/2)

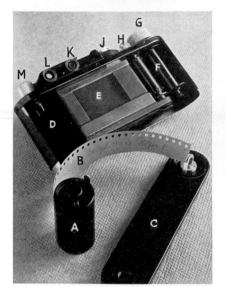

Fig. 62—The back of a Leica cut away to show the main components. The camera shown is a Model II

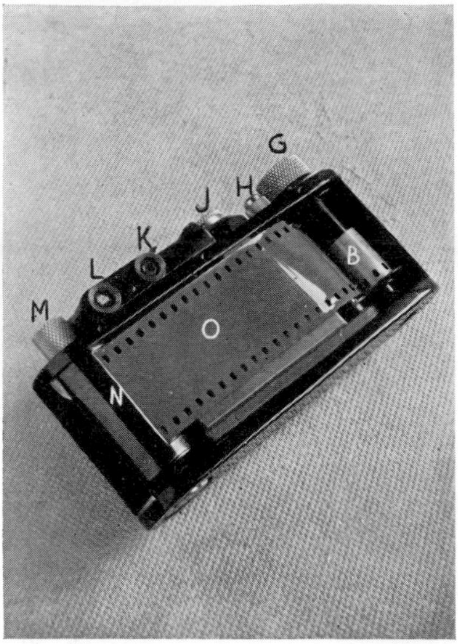

Fig. 63—The Leica loaded with film. The cassette is automatically opened by locking the base C to the camera

A = Cassette holding unexposed film
B = Leading end of film
C = Base of camera (removable)
D = Space for loaded cassette
E = Picture opening, showing blind of focal-plane shutter
F = Take-up spool
G = Winding knob

H = Shutter-release button
J = Shutter-speed dial
K = Viewfinder
L = Built-in rangefinder
M = Rewinding knob to wind the film back into the cassette after exposure
N = Mouth of cassette
O = Film

is necessary: before releasing the shutter, you should make up your mind definitely whether the picture is really worth taking. Otherwise, you will only make a great number of snapshots of very poor quality. Beware of the average-quality snapshot! Let it be your aim to make only really good photographs.

A rear ground-glass screen cannot be used with miniatures, except perhaps in conjunction with some special copying device, and for this reason they are equipped with good viewfinders. Very ingenious devices have been designed to ensure correct focusing; some details of these are given on pages 56 and 57.

An important feature of all these small cameras is that the lenses fitted to them have a very short focal length, the usual figure being 5 cm, or 2 in. Such lenses are able to give, on the one picture, sharp images of both near and distant objects; in technical language, they have great depth of focus. That is why they are particularly suitable when pictures must be made rapidly of objects at varying distances from the camera, for they do not need re-focusing every time. With the bigger cameras exact focusing is much more essential.

The lenses in the more elaborate miniatures are attached to the camera by either a screw-in or bayonet fitting. They can be removed in a moment to be replaced by other lenses designed to serve special purposes. Telephoto or long-focus lenses which give a large picture of a distant object, high-speed lenses for night photography, or wide-angle lenses to include more of a near object, each can be used in turn. More about this will be found in the chapter on lenses.

Lenses are only interchangeable in the more expensive miniatures.

The Miniature Reflex

An ideal combination of the advantages of the miniature with the reflex principle is found in the miniature reflexes, such as the Kine-Exakta or the Swiss Alpa. These cameras have the advantage of complete absence of parallax; that is to say, the focusing screen always shows exactly what will be recorded on the film. Focusing is done with the same lens that takes the picture. To make the picture easier to focus, either a special magnifying screen is used or, more usually, a pentaprism is fitted over it. This gives eye-level viewing of the screen, and the picture seen is both the right way up and the right way round, even when the camera is turned on its side for upright pictures. This is the ideal camera for colour photography, because colours, as well as sharpness and composition, can be judged on the screen.

With the simpler models, the picture on the ground glass inevitably becomes a little darker if the lens is closed down to a small aperture. With such

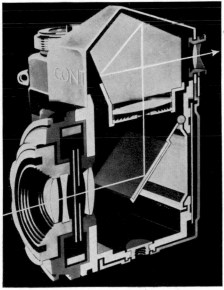

Fig. 64—The interchangeable lens in the more expensive miniatures allows the use of wide-angle and telephoto lenses

Fig. 65—Contaflex eye-level miniature reflex, with picture on the focusing screen seen the right way round through the pentaprism

4

cameras it is very advisable to use a leather hood (Fig. 91), for by excluding all strong light it makes the picture much easier to see. In most modern single-lens reflexes, however, focusing is always done at the widest aperture, and the stop to be used for the actual exposure is set by turning a ring that does *not* operate the diaphragm, but merely sets a stop against which it can be closed. After focusing, and before exposing, the stop-ring is turned, purely by feel, as far as it will go, so setting the stop to the preselected

Fig. 66—The Contax miniature camera shown with the 13·5 cm long-focus lens and special viewfinder applicable to different lenses. No lens hood is shown, but one should be used with every lens

Fig. 67—Miniature reflex (Kine-Exakta) in use. The effect of colour in colour photography can be studied particularly well on the ground glass

Fig. 68—The same camera used at eye-level with optional pentaprism. The picture is seen right way up. Specially useful in crowds and for sports pictures

Fig. 69—" SLING IT AWAY!"   Four pictures taken in two seconds by a Robot camera

opening. This can be done without taking the eyes or the mind from the picture on the screen. In some more expensive cameras, the action of pressing the release frees a spring that closes the iris to the pre-set opening.

These miniature reflexes share with the standard miniature the advantage of interchangeability of lenses, and will take even those of very long focus.

The Robot Camera

After Barnack's Leica had made such headway, a number of other cameras came out using the same miniature size. Among the best-known of these are the Zeiss Ikon Contax and the series of Kodak Retinas, which have also developed into a complete system of camera and accessories, while among the many less ambitious instruments are the Voigtländer Vito and the Agfa Silette.

A further step in construction came with the Robot, which embodies a clockwork motor that moves the film along and resets the shutter automatically after each exposure. This enables the user to make a complete series of pictures in an unbelievably short time, simply by pressing the release repeatedly, which is most valuable for press and sports photography, and for makers of bird pictures, who can arrange to operate this camera electrically from a distance. The original Robot gave a square picture, 24 × 24 mm in size, on 35 mm film but there are now also models for the more usual 24 × 36 mm size.

For the sake of speed in action, lever wind is now tending to replace film wind by knob, and in many cameras winding on the film also cocks the shutter.

Fig. 70—(Left) The Robot takes 50 pictures each 24 × 24 mm. Film movement is by means of a built-in motor, immediately after exposure. (Right) Robot with serial release, for pictures of birds and so on from a distance

45

Fig. 71a—(Left). The Minicord, an Austrian-made sub-miniature for negatives 10 mm sq on 16 mm film

Fig. 71b—(Below). Minox sub-miniature for pictures 8 mm × 11 mm on 16 mm film. Shutter to 1/1,000th sec, f/3·5 lens, focusing to 8 in, 50 exposures at one loading

Rapid advances are still being made in the construction of miniature cameras. Built-in exposure-meters are becoming common, and the latest advance in this field is a coupling between exposure-meter and shutter. Altering either shutter-speed or stop causes an auxiliary needle in the exposure-meter to move: when this coincides with the ordinary needle (that operated by the light) the exposure-value (see page 50) is correctly set. A few cameras (Adox 300, Hasselblad, Mamiyo magazine camera) have interchangeable film holders, each of which holds cassette, film-channel, and take-up spool. With these it is easy to switch from black-and-white to colour film and back again in a few moments, with no loss of film or risk of scratches due to rewinding the film and reloading with it later.

Even the miniature is no longer the smallest camera; there are the sub-miniatures. These mostly use 16 mm film, and give negatives about 10 × 10 mm. So far even the best of them (beautifully built precision instruments) will not give really sharp pictures much over 9 × 12 cm, when sharpness breaks down and graininess appears.

Use and Care of Your Camera

After all this discussion on cameras we must repeat once more that the quality of the picture is not decided so much by the camera as by the ability of the man behind it. It is *his* eye that sees the subject and *his* control of technique that creates, in combination with the camera, the striking picture he desires.

The camera to choose is one of the general type best suited to the kind of work you wish to do. It need not be elaborate or complicated unless you want to take really difficult subjects, but it must be well made and accurately adjusted. Used for subjects within its scope, a first-rate simple camera will give pictures as good as can be got with the most expensive camera made, whereas an ill-constructed or badly adjusted camera, no matter how many refinements it may have, will give disappointing results with every subject, even the simplest.

With every camera the maker includes an instruction booklet. Think of this as a special letter, written to you personally, by the man who designed the camera. It explains with the utmost care how the camera works. Read it several times, and practise every manipulation until you have really learnt to know your camera. You should know the function of every little button or knob, and who can help you more effectively than the designer of the camera himself? First learn to load your camera smoothly and easily. Under no circumstances apply force. Ask your dealer for a piece of fogged miniature film, or even an old roll film, to practise with. Later on your smooth, easy familiarity with your camera will demonstrate the truth of the saying that practice makes perfect.

If you buy your camera secondhand, as so many do nowadays, you may get no instruction book with it. The mechanism of a simple camera you can

Fig. 71c—The Agfa Ambi-Silette, a miniature camera with interchangeable lenses in which the diaphragm shutter lies behind the lens. The entire lens is removed and replaced, not only the front component as in some other designs. A built-in viewfinder shows the correct field for 35, 50 and 90 mm lenses

47

puzzle out for yourself with the aid of this book, but for some of the more elaborate cameras there are " Camera Guide " booklets. Ask your dealer whether there is one for your camera.

Do not keep your camera in a place that is either too warm or too cold; but above all keep it dry. The best plan is to keep the camera in its leather case in a special corner of a bookcase or cupboard; don't keep it in the dark-room where moisture can cause trouble. Always keep the lens covered when the camera is not in use. You should occasionally look through it, and, if it is found to be dusty, wipe it with an old clean handkerchief. Do not use wash-leather, as this may contain sharp particles of grit, which might cause scratches on the surface of the glass. A lens hardly ever gets dirty inside, so it is seldom necessary to dismantle it. If an overhaul is needed, the lens should be sent to its makers or to a competent repairer. But never experiment with it yourself. After an " overhaul " at home, the attentions of an expert are likely to be very urgently needed!

Put a strip of paper in the camera case, with a note on it of the precise film the camera is loaded with. This avoids any doubt that may arise if the camera is not used for a few weeks. It is a sound plan to leave the camera in its case as much as possible when out of doors. This is specially important when using it on the beach, because fine grains of sand are easily blown into the corners of your camera, resulting in unsatisfactory working or even jamming of its more delicate parts. It is also a bad plan to leave your camera in the sun. Instead put it, in its case, in a shady spot.

A. MATEUR

33 Focus Street
BLACKBURN

It is a good idea to have your name and address engraved on your camera. Also, make a note at home of the numbers of your camera and lens or lenses, so that in case of loss or theft you can describe your camera to others.

It is well worth while to insure your camera. The best insurance, however, is your own carefulness, especially when travelling, when a camera is so easily left lying about or slung on the back of a chair in a restaurant.

CAMERA SHUTTERS

A Sound Rule: 1/50 Second, or Use a Tripod

There are two kinds of shutter:

(a) The between-lens or diaphragm shutter that works close to, or in, the lens; and

(b) The focal-plane shutter working immediately in front of the film or plate.

The shutter is designed to allow the light to reach the film or plate for exactly the right length of time, at precisely the right moment. It is essential to know the exact length of time the shutter is open: this is the *exposure time*. A between-lens shutter is composed of a number of blades, opening for a longer or shorter time. The shutter is driven by a spring, and its time of opening is controlled by a clockwork mechanism.

Most shutters offer three possibilities: T, B, and I.

Button for
delayed action

Setting
lever

Socket
for wire release

Release

Scale of
exposure times

Scale of
stops

Stop
adjustment

Fig. 72—The Compur between-lens shutter,
giving Time, Bulb and Instantaneous exposures
from 1 to 1/200 sec with delayed action. The
front component of the lens has been removed

" Z " or " T " stands for the German "Zeit" or English " Time ". When
the release is pressed, the shutter opens and stays open. When the release
is pressed again, the shutter closes. This " time " movement is for giving
long exposures—for instance, when taking interiors. In such cases, exposures
may be as long as a quarter of an hour, or even much longer.

" B " stands for " Bulb ". This expression comes from the old type of
shutter, still used by some professional photographers, which was opened
by pressure on a rubber bulb. When he pressed the bulb, the shutter opened;
when he let it go again, the shutter closed. The modern between-lens shutter
behaves in the same way, press the release lever and the shutter opens, relax
the pressure and the shutter closes. This is for the shorter times of exposure,
of five seconds or so, needed when photographing such subjects as still life.
It is essential that the camera be provided with a good, flexible wire release.
This wire release prevents any movement of the hand from being transmitted
to the camera.

" M " or " I " stands for the German " Moment " or English " Instantaneous ". Originally the term was applied only to fairly fast snapshot exposures;
now it is extended to cover any exposure the length of which is controlled by
the shutter mechanism itself. At this setting the shutter opens for the time for
which it is set. On the cheaper cameras we usually find $\frac{1}{25}$, $\frac{1}{50}$ and $\frac{1}{100}$ second.
But the longer " instantaneous " exposures of 1, $\frac{1}{2}$, $\frac{1}{5}$, $\frac{1}{10}$ and $\frac{1}{20}$ second
are also very valuable. They are shown on the dials of the better shutters,
such as the Compur shutter illustrated (Fig. 72). With this type of shutter
the shortest exposure is usually $\frac{1}{200}$ or $\frac{1}{300}$ second; but still shorter times,
up to $\frac{1}{500}$ second, are possible with the Compur-Rapid. The very shortest
exposures, such as $\frac{1}{1000}$ second, which are needed for fast action pictures, are
not possible with the ordinary between-lens shutters.

49

If we retard the movement of the shutter by a finger on the setting lever, it can be seen that the blades open slowly from the centre, remain open for a while, and then close again. The shutter does not reach its full opening instantaneously, but consumes some time in opening and once it is open, it needs time to close. During this time light is lost; consequently the more quickly the shutter opens and closes and the longer it remains fully open, the higher its efficiency.

Some of the latest photo-electric exposure meters indicate also stop and shutter speed, a single figure containing both and called the exposure value. In a poor light the meter may indicate 4, in a brilliant light perhaps 18. These figures refer to the lowest scale on the latest Compur shutter shown in Fig. 73. If the meter indicates an exposure value of, say, 11, then the stop-adjusting lever is moved to bring it to 11 on the scale. If the shutter happens to be set to 1/125 sec, the stop will then be f/4, but if the shutter had been set to 1/15 sec, the stop would be f/11. When the stop-lever is released it locks to the speed ring, so that when the latter is turned, stop and shutter speed change together in such a way as to keep the amount of light reaching the film unchanged. If the exposure is correct for any one of these settings, it is correct for them all. The advantage is that, without any mental calculation, a short time of exposure with a large stop, or a larger time with a small stop, can be used at will; the former for fast moving objects, the latter for a subject calling for extensive depth of focus. An exposure value of 11, in fact, corresponds to every one of the combination of stops and shutter speed shown in this table:

f/2	f/2·8	f/4	f/5·6	f/8	f/11	f/16	f/22
1/500	1/250	1/125	1/60	1/30	1/15	1/8	1/4

Fig. 73—An "exposure value" Compur shutter with the E.V. scale at the bottom. In other models the scale is on the side or elsewhere

Fig. 73a—Prontor S.L.K. shutter, coupled to an exposure-meter built into the camera

Fig. 74—Focal-plane shutter in a large camera: the slit travels downwards across the plate or film

Fig. 75—The focal-plane shutter is ideal for sports subjects: this one had an exposure of 1/1000 sec

Intermediate positions are also possible—the exposure value may if desired be set to, say, $10\frac{1}{2}$.

To achieve this interlocking it has been necessary to graduate the shutter with speeds such that each is half or double the next, since the step from one stop to the next doubles or halves the light passed.

The Focal-plane Shutter

The photograph in Fig. 74 clearly shows the operation of the focal-plane shutter. Close against the sensitive material a fabric blind, in which a slit has been left open, passes across it at high speed. With the older types of reflex and press cameras this curtain consisted of rubberized black cloth, which is also used in the Leica and most other miniatures, whereas the blind of the Contax shutter is of metal. The fault common to all lens shutters, namely loss of light while opening and closing, does not occur to the same extent with the focal-plane shutter.

Provided the blind is close enough to the film, the full light of the lens instantaneously reaches, and is instantaneously cut off from, each part of the film in turn.

The faster the blind is made to run, and the narrower the slit in it is made, the shorter is the time of exposure. The shortest exposure given by the average focal-plane shutter is $\frac{1}{1000}$ second, but still higher speeds, up to $\frac{1}{2000}$ second, are sometimes encountered. The cloth of a modern focal-plane shutter will withstand both extreme cold and heat. However, if your camera has a focal-plane shutter, *never* turn the lens to the sun. Focused on the blind by the lens, it may easily burn a hole in the cloth, and there have even been occasions when it has set the film on fire, with disastrous results to the whole camera!

The direction in which the blind of a focal-plane shutter runs is highly important. In the sketch of Fig. 76 the film is shown; in front of it is a focal-plane shutter, with a narrow slit, running from right to left. Note the arrow

51

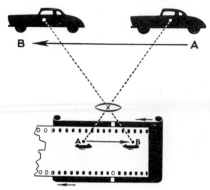

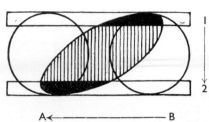

Fig. 76—Relation between the direction of movement of a car and the direction in which the shutter runs. The car should run in the same direction as the shutter, the picture of the car thus running against the moving slit of the shutter. This is desirable for maximum sharpness

Fig. 77—Some distortion of moving objects occurs with focal-plane shutters. When the slit is in the top position I, the wheel is at B. The lower part of the wheel (at the top in the image) is then pictured. When the wheel has travelled to A the slit has arrived at position 2. There the upper part of the wheel (bottom in the image) is recorded. The wheel as a whole is oval and lies at an angle

indicating direction. We photograph a passing car, moving from A to B. When the car is at A, its image, formed by the lens, falls on the film at A. The car moves across to B, causing the image of the car to move from A along the film to B. The image and the shutter-slit meet during their movement, and pass each other very rapidly. But if the car were running in the opposite direction, its image would run over the film more or less simultaneously with the shutter-slit, resulting in a blurred picture. To avoid this, try to snapshot moving objects when they are moving in the same direction as the shutter.

If a moving car is photographed with a focal-plane shutter running from the top downwards, as in Fig. 77, we may get an ellipse-shaped picture of the wheel, which in practice is usually acceptable because we have become used to

Fig. 78—The car was travelling fast enough to move several inches during the time the shutter was open

Fig. 79—When the camera is swung round to follow the car, the background becomes completely blurred, but the car is recorded sharply

seeing speed pictured thus. Even artists have made use of this distortion to suggest speed.

It is safe to say that a sound training in general camera handling is much more important than any theoretical considerations about the running direction of the shutter, for mistakes in this respect only occasionally result in a blur.

Snapshot pictures are not always sharp. We can blur any picture by moving the camera during exposure. Unconscious camera movement is in fact the most common cause of blurred pictures—especially of those that are only slightly blurred. It is *essential* to keep the camera entirely motionless as the shutter is fired. An exception to this rule is in taking racing cars or other rapidly-moving objects. The camera is swung round to follow the object, which is kept in the centre of the viewfinder. The background then becomes blurred, but the car is rendered sharply. (See Fig. 79.)

Moving Objects

Photographing a cow slowly strolling in a meadow is a very different problem from photographing a racing car as it flashes by. The distance between these moving objects and the camera is of basic importance, as also is the direction of the movement with respect to the camera. If a car moves across the lens, the displacement of the image on the film in a certain time is much more than when the car, at the same distance, is moving straight towards the camera. The eye does not see very much movement then, only a gradual increase in size. Always try, therefore, to photograph an object when it is moving directly towards or away from the camera. Failing this, the object may be photographed when moving at an angle of 45 degrees, but only when the light is favourable, and coming from the side of the camera.

SHUTTER SPEEDS FOR MOVING OBJECTS

Aircraft (much more than 50 ft)	..		..	1/500 second or faster	
Express train ..	..	..	..	1/500	,,
Seagull	..	..	..	1/500	,,
Racehorse	..	..	..	1/250	,,
Motor car (40 m.p.h.)		..	..	1/250	,,
Runner	..	..	..	1/200	,,
Motor boat ..	..	..	..	1/200	,,
Trotting horse	..	..	..	1/200	,,
Tram or bus ..	..	..	..	1/100	,,
Rowing boat ..	..	..	..	1/50	,,
Pedestrian	..	..	..	1/50	,, or faster

The table above lists various common moving objects, and gives the shutter speed necessary to use with each to make sure of a sharp picture. The speeds given are based on a distance of approximately 50 ft between object and camera and apply to the least favourable case, when the movement is directly across the line of sight of the camera. They may be lengthened somewhat when the movement is straight towards the camera or at a sharp angle. At the same time, it is worth noticing that slight movement of part of a subject, such as

53

Fig. 80—Body release on Agfa Silette. Smooth working is necessary to ensure absence of camera-shake as the shutter is fired

the feet in the case of a runner, causing a slight blur on the picture, may be very helpful in suggesting movement, though his body should be clearly defined.

The shutters on cameras of well-known makes may be relied upon to give the exposure times marked. If anything goes wrong with the shutter, it is soon detected by the change in the sound it makes when released.

Instruments for measuring shutter speeds have been made, but are usually very elaborate. It is easy, nevertheless, to make an approximate check with the aid of a gramophone motor. A small piece of white paper is stuck on the edge of the turntable, and the motor is placed in sunlight. The turntable is then photographed at various shutter speeds. As the turntable should turn at 78 revolutions per minute, the time of exposure may be calculated fairly accurately from the length of the blur of the white strip as it appears on the negative. This check is, however, unnecessary with cameras of well-known makes, for they are all thoroughly tested before leaving the factory. High accuracy is in any case unnecessary, for a *slight* error in exposure time is entirely taken up by the latitude of the emulsion. It simply does not matter whether the exposure given is $\frac{1}{25}$ or $\frac{1}{30}$ second.

How to Use the Shutter

Every beginner should train himself to release the shutter smoothly and evenly. Dozens of pictures fail in competitions because of blur caused by moving the camera at the moment of exposure. This is perhaps the commonest fault of all.

There are right and wrong ways of releasing the shutter. The wrong one is by giving a sharp push, which results in the immediate response of the shutter—and shakes the camera. The right way is to increase the pressure of the finger slowly and continuously until the shutter fires. The pressure should be increased so gradually that you are not quite sure, to a tenth of a second or so, exactly when the shutter will be released.

When making exposures with the camera in the hand, it is a good plan to release the shutter just after breathing out. This prevents the camera from being shaken by your own breathing. When using a tripod, it is essential to use the wire release to prevent vibration of the hand from being transmitted to the camera; the release, if not pulled tight, will absorb any vibration.

The Body Release

Release buttons or triggers that are not situated on the shutter itself but on the body of the camera are usual, and are called body releases. Placing them on the body is an advantage, because if the shutter release of a folding camera is close to the lens, the movements of the hand involved in operating it make

54

it very likely that the camera will dip down at the instant of exposure, while with the release on the body a much firmer grip on the camera is possible, giving a much steadier action. All modern cameras, except the cheapest, have a body release. When choosing a camera, check that the release moves smoothly. Some of the cheaper cameras are not good in this respect, and in consequence are liable to give blurred pictures.

VIEWFINDERS

It is essential to know exactly what parts of the subject will appear on the negative. The perfect finder will include neither too much nor too little. The focusing screen of the stand camera comes up to this standard, for what is seen on the ground glass will automatically appear on the plate or film, which, in its dark slide, is put in the place of the ground glass. Consequently, for accurate, careful work, the ground glass is ideal. But a film camera, whether roll-film or miniature, cannot be fitted with a focusing screen, for its place is permanently occupied by the film, and so we have to use a viewfinder. This ought to show exactly the same picture as that found on the film, but it seldom does.

A good viewfinder should show a sharply-outlined picture, large, upright, not reversed from left to right, and including exactly what will be seen on the film. It is possible to fulfil all these requirements. The once widely used viewfinder, the " brilliant ", with its little sloping mirror (see sketch) is the least perfect type, especially when it is small. The eye-level tubular finder, as fitted to most of the better-grade modern cameras, is a great improvement on the brilliant, which makes it necessary to use the camera at waist level, but for reasons of space the tubular finder is usually rather too small. The older type of folding direct finder, for use at eye level, is better in this respect, but either can be accurate if well made.

Best of all is the ground glass as fitted to the single-lens reflex (Exakta; Agiflex) which always shows correctly what will be on the negative (see Fig. 54). The picture is, however, reversed from left to right, but one soon gets used to that. A further advantage is that parallax cannot possibly arise.

Fig. 81—(Left) Albada or " sports " viewfinder. (Right) The view through an Albada finder is seen life-size, with a white frame marking off the exact limits of the picture

55

Fig. 82—The universal viewfinder on the Leica shows the picture-field for lenses with focal lengths ranging from 3·5 to 13·5 cm. By turning the ring, a mask limiting the field of the picture is opened or closed to show what is included by the lens in use. To provide the accuracy needed with lenses of very long focus the Ploot reflex attachment is used

Parallax

The upper lens of a twin-lens reflex (Fig. 53) is called the finder lens. Compared with the taking lens, it has the same focal length, often a wider aperture, and—on that account—less depth of focus, which makes for very accurate focusing. However, the lens is more than an inch higher than the taking lens. So it "sees" the subject from a different point of view. The result of that difference is called parallax. The difference is small, but may nevertheless be troublesome in taking close-up pictures. The error can be rectified by pointing the camera a trifle higher than is apparently necessary according to the finder.

Depth of focus is not shown by the finder lens, because its aperture is wider than that of the taking lens. The depth of focus will therefore always be greater than is shown on the reflex picture; to find it exactly, which is not often necessary, reference has to be made to a table.

Of the many varieties of optical viewfinder, the Albada finder, designed by the Dutch scientist van Albada, and fitted to the Contax and some other cameras of the same make, is perhaps the best. It shows the limits of the

Fig. 83—The miniature as a reflex: this is the Contax with a reflex attachment between the camera body and a wide-aperture long-focus lens (Sonnar, 18 cm, f/2·8). The picture is viewed through a five-times magnifier. When exposing, the mirror hinges up first and then the focal-plane shutter fires. Some kind of camera support is essential with these lenses of very long focus

picture just as sharply as the picture itself, making it an ideal instrument not only for sports pictures but for all branches of photography. The picture is seen clearly in natural size, making it possible to keep both eyes open. " Floating frame " or " bright-line " finders, though optically quite different, share the same advantages.

The more expensive miniatures have different viewfinders for lenses of different focal lengths. Parallax can be corrected by tilting the viewfinder down to direct it at the object focused upon. However these viewfinders are hardly

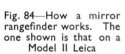

Fig. 84—How a mirror rangefinder works. The one shown is that on a Model II Leica

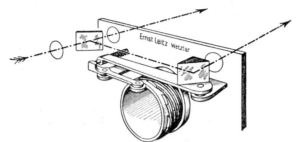

accurate enough for tele-lenses, and this is the reason why the manufacturers have reverted to the ground-glass picture, and make use of reflex attachments.

Taking all in all, there can be little doubt that the single-lens reflex provides the best viewfinder. The subject is both clearly seen and sharply focused on the screen.

For exactly the same reasons, the combined viewfinder and rangefinder is the most nearly complete equivalent of the ground glass of the reflex. With this combination, a small bright spot is seen in the viewfinder picture, and within this the subject, if the lens is out of focus, is seen clearly but doubled, as two overlapping images. By altering the focusing adjustment of the lens one of these images slides over the other, and when the two images of some particular object fuse together to make a single clear image, the lens is exactly focused on that object.

RANGEFINDERS

Though it is by no means easy to make a rangefinder with the high precision needed, its principle is quite simple. The schematic drawing of Fig. 84 shows two rays of light from the subject passing through the two rangefinder windows, one towards the left and one towards the right of the camera. The angle between the two rays is a measure of the distance of the subject. The right-hand ray falls on a mirror or prism that reflects it to the left, where a semi-transparent mirror reflects it into the eye-piece. The ray reaching the left window passes directly *through* this mirror, and also enters the eye-piece, so that both rays are seen at once. The eye therefore sees two pictures of one object. If now the prism at the right, which is mounted on a pivot, is made, by a system of levers, to turn slightly as the lens is moved in and out for focusing, the whole mechanism can be adjusted so that when the lens is focused on an object the two images of that object exactly coincide.

57

This is the principle of the coupled rangefinder, which works most accurately. When combined with the viewfinder, the handling of the camera is hardly less simple and certain than that of one using a focusing screen, and has the additional advantage of greater rapidity and ease in use. Nevertheless, a camera fitted with a coupled rangefinder and a separate viewfinder is exceedingly satisfactory too.

Instead of the tilting mirror or prism, a more elegant solution of the problem has been achieved in some cameras by means of revolving wedges or a prism of variable angle. These need less precise construction, but the effect remains the same. A much less expensive plan is to use an uncoupled rangefinder, which may be built into the camera or just clipped on. It measures the distance, and then the lens-focusing is set to match. It is slower in use than a coupled rangefinder, but no less accurate.

A number of miniature cameras, including the Contax, Leica and Reid, as well as several less expensive instruments, allow of the easy interchangeability of lenses, which are all coupled to the same rangefinder. This advantage is shared with the single-lens reflex cameras, in which any lens that may be fitted throws its image on to the same ground glass.

The Leica has a bright-line finder: the whole of the field corresponds to the 3·5 cm wide-angle lens, and the bright line outlines the field of the normal 5 cm lens. On replacing this with a 9 cm or 13·5 cm lens a new bright line, correct for the field of the lens in use, makes its appearance. There is automatic parallax correction, and the rangefinder spot is always in the centre of the field.

CAMERA ACCESSORIES

Camera Cases, Dark Slides, and Film Adapters

A good case to protect the camera against rain, sun and dust is most essential. A very convenient type is the " ever-ready " case (Fig. 85), from which the camera does not have to be taken for use.

The miniature camera uses cassettes which the user can refill with 35 mm film, bought either in 36-exposure lengths ready cut and trimmed, or in uncut lengths of up to 100 ft or even more. Non-reloadable cassettes, ready loaded with film, can also be bought; the cassette is meant to be thrown away after use, but many people keep and refill them. A good supply of cassettes is a very great convenience.

For plate cameras, dark slides each holding one or two plates are used, but an adapter for roll films is a very desirable extra. The " ammunition " for roll-film cameras is too familiar to need describing, but a few such cameras, with the aid of a special back, will take plates in dark slides; and for one camera, the Rolleiflex, special accessories to enable 35 mm film to be used (Fig. 87) can also be obtained.

Store empty dark slides or cassettes in a box in order to keep them safe from damage. The fronts of dark slides should be removed to keep the plush springy. Loaded slides and cassettes should be kept with the camera ready for immediate use.

58

(Above) Fig. 85—Ever-ready case. When the cover is hinged down, the camera is fully accessible for use

(Top right) Fig. 86—Plaubel roll-film adapter

(Right) Fig. 87—Rolleiflex accessories. Top, special back and dark slide for using plates. Bottom, accessories equipping the camera for 35 mm film

The cassettes for miniature cameras *must* be loaded correctly. Read the instruction booklet for your camera carefully. Practise with a length of old film until the cassette can be loaded easily; then try to do it blindfold or in the dark. Once you have learnt this you will be able to load your cassettes with film in your own darkroom from film bought in uncut lengths 15 or 30 ft long. To load a cassette from film bought in this way costs hardly more than half as much as a ready-filled cassette, and even a ready-trimmed " darkroom loading refill " costs only a few coppers more than a 36-exposure strip cut from the length. Naturally it is much easier to handle than bulk film.

The standard 35 mm cassettes consist of a spool surrounded by a casing in which there is a slot for the film to pass through. To prevent entry of light this slot has a velvet-lined edge, which is not always free from dust. Users of Leica, Reid and Contax cameras should use the all-metal self-opening cassettes made for these cameras: these have no plush or velvet, and cannot cause scratches. Cassettes on the same principle (Shirley-Wellard) can be used

Fig. 88a—Modern tripod (Schiansky) with centre pillar, enabling the camera to be raised or lowered easily.

Fig. 88b—Studio-type tripod, sturdy, adjustable and compact, ideal for home use

in quite a number of cameras intended for standard cassettes. Colour film is also sold in standard cassettes and most makes cannot be bought in uncut lengths, although refills can be had in one or two makes.

There are holders for roll film that fit on to the back of a plate camera in place of a dark slide, converting it into a roll-film camera which still allows the focusing screen to be used when desired. Such adapters are seldom seen in sizes other than $3\frac{1}{4} \times 2\frac{1}{4}$ in, and adapters of this size are often used on quarter-plate or 9 × 12 cm cameras. Adapters for film-packs (12 flat films in a daylight-loading package) are also sometimes used, but film in this form is so very much more expensive than in the more usual roll that film-packs are now very seldom met. Indeed most makers have not resumed production of them since the end of the war.

Tripods and Other Supports

One of the most important accessories is the tripod. A strong, simple tripod is best. This is indispensable for many subjects. Few tripods are sturdy enough to render real service. A 16 mm ciné-camera tripod with a revolving top is excellent. There are also wooden tripods with legs in two parts, one sliding within the other. These are usually very steady. A revolving tripod head on a tripod of this type makes a really excellent combination. Still better and heavier are the studio-type tripods with revolving heads, many of which have an adjustable centre column (Fig. 88).

Always take a pocket tripod or some kind of camera support out with you whenever you take your camera. This often helps you to take a photograph that otherwise would be impossible (see Fig. 280).

The " unipod ", as Fig. 90 shows, is a single long leg, usually telescopic for portability. When slow exposures (up to $\frac{1}{4}$ sec) have to be given, but a tripod

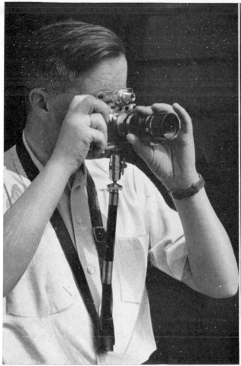

Fig. 89—Chest-pod with ball and socket head. A chest-pod is the minimum support you should use for exposures of 1/20 sec or longer

Fig. 90—The unipod: one stage steadier, but one stage less convenient, than the chest-pod

cannot be used, it often saves the situation.

Many pictures taken at shutter speeds between $\frac{1}{2}$ and $\frac{1}{50}$ second are blurred through camera movement. A " chest-pod " (Fig. 89) is a great help in such work, and is especially valuable with miniature cameras, particularly when using long-focus lenses, the enlarged images of which are blurred by even the slightest camera shake. When using a chest-pod or unipod, but especially with the former, it is a good plan to lean against a wall or other support whenever possible, as this prevents swaying of the body.

The Lens Hood

Never forget your lens hood. Use it for every exposure you make. It keeps stray light from the lens, and by so doing makes every picture clearer and brighter, especially with a bloomed or coated lens. For the same reason, keep your lens well cleaned.

Fig. 91—A leather extension hood in use over the focusing screen

61

Fig. 92—"DAWN". An attractive study in light and shade, taken near Exeter

Light and Your Subject

Amidst all these technical pages about finders and other details comes a personal word from the author to the reader. The best of viewfinders will be of no use to you if you are blind to subjects that will make pictures. Your perceptions must be as sensitive as the film in your camera.

If a lovely sunset does not move you, or you are not yet awake to the beauty in the play of light on the fair head of a child, let me urge you to wait awhile with your pictures and learn to see first. Watch the mist rising towards evening, or sunlight glittering on a moist cobweb. Wander through country lanes, enjoying atmosphere and silence, and gradually you will see subjects that never attracted you before. Maris, a great Dutch painter, once said: " I do not paint cows, I paint light falling on their backs! " He saw in terms of light, and you must learn to do this too.

Notice how a building can look bright and friendly one day and stern and gloomy the next, simply as a result of a change in lighting. Pay attention to the relation between light and shadow. Look at a subject with light falling on it from the side, then from the front and then from behind. See the difference between light and shadow on a cloudy summer day and on a day with clear blue sky. Open your eyes to the beauty of changing light as it grows from early morning to bright midday and fades again in the quiet evening. Visit picture galleries, and see what great painters can do with light. Associate with artists, and learn from them.

In such ways you can really progress in photography, and in the end make truly artistic pictures.

4 LENSES

IN this chapter we will discuss what the photographer needs to know about optics—always keeping an eye on practical needs. Camera lenses are intended for taking pictures, not as excuses for doing arithmetic. Yet one has to know something about one's lens in order to make the most of it. It is not our aim to discuss the aberrations or faults of lenses, but to help the amateur to *use* the lens, and in doing this we shall try to deal with lenses clearly, simply, and without any formulae or other complications. We will study them with the help of photographs.

The whole matter can be put quite simply, but the following points should be carefully noted as they will constantly be reappearing. As early in this book as Fig. 3 we saw what was meant by focal length. The boy with his burning glass, which of course is a lens, moves it to and fro until the image of the sun appears small and brilliant. The distance from the lens to this point is called the focal length, indicated by the letter f. Every lens has its individual focal length, which is a fixed property of the lens and does *not* vary, as beginners sometimes think, as the lens is moved towards or away from the film in focusing.

The normal lens of a miniature camera taking pictures 24 × 36 mm has a focal length of 2 in (50 mm); it is inscribed "f = 50 mm." The lens of a 2¼ × 3¼ in camera usually

Fig. 93—Sun, lens, focus and focal length f

has a focal length of 100 mm (4 in) and is marked "f = 100 mm."

If we photograph a church tower, first with one camera and then with the other, we shall find that the tower is exactly twice as high in the 3¼ × 2¼ picture as in that taken with the miniature. In other words, the size of the image is in direct proportion to the focal length; and with a lens of twice the focal length the picture will be twice as big. If we used a professional camera with a 500 mm (20 in) lens, then the tower on the ground glass would be ten times as large as the image of it on the miniature negative taken with the 50 mm lens.

If we put the lens of a small camera, for instance a 50 mm lens, on a large camera (Fig. 94), we shall see on the ground glass a bright circular picture which darkens towards the edges. From that bright part we select a part to make the picture. The circle of illumination, as it is called, is larger the greater the focal length of the lens. The image is best in the centre, so the portion chosen will always be central. It is clear that a square shape will be best if it is desired to use the greatest possible area of the available image.

Fig. 94—A 50 mm lens in a 9 × 12 cm camera gives this circular picture. Of the centre part, a section measuring 24 × 36 mm is used for the picture in the miniature camera. All lenses yield a circular field, of which a larger or smaller part is used for the rectangular or square picture

Standard Focal Lengths

For every different negative size there is a standard or " normal " focal length; except in a very few special cases, any camera one may buy will have a lens with focal length as shown in the following table:—

Miniature cameras	f = 50 mm. Picture size 24 × 36 mm
Miniature cameras for roll films ..	f = 50 mm. Picture size 3 × 4 cm
V.P. cameras	f = 75 mm. Picture size 4 × 6·5 cm
6 × 6 cm folding cameras, twin-lens reflexes, and most single-lens reflexes	f = 75 mm. Picture size 6 × 6 cm
2¼ × 3¼ in (6 × 9 cm)	f = 105 mm
3¼ × 4¾ in (9 × 12 cm)	f = 135 mm (usually) or 150 or sometimes 180 mm

Angle of View

If we make two pictures from the same point, one with a miniature and the other with a 6 × 6 cm reflex (Figs. 95 and 97), the miniature will include less of the subject than the reflex. This is because of the difference in angle of view.

The square picture of the reflex shows more, not only at the top and bottom, but also at the sides. The angle of view depends on the focal length of the lens in relation to the size of the picture.

Fig. 96 shows the same view again with the statue looking very far away. This is a miniature picture taken with a wide-angle lens, which, as its name implies, includes a wide angle of view, so taking in more of the subject than does a normal lens. The wide angle is due to its shorter focal length of 35 mm. In the sketch below the photograph, the size of the picture, namely 24 × 36 mm, is shown. The lens is only 35 mm away from the film, so that, as the dotted lines show, the 3·5 cm wide-angle lens covers a fairly large area. The 50 mm lens covers a somewhat smaller angle, because its focal length is a little longer. The 90 mm lens includes still less of the subject, but since in every case the picture formed by these lenses is received on the 24 × 36 mm film, it is evident that if the picture taken with the 90 mm lens includes less, each individual object must be shown as being larger (Fig. 98). It is like looking through a

Fig. 95—Taken with a twin-lens reflex, using a 7·5 cm lens and 6 × 6 cm film. Figs. 95 to 98 are all taken from the same point in front of Buckingham Palace

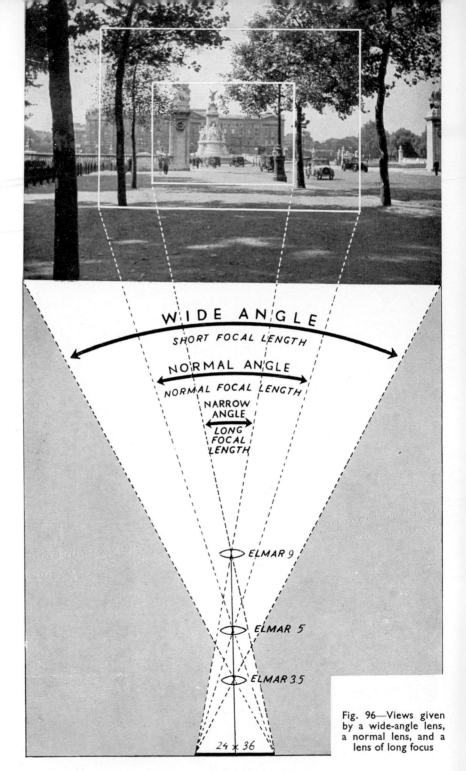

WIDE ANGLE

SHORT FOCAL LENGTH

NORMAL ANGLE

NORMAL FOCAL LENGTH

NARROW ANGLE

LONG FOCAL LENGTH

ELMAR 9

ELMAR 5

ELMAR 3.5

24 × 36

FILM SIZE

Fig. 96—Views given by a wide-angle lens, a normal lens, and a lens of long focus

Fig. 97—Taken with a normal 50 mm lens

Fig. 98—The long-focus lens (f=90 mm) includes less of the surroundings, but enlarges individual objects

telescope, through which only a small part of the landscape is seen, but that small part is enlarged.

Hence the following rule:

> *Long-focus lens: includes little, but makes it large.*
> *Wide-angle (short-focus) lens: includes much, but makes it small.*

This is clearly seen in Fig. 96, which shows what is included on a 24 × 36 mm negative with the 35 mm wide-angle lens, the 50 mm normal lens and the 90 mm long-focus lens. On the first picture the statue in the centre is small, but more than the whole palace is included. With the long-focus lens the statue appears larger, but the trees left and right are now left out. Notice that the square reflex picture (Fig. 95) covers a good deal, the lens having a more or less wide-angle effect.

It is clear that when using lenses of different focal lengths on one camera the viewfinder must be adjustable to show the different fields of the various lenses accurately.

Choice of Viewpoint

(A fly on your spectacles can blot out a cathedral!)

The choice of viewpoint is of great importance. Imagine that we stand in the garden of a big building, and that in the garden is a sundial. The building, naturally, is big and the sundial small. Fig. 99 gives an impression of their relative sizes. For the first experiment we place the camera quite close to the sundial. The resulting photograph shows a large image of the sundial (Fig. 100), but the building has shrunk so far that it is hard to recognize it. In the next picture (Fig. 101), the sundial is shown much smaller, but the house here seems much bigger again.

The camera does not lie. Fig. 101 is the result of placing the camera much farther away and using a lens of long focus. The relative sizes of the different parts of the picture have in consequence been altered completely. This is *not* because of the change of lens, as is sometimes thought, but purely because of the change in viewpoint. If, from the viewpoint chosen, the top of the sundial is seen against the window (Figs. 99 and 101) or its centre against the roof (Fig. 100), the lens can but photograph it so. If we had used the lens of shorter focus in the position from which Fig. 101 was taken, the relative proportions would have been exactly as in Fig. 101, but the picture would have included more, as can be seen by comparing Figs. 101 and 99.

It should now be clear that, by placing the camera at different points and using lenses of different focal length—or even by enlarging up part of a negative if we have no long-focus lens—we can control the relative sizes of the various objects included in our photograph. By so doing we can control also the message and spirit of the picture we are making. *Choice of viewpoint is vitally important.*

The next two illustrations (Fig. 102) of the windmill tell the same story. In one (with the horse) the tree is near and large, while the much more distant windmill is small. Further, we get the impression that the field where the

Fig. 99—The garden in which the two photographs below were taken

Fig. 100—A large sundial and a small house　　Fig. 101—A large house and a small sundial

THE SAME TREE

Fig. 102—The relative sizes of foreground and background on the camera position. (Left) Taken with normal lens, camera not far from tree. (Right) Taken from much farther away with a tele-lens

horse is grazing is quite large. For the next picture the camera was taken back a good way and a lens of longer focus was used. As a result the windmill has been made to appear large, the tree seems much smaller, and the field has apparently shrunk to a breadth of a yard or two. Once again, it is all a question of choice of viewpoint.

On the whole it can be said that such differences mostly occur when using wide-angle lenses, as they exaggerate perspective. A wide-angle lens used to photograph an ordinary room has the unpleasant effect of making subjects close by appear unnaturally large while those farther away are shown small. So a wide-angle lens should be used only when there is no alternative; that is, when it is impossible to get the camera far enough back to include all that is wanted in the picture.

This leads to a special warning: do not take portraits with a short-focus lens. As we have already seen, they include a great deal of the subject, but show it all very small. To obtain a large picture of a head using a short-focus lens, the camera has to be brought close up to the sitter. The result is that the parts of the face which are nearest to the lens, such as nose and mouth, are shown quite large, while the features farther away are shown too small in comparison. These differences of scale throw the face out of proportion, and this effect is clearly noticeable in a portrait taken from too near a viewpoint. With the camera farther away, we shall get a much more natural picture.

70

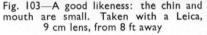

Fig. 103—A good likeness: the chin and mouth are small. Taken with a Leica, 9 cm lens, from 8 ft away

Fig. 104—Mouth and chin too big as a result of using a reflex with portrait attachment. The camera was less than 3 ft from sitter

Fig. 105—A neck like a giraffe

Fig. 106—That tiny Leica !

Fig. 105 was taken with 6 × 6 cm reflex close to the horse's head. The distortion vanishes when the eye is brought to 3 or 4 in from the print. Any photograph is seen in true perspective if the eye is at a distance from it equal to the focal length of the lens used. (For enlargements, multiply focal length by enlarging factor.)

When using, for example, a 6×6 cm reflex, the lens of which includes rather a wide angle of view, we have to take the camera well back from the sitter and be content with a small portrait with many unimportant items around it, and then enlarge just as much of the negative as we want, omitting the rest. Or we can use a miniature or a stand camera with a lens of focus long enough to fill the negative with just as much of the head and shoulders as we wish to include. We shall then not be troubled with distortion. *Never* use a portrait attachment for taking portraits.

This over-accentuation of perspective through too close an approach to the subject is not limited to portraits, as Fig. 105 shows. The camera was too near, so the horse is shown with a ridiculously large head and a very small body. Such subjects should always be taken from farther away, either enlarging only the centre of the negative, or excluding unwanted objects in advance by using a long-focus lens.

Of course this effect can be turned to account for comic pictures, as the photograph (Fig. 106) of the Leica shows. The Leica is larger than the owner's head, and yet we all know that in reality it is a very small camera. It is clear how the effect was produced; the Leica was held in a hand stretched out so far towards the camera as to make it large in comparison with the head behind it.

Focusing

There is a bottle on the table (Fig. 107) which I want to focus sharply on the ground glass of a stand camera. Light rays from the bottle pass through the lens and converge to a point at a certain distance behind it. If the ground glass is placed exactly where the rays converge, the image will be sharp (see middle picture). If the ground glass is placed just nearer to the lens than this point of sharp focus, it will cut the cone of rays a little short of its tip, as shown on the left, and there will be a circle of light, instead of a point, on the screen. This is called a circle of confusion and because of it the image is unsharp. If the focusing screen is placed just behind the point of the cone, as shown on the right, then again the rays do not converge on to the screen, and once more the image is blurred.

Fig. 108 shows the principles of focusing in rather greater detail. Here there are three things, all at slightly different distances from the camera: a Leica, a cactus in a pot, and (farthest from the camera) the bottle. We see the lens again, and behind it the focusing screen in three positions. First the camera is focused accurately on the object nearest to the lens, which is the Leica; it should be noticed that, of the three positions, this is the one with the focusing screen farthest from the lens. This is position 1. Next comes position 2. This time the camera is focused on the cactus, and it will be seen that the screen is nearer to the lens. Now the last position, 3. Here the camera is focused on the bottle, and for this the screen has to come still nearer the lens —but meanwhile the cactus and the Leica have become blurred.

From these experiments it is clear that every different distance between object and lens necessitates a corresponding different distance between the lens and the focusing screen or film. An easy way to remember this is to imagine a big fierce dog in front of the lens and a nervous little one behind. If the big dog moves away from the lens, the little one plucks up courage to come a little nearer; if the big dog approaches, the little one backs away again.

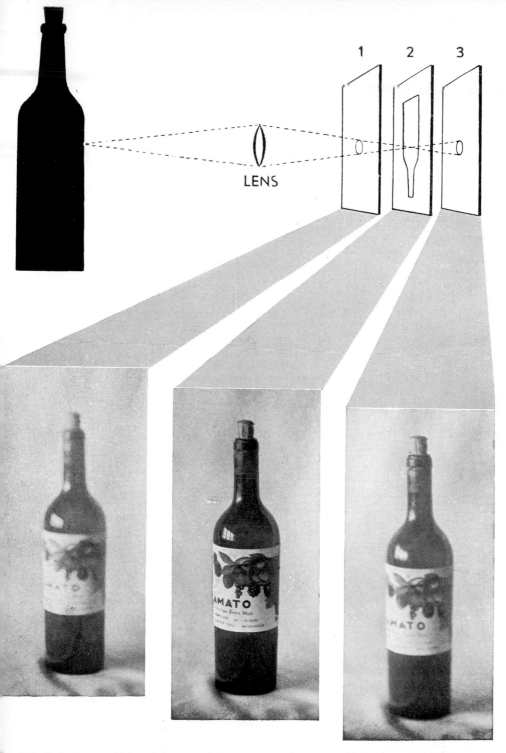

LENS

Fig. 107—Only in one position of the ground glass is the bottle sharp. In all other positions the ground glass cuts the beam of light rays, with the result that there is a big patch of light—a circle of confusion

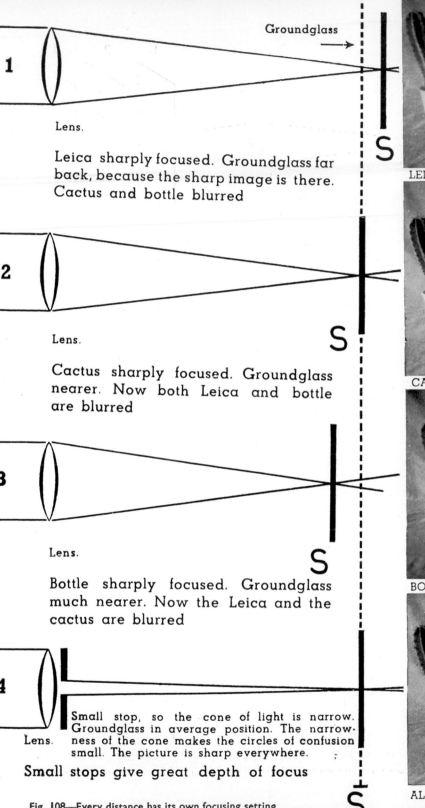

1

Lens.

Groundglass →

Leica sharply focused. Groundglass far back, because the sharp image is there. Cactus and bottle blurred

2

Lens.

Cactus sharply focused. Groundglass nearer. Now both Leica and bottle are blurred

3

Lens.

Bottle sharply focused. Groundglass much nearer. Now the Leica and the cactus are blurred

4

Lens.

Small stop, so the cone of light is narrow. Groundglass in average position. The narrowness of the cone makes the circles of confusion small. The picture is sharp everywhere.

Small stops give great depth of focus

Fig. 108—Every distance has its own focusing setting

LEICA SHARP

CACTUS SHARP

BOTTLE SHARP

ALL THREE SHARP

The distance between lens and screen can be varied just as well by moving the lens as by moving the screen to and fro. This is in fact the method used in most cameras.

How can we get all the three objects of our still-life picture sharp at once? This is where the stops come in: we just stop down. That is, we reduce the size of the opening in the lens. It may be thought that the stops are for controlling the amount of light entering the camera: that on the beach one would use a small stop, while in a shady place the lens should be set wide open. This is good advice for a box camera with only one shutter speed, but in all other cases the stops should be thought of as a control of depth of focus, and only secondarily as a control of light.

Position 4 in Fig. 108 shows what happens when the lens is closed down to a small aperture; all three objects at once are sharp on the screen. The camera is focused on the middle object, the cactus, and the lens stopped down to about f/36. Now the circles of confusion are so small that there is sharpness enough both behind and in front of the position of precise focus.

This then is what the stops are for: to give depth of focus.

For sharp rendering of objects both far and near, use a small stop.

Lens Speed

There are several figures on the front of a lens. The Elmar lens of a Leica, for example, is marked "f/3·5, f = 5 cm." This last, f — 5 cm, means the focal length of this lens is 5 cm and the other figures indicates its speed.

What does speed mean as applied to a lens? If we look at the focusing screen of a camera while reducing the stop, we shall see the image growing darker. This is obvious, as a big opening passes more light than a small one. The more light a lens passes, the faster the shutter can be run in taking a photograph: a lens that passes plenty of light is called a " fast " lens, or one of high " speed." The number 3·5 on the Elmar shows exactly how fast it is when wide open.

This speed depends partly on the area of the lens and partly on its focal length. To make this clear, let us take the simple example of a room. This room has a small window by the light of which a book can be read at a distance of a yard or so, but at the back of the room it is too dark to read. If a bigger window is put in, the book can be read there quite well. So both the size of the window and the distance between it and the book affect the amount of light there is to read by. The amount of light can, in fact, be measured by the ratio of the area of the window to the distance from it of the book. The book that could be read at a yard from the small window can equally well be read at four yards from one of four times the size. It is the same in the camera. Of two lenses with the same focal length and different diameter, that with the smaller diameter will pass less light.

Think of two rooms, one with a window a yard square and another with a window two yards square. If a book is placed at a distance of one yard from each, the second book will be four times as brightly lit as the first, for in the first case there is one square yard to illuminate the book, and the second four square yards.

The same thing holds for lenses. The amount of light passed by lenses is proportional to the squares of their stop numbers. If one lens is marked

6

AT ONE YARD
FROM THE WINDOW:
VERY EASY TO READ

AT ONE YARD
FROM THE WINDOW:
EASY TO READ

FURTHER FROM THE WINDOW
STILL ENOUGH LIGHT

FURTHER FROM THE WINDOW: DARK

Fig. 109—Showing that both area
of window and distance from
control the light received

f/3·5 and a smaller lens f/8, then the exposures needed are proportional to the squares of these numbers, being 3·5 × 3·5 = 12·25 and 8 × 8 = 64; that is, a proportion of 12·25 to 64 or 1 to 5.

With the f/8 lens the exposure must be five times as long to give the same result on the negative. (The picture taken at f/8, however, is sharper, especially in depth.)

Though the movement of the iris diaphragm of a lens is continuous, so that it can be set at every possible value between the highest and the lowest, there are certain " stopping points " recognized for convenience. The standard series of stop numbers has been chosen so that at each stop from one to the next the amount of light passed is halved, and the exposure consequently has to be doubled. This gives us the following table:

Stop number	1	1·4	2	2·8	4	5·6	8	11	16	22	32
Relative exposure	1	2	4	8	16	32	64	128	256	512	1,024

These are the numbers usually met with, but naturally any in-between number could be used. Some lenses do not " begin " with one of these numbers, but with f/3·5, f/4·5 or f/6·3. To find how much longer to expose with an f/4·5 lens than with an f/4 lens, square both numbers and compare the results. In this case we get 4·5 × 4·5 = 20·25 and 4 × 4 = 16, giving a proportion of 20·25 to 16, or about 5 to 4. So if $\frac{1}{5}$ second is the right exposure at f/4, $\frac{1}{4}$ second will be needed at f/4·5. Similarly, the exposures at f/3·5 and f/4 are in the proportion 3 to 4, at f/6·3 and f/5·6 in the proportion 5 to 4 again. Such comparisons can be made between any pair of stop numbers.

In considering any individual lens, it is easy to see that as the stop is opened more light is passed and less exposure is needed. In comparing two lenses

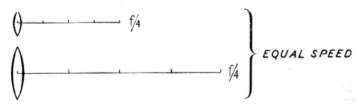

Fig. 110—The stop number depends not only on the diameter of the lens opening, but also on the distance from the lens at which the image is formed. Although one of the lenses shown above is larger than the other, the images they form are equally bright. They both work at f/4

of different focal lengths the relationships, though less obvious, are equally simple. If the focal length of the second lens is greater, the image formed will be bigger, so the light must be distributed over a larger area. Therefore a lens with a diameter of 10 mm and a focal length of 80 mm has the same speed as a lens with a diameter of 20 mm and a focal length of 160 mm. Both lenses work at a stop of f/8, for f numbers are determined as in Fig. 110. *The diameter is divided into the focal length.*

It follows that the tiny lens of a 16 mm movie-camera may be a good deal faster (that is, work at a smaller f number) than a great barrel of a lens on a professional's big portrait camera.

Sometimes one comes into possession of an old lens with no stop numbers marked on it. In that case, the approximate focal length must firstly be found; this is done by putting the lens into a camera and focusing on a distant object. The distance between the focusing screen and the diaphragm is approximately equal to the focal length (except with a telephoto lens).

Suppose this is found to be 8 in. Then measure the diameter of the diaphragm; perhaps this is $1\frac{1}{4}$ in. The f number will then be $8 \div 1\frac{1}{4}$ or approximately f/6·3.

Depth of Focus

The experiments in focusing (Fig. 108) showed that the cone of light becomes narrower when the stop is made smaller. The circles of blur on the focusing screen also become smaller and sharper. If they are as small as $\frac{1}{10}$ mm, or $\frac{1}{250}$ in, each circle appears to be a point.

Reducing the aperture, or " stopping down," as it is always called, gives a greater depth of focus. Our reference tables (page 265) include tables of depth of focus for lenses of the usual focal lengths. It will be noticed that beyond the point focused the depth is considerable; on the camera side it is small.

That depth of focus is greater beyond the point of sharp focus is made clear in Fig. 111. Three objects are shown; a church tower in the distance,

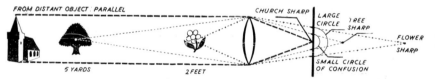

Fig. 111—Why depth of focus is greater towards the distance

from which the rays falling on the lens are parallel, then there is an object some 12 ft away, and finally one very close to the lens. The focusing point for the near object lies much farther back than that for the object at 12 ft. That this distance increases rapidly as the object approaches is an optical law. The closer the object is to the lens, the farther behind the lens is the sharp image, as can be seen at once simply by looking at the focusing scale of a camera (one is shown in Fig. 112). For focusing on an object at a distance of 15 or

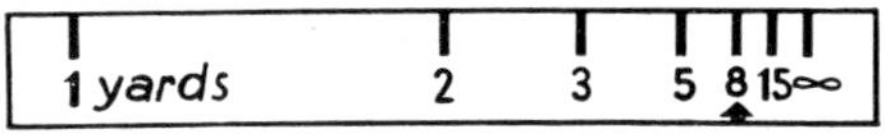

Fig. 112 — A focusing scale

8 yards the lens is advanced but little from the infinity point (marked ∞) correct for distant objects.

When focusing on an object at one yard it has to be advanced much farther. In the first position of the ground glass the circles of confusion, where the

78

TWO FOCUSING RULES

For everyday use, elaborate tables of depth of focus are not wanted. So, as depth cannot be ignored, here are two suggestions. With a touch of red paint make a special mark on the focusing ring of the camera at the distances 9 m and 4 m (30 ft and 12 ft).

RULE 1

To get both the background and a near object sharp set the focusing to 9 m (30 ft) and stop the lens down to f/8.

For General Work:

If your camera is:	You will get sharp focus
A miniature	From 12 ft to infinity
6 × 6 or V.P. size ...	From 15 ft to 200 ft
3¼ × 2¼ with 10·5 cm lens	From 16 ft to 70 ft

This is effective for most subjects over 10 ft away; especially landscapes, street scenes, and buildings.

RULE 2

For near subjects set focusing to 4 m (12 ft), and stop down to f/8.

Close-up Subjects:

The zone of sharpness then extends:	
With a miniature ...	from 7 ft 6 in to 30 ft
With a 6 × 6 or V.P. camera	from 9 ft to 20 ft
For 3¼ × 2¼ camera with 10·5 cm lens	from 10 ft to 16 ft

Drill yourself thoroughly in these two rules. They will help you enormously. You will take a sharp picture while others are still fumbling with their focusing. Always use f/8.

1. Meniscus

Shows every possible aberration. Usable at f/13

2. Achromat

Combination of two lenses. Corrected for colour. Works quite well at f/11

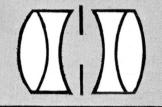

3. Aplanat or Rapid Rectilinear

Two achromats, one each side of the diaphragm. Many aberrations eliminated but not astigmatism. f/7.7.

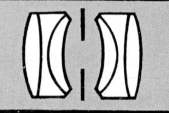

4. Double anastigmat

Fully-corrected lens. Maximum aperture f/6.8. Each half can be used separately as long-focus lens

5. Triplet

Anastigmat of high resolution. Tessar–Elmar type f/3.5

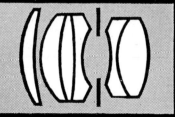

6. Ultra-fast miniature Lens

Sonnar-type with excellent corrections Aperture f/1.5 to f/2

Fig. 113a—A modern Synchro-Compur shutter with automatic depth of field indicator. The red pointers at ∞ and 4 m, which separate or come together as the stop is closed or opened, indicate the depth, for any distance, on the focusing scale itself

screen cuts through the cone of rays, become bigger and hence less sharp. It is for this reason that objects near the lens are blurred.

Lens Quality

If the amateur wishes to compare two lenses, a simple but effective plan is to put the two cameras in turn on a tripod and photograph from the front a house with a flat facade, choosing a time when sunlight is coming from the side.

This will show whether the lens yields a picture sharp right into the corners. Pictures taken with the camera in the hand are not reliable on account of the possibility of camera shake.

Stops and Tones of Prints

There is a curious misunderstanding one often comes across to the effect that the overall depth of tone of the picture is influenced by the choice of stop. It is thought that a photograph taken with a large aperture gives a print which is clearer and brighter than one taken with a small stop, and that a negative taken with a small aperture is more contrasty than one taken with a big aperture.

This misunderstanding apparently comes from the fact that when a large aperture is used the picture on the focusing screen is clear and bright, while it darkens as the iris diaphragm is closed. However, it is a mistake to believe that using a small diaphragm results in a darker print. It is true that if the exposure is not increased to compensate for the smaller stop, the negative will be underexposed and the print may indeed be dark; but if the exposure has been correctly lengthened to allow for the small stop (see table on page 77) the tone values of the picture remain exactly the same as when using a bigger aperture.

Evenness of Illumination

It is important that the corners of the film or plate should receive as much light as the centre. In pictures taken with box cameras dark corners are often seen. An example is shown in Fig. 115, where it is evident that the lens had

Fig. 114—Much can be learnt of the quality of a lens from using it in photographing a house, so long as the camera is carefully focused and the exposure made from a tripod

Fig. 115—The manufacturer of the camera with which this picture was taken used a lens with too small a circle of illumination. (See Fig. 94)

too short a focal length and that the manufacturer used too large a portion of the available circle. This results in dark corners. Any fault of this sort is especially to be avoided in colour photography, because if the corners receive less light, the colours there will be incorrectly rendered.

It should be noted, however, that dark corners are not always the fault of the maker of the lens or camera. A lens hood that is a little too long, or a little too narrow, is quite capable of cutting off some light from the corners of the picture. Sometimes a hood is satisfactory when used alone, but gives dark corners when made longer by being used over a filter. If two corners only are dark, the usual cause is a lens hood put on crookedly.

The designer of a modern lens pays close attention to the distribution of light. In general, the illumination is more even with a small stop than with a large one.

Coated Lenses

Sometimes we are surprised at the excellent results a beginner achieves in taking difficult subjects with a box camera. Users of expensive cameras go to great trouble to get similar results and often fail.

The box camera user's advantage in such cases lies in the simplicity of the lens he uses, for it has only one glass and works at a small stop. Naturally such a lens passes very little light, but in some directions this is an advantage. Complex lenses (see examples on page 80) are built up from several separate pieces of glass.

Now it is well-established that about 6 per cent of the light reaching each glass-air surface is lost by reflection, so it is clear that such a lens is in practice not so fast as its f number suggests: 6 per cent is lost at the first surface, leaving us 94 per cent; 6 per cent of that 94 per cent is in turn lost at the

Fig. 116—Patches of light, due to reflections within the lens, often appear when a picture is taken against the light.   (Sonnar f/1·5)

Fig. 117—The patches of light do not appear when a coated lens is used.
(Coated Sonnar f/1·5)

second surface, so that only 88·4 per cent of the light received passes through the first component glass. When using a lens with five separate glasses, about 46 per cent of the " incoming " light is sacrificed to " income-tax." Only 54 per cent remains.

Modern technique has found a way of reducing this loss. Exceedingly thin films are applied to the surfaces in the form of a transparent coating that appears blue-violet by reflected light. At a surface so " coated " (or " bloomed ") the loss is reduced from 6 per cent to 0·38 per cent. An appreciable increase of effective lens speed is thus achieved, for practically all the light that was previously reflected now passes through the lens.

An even more important advantage of the coated lens is the absence of internal reflections. With an ordinary lens, part of the light reflected forward from one surface is re-reflected into the camera by another surface, so degrading the whole picture by scattered light. If the subject includes any very bright object, it often happens that one such pair of reflections forms on the film a second image—usually a blurred one—of the object in question. This appears on the film as a blurred light circle (see Fig. 116) known as a " ghost " or " flare spot." Such effects are most often found when photographing against the light.

With a coated lens this trouble arises much less often, as the comparison pictures of Figs. 116 and 117 clearly show. The fewer surfaces a lens has, the less the chance of encountering flare or ghost images; the old type of double anastigmat (see drawing 4 facing page 81) is largely free from them. A miniature lens with eight surfaces is more likely to give flare than one with six surfaces.

The introduction of coating has made it possible for uncemented lenses with many surfaces to be designed without incurring this annoying and troublesome fault.

Interchangeable Lenses

For cameras with focal-plane shutters, lenses of other focal lengths are usually available for interchange with the normal lens. That, indeed, is why the focal-plane shutter was chosen. But it has its disadvantages (often no slow speeds, seldom reliable speeds between $1/5$ and $1/25$ second; inconvenient with flash), and to avoid them many modern cameras use a Compur-type shutter, even though this necessitates special lens-design. In some cameras the whole lens is mounted in front of the shutter, but always with its back glass almost touching the shutter leaves. It is then as easy to change lenses as with a focal-plane shutter.

More recently three makers (Schneider: Rodenstock: Zeiss) have produced lenses in which the shutter-leaves lie, as usual, between the components; to change focal lengths the front component (those glasses lying in front of the shutter) is removed and replaced by another giving either a wide-angle or a long-focus lens.

Bubbles in Lenses

Many an amateur with an expensive lens worries about the air bubbles it contains. There is no need for this, as these bubbles are almost unavoidable

84

in some kinds of optical glass. They cause no loss of sharpness and practically no loss of light. Professor Abbe, who introduced the optical glasses that made anastigmats possible, once had to deliver a large astronomical telescope. A member of the inspection committee made a remark about an air bubble in the lens. Abbe became so angry that he stuck a postage stamp on the centre of the lens and then asked the wiseacre to look through the eyepiece. He saw no sign of it. Bubbles in a lens make no more difference than did the stamp on the telescope.

Fig. 117a—Rodenstock Heligon lens with fixed back component and three interchangeable front components. Combinations given are 80 mm f/4, 35 mm f/5·6, and the normal lens is 50 mm f/2

Supplementary Lenses

The focal length of any lens can be altered by the use of a supplementary lens. These are ordinary spectacle glasses fitted in a mount to slip on to the front of the camera lens. Focal length can be increased or decreased at will by choosing a diminishing (negative) or magnifying (positive) supplementary. Supplementary lenses are sold to fit certain cameras, but one can quite well buy spectacle glasses of various focal lengths from any optician who knows something about photography.

There are special supplementary lenses calculated for lenses of particular makes, including the Distar and Proxar lenses made by Zeiss, the Voigtländer Focars, the Leitz supplementaries for the Leica, and others. Proxar lenses are positive and shorten the focal length, while Distar lenses are negative and lengthen it. The latter can only be used on those bellows cameras in which the lens can be moved well forward of its normal position. With miniature cameras, 6×6 cm reflexes, and the ordinary roll-film camera Distars in consequence cannot be used. But Proxars can.

A positive supplementary shortens the focal length of the lens to which it is attached, and is mostly used when the object is too near the camera to be

85

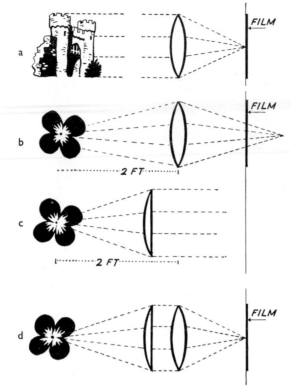

Fig. 118—Close-up focusing with a supplementary lens

focused sharply without extra aid. About 3 ft, or sometimes 5 ft, is as near as most cameras will focus.

Suppose it is desired to photograph a flower at a distance of 2 ft. Fig. 118a shows the light rays from a distant object converging on the film in the focal plane. The flower, however, is at 2 ft distance so that its image falls well behind the film (see Fig. 118b) and is unsharp.

To get the rays from the flower to meet in the focal plane they must be made parallel, like those from the distant object, before they reach the lens. This is easily done with a positive lens having a focal length equal to the distance between the flower and the camera lens; in this case 2 ft. Then, as in Fig. 118c, the rays from the flower will be rendered parallel. This exactly duplicates the state of affairs in Fig. 118a; the rays falling on the lens are parallel again and are once more refracted on to the film in the focal plane (Fig. 118d). The flower is sharply focused. It will be equally clear that if the flower were 1 ft away a positive lens of focal length 1 ft placed in front of the camera lens, the latter being focused at " infinity," would again give a sharp image of the flower.

It is important to notice that the quality of a lens is impaired by the use of supplementary lenses, and the image less sharp. Further, depth of focus becomes very small. The use of a small stop will help to rectify both these faults. Focusing with a supplementary lens in place can, of course, be done on the ground-glass screen when using a suitable camera, but most modern cameras have no focusing screen, so that special methods of focusing must be used.

For miniature cameras there are additional accessories such as the Contameter for the Contax, or the Nooky for the Leica, but close-up focusing with reflex cameras, either twin-lens or single lens, is quite simple, as the ground glass can again be used. With a twin-lens reflex a pair of matched supplementaries is used, one over each lens.

Fig. 119—The Nooky: an accessory for close-up focusing with the Leica

Fig. 120—A picture made with the Nooky. A small stop is essential for sharpness

Portrait attachments are supplementary lenses for near focusing, and were originally introduced for taking portraits with box cameras of the simplest type. One that gives sharp focus at 7 to 10 ft is a good investment for those whose cameras have no focusing movement, yet wish to take portraits. If the camera will already focus as near as this a portrait attachment to make it focus nearer still should on no account be used with it; at least, not for portraiture (see page 70). However, these attachments can be invaluable for other close-up subjects.

For some cameras with coupled rangefinders, optical devices of one pattern or another are available so that the rangefinder can still be used for focusing even when a supplementary close-up lens is in use. These, however, have mostly to be designed for the particular model of camera for which they are to be used, so only one is illustrated here (Fig. 119).

Anyone who is thinking of specializing in close-up work will do best with a camera so made that the actual image formed by the lens is seen on a focusing screen. If it is essential to use a miniature camera, as it might easily be if the only available enlarger will take nothing larger than miniature negatives, a single-lens reflex is the only possible type, and even in this rather restricted field it is best to choose one with a focal-plane shutter and a detachable lens. With this equipment, close-up focusing is easy, for one can insert an extension tube between lens and camera body for very near work. The picture seen on the screen is exactly that which will be recorded on the film; no allowance for parallax has to be made, as with the twin-lens reflex, in which viewing and

87

taking lenses survey the subject from different points of view. At a distance of a foot or so, this difference in viewpoint can be very important; it is not only a matter of equalizing fields of view, so that screen and negative contain the same part of the subject. The viewing lens may see the top surface of a small object where the taking lens sees only the front, and in any case the relationship of the object to its background is bound to be different from the two viewpoints.

For a few cameras of rangefinder type, reflex attachments can be had, but they can only be used with long-focus lenses, and so are rather limited in their application.

Where negative size is not important, a folding plate camera, still obtainable second hand at a very moderate price, will do as good work in this field as the most elaborate miniature, and it requires no accessories to help it. Its sole real disadvantage is that it is rather slow in use, but for most subjects taken in the home this does not matter.

Care of the Lens

The cap should be kept on every lens when the camera is not in use. Check that the lens is free from dust before making an exposure. If necessary, dust it. This may be done with a very soft camel-hair brush. Lenses should never be cleaned with wash-leather, as it sometimes contains pieces of grit. An old well-washed piece of fine linen, such as an old handkerchief, is better. Never use a handkerchief in current use.

In a damp climate little blue or iridescent patches, or even an all-over blue tint, sometimes appear on a lens due to the weathering of its surface. This is known as " bloom," and is usually completely harmless. At an early stage it is even an advantage, for the surface layer is closely similar to that artificially deposited on the modern coated lens (see page 82). But when the surface of the glass has deteriorated really badly, the lens must be returned to the makers for re-polishing.

Extra lenses for miniature or other cameras are best kept in their own special cases, or in the cardboard boxes in which they were supplied.

5 PLATES, FILMS AND FILTERS

PLATES and films form the sensitive material on which the image is thrown by the camera's lens.

In Fig. 121 the old-fashioned plate is shown with the two kinds of sensitive material now most popular: the roll film and the miniature-camera cassette of 35 mm film. The plate is often considered out of date, but is at the same time highly modern when it comes to producing a negative full of sharp detail. In our two-camera system plates hold an honoured place. The best size is quarter-plate ($4\frac{1}{4} \times 3\frac{1}{4}$ in) or 9×12 cm.

Roll films are used by millions for taking snapshots to serve as mementos. The sizes most widely used are the 127, or V.P. (Vest Pocket) size for pictures $6 \cdot 5 \times 4$ cm, and $3\frac{1}{4} \times 2\frac{1}{4}$ in. In the latter size there are two different spools, 120 and 620, the latter, which is more compact, being for special cameras. As few cameras will take both interchangeably, it is important to get the right one.

35 mm Film

Originally 35 mm film was only a cinema film but since the introduction of the Leica it has become widely used in miniature cameras. This film can be had in daylight-loading cassettes, filled and ready for use, in uncut lengths in tins holding up to 100 ft, for loading into cassettes, or ready-cut and trimmed in 36-exposure lengths of $1 \cdot 60$ m (5 ft 4 in). The longer lengths are the most practical and cheapest. For the necessary trimming of the end to shape, the trimming template (Fig. 122) will be found very convenient.

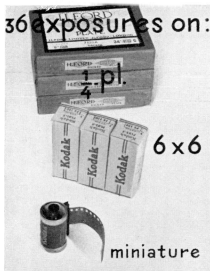

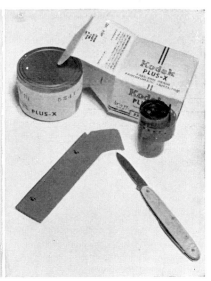

Fig. 121—The sensitive materials most frequently used: plates, roll films and miniature film

Fig. 122—A tin (5-metre size) of 35 mm film, a loaded cassette, trimming template and knife

Cut Film for Bigger Sizes: $2\frac{1}{4} \times 3\frac{1}{4}$ to 8×10 in

In cut film the base is made of thick celluloid instead of glass. Its chief advantages are unbreakability and light weight, for the sake of which this material is widely used in plate cameras by professional photographers. For the ordinary amateur, however, its only use is in the form of positive film (see page 180).

Some General Points

Beware of light is a safe rule in handling any negative material. The camera should never be loaded in full sunlight, but always indoors; but if this is impossible keep it at least in the shadow of your own body. Keep your camera cool and dry, not in a place where moisture, gas or steam can penetrate. The darkroom is unsuitable; use in preference a cupboard in the sitting room.

Keep your stock of unexposed films in a tin. Put the date on the outside immediately after purchasing, and use the films in the order in which they were purchased. The date of its expiry will always be found on the cardboard container in which the film is bought. This date is a year or two later than the date of manufacture. This gives more than enough time to use it, but in most cases the film remains usable for as long again. There is no expiry date on plates, but they will certainly last a few years. Paper does not usually keep so long; it can be relied on for one or two years at most.

Getting good results in photography is to a great extent a matter of habit. All makes of plates and films are of good quality, but they all have their different characteristics. These characteristics you have to learn. Choose a film of good make—if in doubt, ask your dealer what he recommends—*and keep to it.* If you do not succeed at first, do not change your film, but learn to know it. Except by chance, you are not likely to do better with another; on the contrary, a change will lose you the experience you have already gained.

FILM SPEED

We all know that there are different kinds of films, fast and slow. Why? Would not one kind of film be suitable for all work?

Look at page 91 with its four pictures. First the still-life, exceedingly sharp and full of fine detail. This was taken with a slow film, for the length of the exposure simply did not matter. It was taken on a film of speed 20° B.S., with 2 minutes' exposure. Here, with a none-too-sensitive film, we have the advantage of extremely fine grain and therefore great sharpness.

For the picture of the child a faster film was wanted as the exposure had to be shorter. The film used had a speed of 27° B.S.; the exposure was $\frac{1}{25}$ second. The grain is still unnoticeable.

Thirdly comes the sports picture, which was a very quick snapshot at $\frac{1}{500}$ second, using a film of speed 31° B.S. Any grain that might appear mattered little; the short exposure was essential.

The stage picture was given an exposure of $\frac{1}{100}$ second with a film of speed 37° B.S. Where very little light is available the fastest possible film is needed. Grain is secondary; to get any sort of picture is all that matters.

The films used here have British Standard numbers, which indicate sensitivity, running from 20° to 37°. The film marked 31° B.S. is more sensitive

Fig. 123—Four subjects and the films used for them:

(1) Still-life on ultra-fine-grain film of 20° B.S.
(2) A child study on fine-grain film of 27° B.S.
(3) " The Amazon " (Kodak Library) on a rapid film of 31° B.S.
(4) A stage picture on ultra-rapid panchromatic film of 37° B.S.

Beside each photograph is the D.I.N. speed scale made in a speed-testing laboratory. (The D.I.N. speed is uniformly 10 units lower than the B.S. speed.)   The arrow indicates the least useful density, and hence the speed of the film

than one marked 27° B.S. This highly-sensitive film is satisfied with a smaller amount of light than the less sensitive film, and still gives a good negative.

Each time the B.S. number of a film is increased by three, the exposure it needs is halved. So in circumstances where a film of speed 17° needs one second's exposure, the relative exposures for films of other speeds are as follows:

B.S. Speed			17	20	23	26	29	32	35
Relative Exposure			1	$\frac{1}{2}$	$\frac{1}{4}$	$\frac{1}{8}$	$\frac{1}{16}$	$\frac{1}{32}$	$\frac{1}{64}$

When light falls on a film and it is afterwards developed, the parts affected by light turn dark. The film contains silver bromide, and from this silver is separated in so finely-divided a form that it appears black—so long, of course, as the amount of light was not too small. One film will yield a deposit of silver with one amount of light while another, less sensitive, may need twice as much. If the speed of the first film is 27° B.S., that of the second is only 24° B.S. Three B.S. degrees less indicates half the speed. Three degrees more indicates double the speed.

It is often thought that the speed of a film—i.e., its sensitivity to light—is as easily measurable as the speed of a moving car. In fact, the measurement of film speed is quite a complex problem, and many methods have been used in the past and then discarded as insufficiently accurate. References to these methods will be found in older books, where film-speeds measured on the H. and D., Scheiner, Watkins, and Wynne systems are mentioned.

The modern method, based on researches carried out in the Eastman Kodak laboratories in America, is that set forth in the Standards issued by the American Standards Association and the British Standards Institution; it gives rise to A.S.A. or B.S. figures. The measurement is based on the least exposure that will give a satisfactory print, so that the speed-number, or " exposure index," closely represents practical needs. A.S.A. and B.S. figures are precisely interchangeable according to the table on page 259; the German DIN speeds are now measured in very nearly the same way, but the actual figure chosen to indicate the speed is always 10 units lower than the B.S. speed for the same film. Weston speeds, as used with the Weston meters, are differently determined, but in practice turn out to be practically identical with A.S.A. speeds.

But in calculating exposure do not forget that different workers like negatives of different character, and that the exposure to be given depends to some extent on the developer to be used. The only perfect plan is to calibrate your own exposure meter in terms of the particular film you use (see page 196). You may find you get the kind of negative that pleases you best by reckoning exposure on the basis of a speed-number considerably higher or lower than the official one for your film.

GRADATION

Put a table near the window, and place on the table the things seen in Fig. 125: a white mortar or dish, a crumpled napkin, a book, and a dark object such as a black hat. Let us begin by studying the subject—a good habit to

Fig. 124—" HIDE AND SEEK "

A very well-lit photograph, with the small model well framed in the curve of the pipe, the inside of which makes an excellent background. Weak evening sunlight, 1/100 sec at f/5·6

Fig. 125—Still-life for the study of tone values. It includes dark, light and intermediate tones

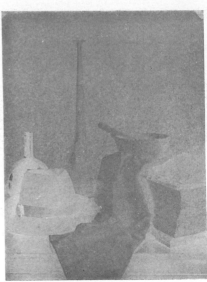

Fig. 126—A harsh negative: there is a
great difference between highlights and
shadows. A failure!

Fig. 127—A soft negative: here, little
difference is found between the various
tones. This is better than Fig. 126, but
more contrast is desirable

acquire. What is the highest light? The reflection of the window in the mortar. Next come the diffusely-lit parts of the napkin. The shadows of these objects are rather darker. Then comes a big difference, with the light parts of the book, and a still bigger one with the dark parts of the hat and brown bottle. There is thus a whole series of tints, from very light to very dark, and this we must reproduce photographically.

We make two negatives of this still-life. Fig. 126 is from a harsh negative: the mortar and the napkin are completely opaque, while the hat is on the contrary so thin that one can see straight through it—not a grain of silver has been developed here. The second negative (Fig. 127) is entirely different: it is greyer, but shows far more detail in the hat as well as in the napkin and mortar. This is a soft negative, and your negatives should resemble it in tone qualities.

Very fast films are by nature inclined to give soft results. Slower films tend to give harsher negatives. A good negative, whatever film it may be made on, will be soft and well-graded, with full detail everywhere in both lights and shadows. A still-life of this kind is a valuable help when learning to " see " contrasts and details in nature. We shall meet this still-life again.

The conceptions " hard " and " soft " must now be explained more exactly. They refer to the relationships between the various tones. There are cloudless mid-summer days when, at noon, the light can be very hard, giving brilliant highlights and deep shadows. Such a light is called harsh—or, better, " contrasty." The very opposite of this is a misty landscape in November, when there are neither brilliant lights nor dark shadows and everything is a

Fig. 128—A subject showing great contrast of light and shade

95

Fig. 129—" MISTY MORNING." A " soft " lighting; little contrast

medium grey. Remember the comparison: hard lighting and soft lighting. Which of them you have to deal with depends on your subject. It makes all the difference whether you photograph an archway with the sun shining into it and brilliant spots of light among dark shadows, or a yacht sailing on a lake with nothing but light tones all around. The one is a harsh subject full of contrast, and the other soft and lacking in contrast. And negatives, as Figs. 126 and 127 show, can have similar characteristics.

Some films or plates incline to give harsh results, others to give soft ones; to use the professional's term, they give different gradation. This difference is due to differences in density. This term refers to the amount of silver on any particular part of the negative. If there is much black silver, the density will be high and little light will be transmitted; if there is not much silver the density will be low and more light will be transmitted.

And now we come to something rather pretty. Refer to Fig. 130: here we have a graphical reproduction of the still-life with hat and dish. On the left there is a scale of density and along the bottom the various objects have been arranged according to their brightness: first the bottle, then the hat, followed by the napkin, then the mortar, and finally the highlights on the mortar. These are the shadows, the half-tones and the light parts of our subject.

As we already know, the shadow in the negative has very little density. We therefore put a cross low on the paper above the word " hat." The light parts of the mortar, and particularly the highlights, correspond to a high density on the negative. Therefore we put a cross high on the paper above these lights. The half-tones have an intermediate density. If we now join these three points, we get a curve. It is clear that the curves corresponding to the two negatives (Fig. 126 and 127) will not be alike. The mortar shows high

96

density on the harsh negative and much less on the soft one. The curve of the first negative therefore rises steeply, while that of the other is flatter.

Read this section again, and make sure you have clearly in mind the difference between a contrasty film and a soft-working one, between hard and soft gradation and between much and little contrast.

There are much stronger contrasts in nature than in our still-life subject with the hat and the mortar. In an interior there may be very dark shadows under a cupboard, a book lying on the table may be much more brightly lit, and the view through the window may be dazzling in comparison. If a plate or film is exposed to such a series of brightness it will show a whole series of different densities. These are shown on the curve of Fig. 131, where the increasing amounts of light are indicated by a candle, a small electric bulb, a bigger bulb, a photographic floodlight, a searchlight, and finally the sun. These stand for tenfold steps, taking us from 1 to 100,000 units of light. If we allow all these different quantities of light to fall on a plate, and then develop it, we obtain a complete curve corresponding to the partial one derived from the still-life subject. It then becomes clear that the curve is not a straight line, but is S-shaped, being long and flat if the plate has soft gradation, but steeper and shorter if its gradation tends to be hard.

It will be clear that the angle the straight central part of the curve makes with the horizontal base-line is a measure of the slope at which the line runs up. If the angle in question is 45°, then the slope is 1 (the tangent of 45° = 1). This number, indicating the slope, is called gamma, and is indicated by the Greek letter γ.

gamma of 0·7 to 0·8 = soft gradation.

gamma of 0·9 to 1·0 = normal gradation.

gamma greater than 1·0 = hard gradation.

The value of gamma obtained in any given case depends very largely on the

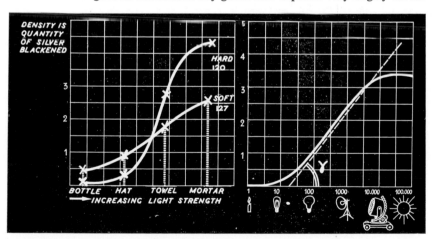

Fig. 130—Gradation curves of the negatives of Figs. 126 and 127

Fig. 131—Characteristic curve of a photographic emulsion

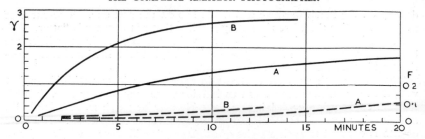

Fig. 132—Variations of gamma (full-line curves) and of fog (dotted curves and scale on right) with development times. The curves refer to the same emulsion with two different developers: A was a fine-grain developer, B a developer for high contrast

duration of development. Long development gives harder negatives, which means a higher value of gamma. Though each individual film has its own gradation—soft, normal, or hard—much control can be had by varying development.

Make sure you have grasped this section—read it over once or twice more if in doubt—for it is of fundamental importance. The first essential of good photography is to learn to recognize the contrasts of light in the subject, so that, having also learnt the characteristics of the film used and how to control them, perfect studies of the light effects in nature can be made, with clear deep shadows, beautifully modulated half-tones, and bright sparkling lights all glowingly rendered. All this depends on exposure and development.

So much technique can do. But the choice of subject is your responsibility. It is only fair to warn you that without keen perception you will not get far, so go out into the country and try to see what exactly it is in a landscape that gives rise to the many different moods they show. There you will find the secret of mastery over the whole wonderful art-technique of the rendering of tone values, this mixture of science and art that we call photography.

Latitude

If the exposure required to yield a good negative is $\frac{1}{25}$ second, and only $\frac{1}{50}$ is given, the negative will not be a complete failure. It will be thinner than

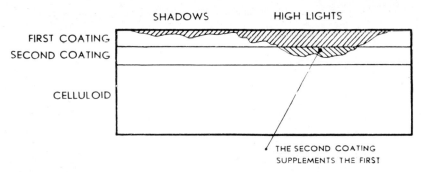

Fig. 133—Cross-section of a double-coated film, showing how the two layers increase latitude

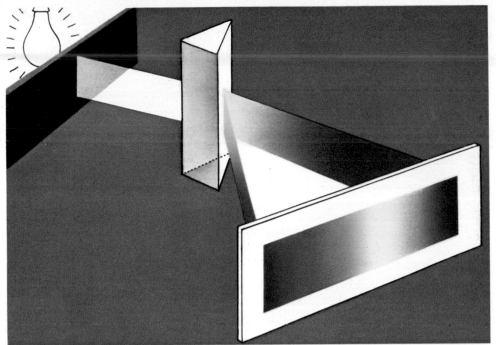

Fig. 134 — A small pencil of white light passes through a glass prism.
This produces a spectrum: a band of pure colours

Fig. 135   This is how the eye sees the spectrum

Fig. 136 — Here we have a correct translation of the spectrum into the
grey tints of photography

Fig. 137 — In the past
flower pictures came out
like this

Fig. 138 — Now we get
this result (panchromatic
plate with yellow filter)

FIG.
139

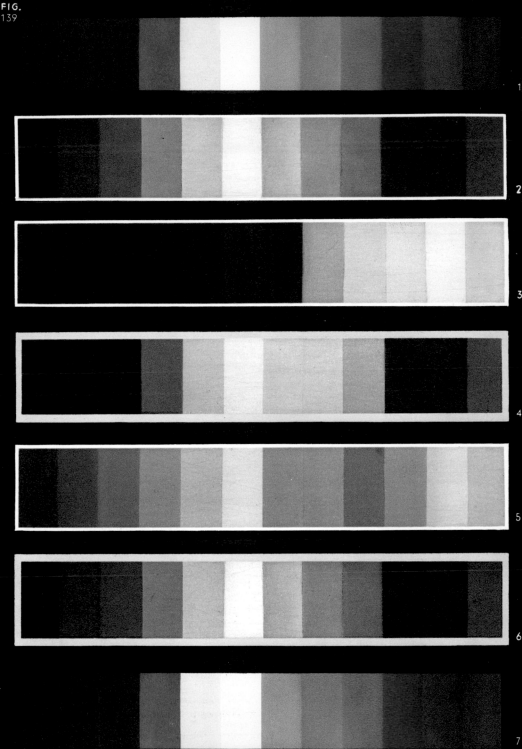

1

2

3

4

5

6

7

Fig. 140 — Photographed on three different types of film, this gives the three black and white versions shown

Fig. 141 — The old-fashioned "ordinary" film saw blue as white, green and red as black

Fig. 142 — An ortho film is better, but red remains too dark

Fig. 143 — A panchromatic film with yellow filter converts the colours correctly into blacks, whites and greys

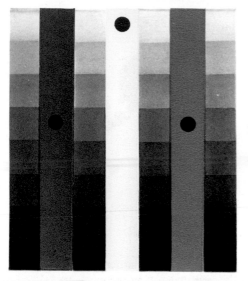

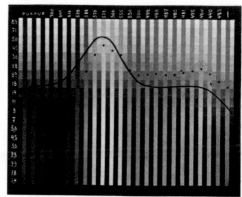

Fig. 145 — The Lagorio chart photographed on an ortho-chromatic film

Fig. 144 — The principle of the Lagorio chart. Yellow is lighter than red or blue

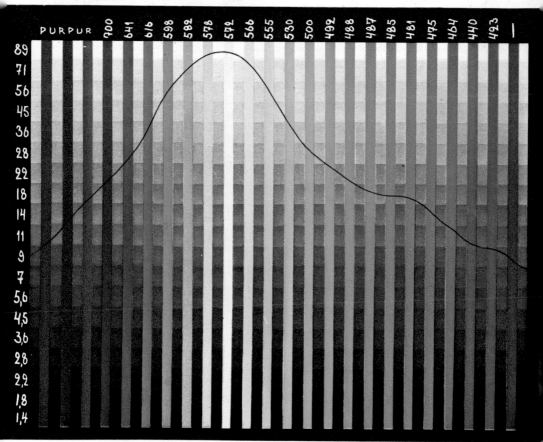

Fig. 146 — The Lagorio chart. The black line indicates where the grey tone appears the same depth as the colour. This is the curve of the eye. If the chart is photographed the curve of the emulsion will appear.

it should be, there will be less detail in the shadows, but it will still yield a very presentable print.

If, on the other hand, the exposure is increased, say to $\frac{1}{10}$ second, even less harm will be done. The negative will be denser, but will nevertheless make quite good enlargements.

There is always a little latitude in exposure, which is the reason that these *small* variations do no real harm. Soft-working films are the best in this respect, as they do not give a very great change in density in response to a change in the amount of light they receive. More contrasty films are less accommodating; the result of a longer exposure is a considerable increase in density. Their response to a shorter exposure is even more marked, the density falling away very fast.

The effect of changed exposure also depends on the subject, or rather on its contrast. If we take a flat subject, such as a misty landscape, a correctly-exposed negative shows little variation in density over its surface. The lights are not very much darker than the shadows. The exposure could quite well be shortened a trifle without losing detail in the less dense parts, or it could be lengthened without making the negative unduly dense all over. The average density would change, but the relative densities of lights and shadows would not alter.

But in making a negative of a contrasty subject, such as an interior with windows, where the shadows show just enough detail and the windows are just short of being too dense, the exposure cannot be altered much. If the exposure were reduced the negative would be thinner and the shadows would lose all detail; if it were increased the highlights would be over-exposed, making the windows absolutely black.

In photographing a subject in which the lights were ten times as bright as the shadow, by varying the exposure we could impress any desired number of units of light (see Fig. 131) on the plate in the shadow region of the subject. The highlights, however, would always give their part of the plate ten times as much light. Give the shadow ten units; the highlights get 100. The curve shows that the difference in density will not be great. Now imagine the exposure increased ten times; the shadows get 100 units of light, the highlights 1,000. But the negative, as the curve shows, will still be perfectly usable, in spite of the ten-times increase in exposure.

But if the light parts of the subject had been a hundred times brighter (contrast range 10 to 10,000, or 1 to 1,000, which might easily be found in an interior) then while ten units of light for the shadows is, as the curve shows, only just enough, the accompanying 10,000 units for the highlights is only just short of being too much. Neither a longer nor a shorter exposure can be given.

Latitude is particularly great when using films with two layers of emulsion. These double-coated films have a first layer of comparatively slow emulsion, and over this a second layer of high sensitivity. With correct exposure only the upper layer is used. If, however, the exposure is longer, the top film may no longer respond to detail, when the lower layer takes over the task, at the same time contributing some density. The negative will become rather dense, but will still show a reasonable difference between lights and shadows. Detail and gradation will not be lost.

These double-coated films are naturally no help against under-exposure, for if exposure is insufficient to affect the upper layer there can be no shadow detail. Most films of speed 29° or 30° B.S. are double-coated, but the slower films, especially the slower miniature films, have only a single layer. For these the exposure must be very accurately judged, for they have comparatively little latitude.

COLOUR SENSITIVITY

During daytime we have light from the sun on the subjects we wish to photograph—our children, landscapes, etc. This sunlight is said to be white. In reality it is a mixture of numerous colours: red, orange, yellow, green, blue and violet. And between these are many intermediate shades: sea-green, cherry-red, olive-green, sky-blue and so on.

A red book is red because it reflects red light: the rest of the white light which falls on it is retained, or *absorbed*. We see this clearly if we make the light show us its component parts. To make it do this we pass it through a triangular glass prism (Fig. 134), and immediately a complete spectrum appears; the coloured band of the rainbow.

Physicists have found that light is an undulatory motion and every pure colour, as in the spectrum, has its own wave-length. The eye sees long light waves as red and short ones as blue light. Red light has a wave-length of about 700 millionths of a millimetre, and blue a wave-length of some 400 millionths of a millimetre. If kitchen salt is put into a gas flame, the yellow colour produced will have a wave-length of 589 mμ (1 mμ = 1 millionth mm). This figure is exact, irrespective of place or time.

All these colours together yield white light. If blue rays are absent from this white light (for example in the evening, when the blue light is markedly scattered by dust and damp in the air), the light will become reddish, as at sunset. Blue and violet are mostly absent from electric light, so that, when compared with daylight, this light appears distinctly yellow.

The response of the photographic emulsion, whether on a film or plate, to these colours is a matter of importance in photography. On the focusing screen and in a finder a scene is shown in colours, but in the photograph these colours will be reproduced as varying tones of grey, black, and white.

How Our Eyes See Colours

Under the spectrum in Fig. 135 is a grey strip, divided into light and dark steps (Fig. 136). This strip is the ideal interpretation of the various colours of the spectrum as tints of grey, with their relative luminosities exactly as the eye sees them. Red is reproduced as medium grey, yellow much lighter, green somewhat darker, blue darker still, and purple a shade lighter than the blue beside it. But the film does not see it thus. The early emulsions gave most untrue colour rendering, for the plate or film was only sensitive to blue, purple and ultra-violet. That is to say, these colours affected it strongly. The plate darkened at the points where blue light fell and remained unaffected where red light reached it. In a photograph of the Union Jack, for example, the blue part was shown as white on the print, and the red part as black. The spectrum, in short, was quite wrongly represented in the grey tones of the print. A yellow daffodil was shown far too dark, since the film was not sensitive to yellow light (see Figs. 137 and 138).

The first indication that it was possible to make emulsions sensitive to light other than blue came in 1871, when Professor Vogel, of Berlin, found that by adding the dye erythrosin to the emulsion it could be made sensitive to yellow and green. It was soon found that many other dyes had similar properties, and research on " sensitizers " has gone on to this day. It is now possible to confer sensitivity to light of any colour at will, even including the invisible infra-red, and panchromatic films, sensitive to light of all colours, including red, are in everyday use.

" Ortho " and " Pan ": How Different Films Reproduce Colours

At the top of Fig. 139 we see a spectrum, which comprises all colours. No. 2 is the ideal reproduction of this in monochrome, and shows how a painter, who can estimate the relative brightnesses of the various colours, would translate them into grey tones. Now, as the early plates were sensitive to blue only, blue was rendered as very light, and yellow, green and red as black; this is shown in No. 3, where the spectrum has been photographed on a " colour-blind " plate. It is clear that under this system the colours of any subject were greatly falsified: red tomatoes and green trees were alike reproduced as black.

A photograph of the spectrum on an orthochromatic (colloquially, " ortho ") plate or film is hardly different from No. 3; although such a plate has been made slightly sensitive to yellow and green it still responds chiefly to blue. But if now a yellow filter, absorbing blue light, is put over the lens, and the exposure suitably lengthened, the yellow and green have time to affect the emulsion, and the much improved rendering shown in No. 4 is obtained. Note, however, that red is still shown as black.

No. 5 shows the rendering given by a panchromatic (colloquially, " pan ") emulsion; this is much better, but blue is again too light; with a yellow filter, however, we at last get in No. 6 a correct rendering of the colours in monochrome (compare No. 2).

The practical application of all this can be seen from the three very different renderings of the little sketch in colour (Fig. 140). To compare ortho and pan emulsions, this sketch can be copied by any reader for his own interest or instruction, or alternatively a natural subject can be chosen, such as a red tomato and a yellow lemon on a tablecloth, with a red book and a very bright blue one behind them. Whatever the subject, if it has the required colours photograph it with an ortho plate or film, and also with a pan film. This test is really well worth trying, and the sort of thing one can expect is seen in Figs. 141 to 143, where the comparison in tone values is most interesting.

In order to reduce the varieties of film made and so keep the price down, some of the leading manufacturers, both British and Continental, have recently ceased to offer orthochromatic emulsions in roll-film form, although at the time of writing there are still one or two ortho films of Continental make on the market. It is no real hardship for the amateur to have only panchromatic films at his disposal; ortho film for miniature cameras has not been made by any manufacturer for twenty years or more, and miniaturists have been perfectly happy without it. If the characteristics of an ortho film are required, it is quite simple to put over the lens of the camera a blue filter so designed that it absorbs all red light. This is a much more convenient way of working than actually using an ortho film, simply because the full sensitivity of the pan film may be wanted for other exposures on the same roll. With filters, a pan film can be given any characteristics desired.

The Need for Filters

As has already been shown, just using a pan film is not enough to ensure perfect rendering of colours. Such a film may yield satisfactory results, but a yellow tinted glass, called a filter, is still needed. It gets this name because, like any other filter, it holds something back and lets something else pass, just as coffee grounds are kept back while the liquid runs through. The task of the yellow filter is similar; it absorbs, and so holds back, blue light, while allowing light of other colours to pass freely. And as white light from which blue has been removed looks yellow to the eye, we call it a yellow filter—though it must not be thought it passes *only* yellow.

The yellow filter is needed because, in spite of the dye-conferred colour sensitiveness of ortho or pan plates and films, the emulsion still remains too sensitive to blue light, even though the manufacturers subdue this blue sensitivity as much as possible. Besides keeping back blue light, the yellow filter absorbs the ultra-violet light that is found in daylight; this light, which is present in the light from a blue sky, must be removed because it can otherwise cause the too-light sky found in most photographs. It follows that a filter should almost always be used for outdoor pictures. When looking at the spectrum of Fig. 139 through a filter one sees its effect very clearly: blue immediately becomes darker.

The Lagorio Chart and the Wedge Spectrogram

Green is a bright colour and blue a darker one. But how bright and how dark? Fig. 144 shows how this question is answered. In the background there are eight steps running from black through a scale of greys to very light. The yellow strip corresponds in brightness with the first step, as all the lower ones are much darker. The blue and red strips, on the other hand, correspond in brightness with the fifth step. If we photograph this drawing, the blue and red strips, in the print, should be the same depth as the fifth grey step, and the yellow strip the same depth as the first. We have then represented the colour values by the correct tones of grey.

This principle has been fully developed by Lagorio, who devised the chart shown in Fig. 146. In this there are twenty-four colours in the form of vertical strips, each separated from the next by a scale of greys. A black line connects up the points at which the colours appear equally bright to the eye as the greys beside them. The line is at its highest for yellow, and lower for red and blue. If we photograph this chart on ortho film and make a print from the resulting negative, the coloured strips will be represented by various shades of grey (Fig. 145). With everything in monochrome, it is easy to mark in points where the greys representing colour have the same depth as the true greys beside them. The curve outlined by these points indicates the colour sensitivity of the film.

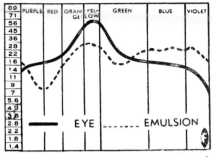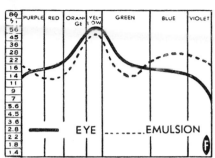

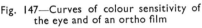

| Fig. 147—Curves of colour sensitivity of the eye and of an ortho film | Fig. 148—Curves for pan film. Pay special attention to the scale of numbers on the left |

It will be seen that the ortho film, the testing of which gave Fig. 145, has by no means the same sensitivity to colours as the eye; the curve of points is far too low in the red and too high in the blue compared with the black line which shows the sensitivity of the eye.

Another method of finding, and showing, the colour sensitivity of a film is by means of a wedge spectrogram. This is obtained by photographing on the film a spectrum, exactly like that of Fig. 139 except that it is intensely bright at the bottom but fades off into darkness at the top. (This is done by placing a wedge on the slit of the spectroscope.) In parts of the spectrum to which the film is highly sensitive, even the dimmer parts affect the film, so that the image extends almost the full width of the spectrum; but in parts containing light to which the film is less sensitive only the brighter (lower) part of the spectrum is strong enough to produce an image. Thus the height of the image at any point in the spectrum depends on the sensitivity of the film to light of the colour at that point; in effect, the image obtained is a ready-made curve of sensitivity, like those shown in Figs. 147 and 148. When the resulting film negative is printed, it gives a print the bottom part of which is white and the upper part black; the height of the white portion, the upper edge of which has a form like the curves just referred to, indicates for each wavelength the relative sensitivity of the film.

If a yellow filter is put over the lens, blue is rendered darker than it is without it. This means that the curve is lowered in the blue and raised in the yellow. In this way we can supply any correction that the curve of the film by itself still needs.

Of what practical value are all these things? Does it really matter if a blue sky is shown somewhat lighter or darker than it should be? Most certainly it does. If the sky appears white in a photograph instead of a pale grey, there can be no difference between it and white clouds. A filter is *always* needed for clouds.

If we photograph a fair-haired child without using a yellow filter, the hair will seem darker than in reality. The use of a colour-sensitive film plus a good yellow filter will give a correct and pleasing rendering.

But whatever the subject, it is only an amateur with artistic inclinations who is capable of observing the tone values of nature and reproducing them

Fig. 149—Spring landscape, taken on panchromatic film without filter. There are some clouds, but they are not very clearly marked

Fig. 150—Taken through a medium yellow filter. The blue sky is shown darker, and the clouds consequently show up better

convincingly in his pictures. Only through intensive study of nature can a realistic reproduction be achieved. Observation is needed to find the reason of Nature's moods, and to gain control of the subtleties of tone rendering which is photography's greatest means of expression.

FILTERS

Since a yellow filter operates by absorbing blue and violet light, it is evident that when a filter is in use less light will reach the film, so it will be necessary to give a longer exposure to get a satisfactory photograph. The extent to which exposure must be increased depends both on the amount of light absorbed by the particular filter and on the colour sensitivity of the film in use, but the " filter factor," by which the normal exposure must be multiplied, is usually given in the directions for use issued with the filters.

It is fairly clear that the higher the colour sensitivity of the film, the less the influence of the filter. If a film were equally sensitive to yellow and blue, and if the blue were totally absorbed by the filter, then the plate would be exposed by yellow light only, and the exposure would have to be twice as long with the filter as without (filter factor, 2). But with a film having great sensitivity to blue and very little to yellow, when the filter had eliminated all the blue we would have left only light to which the sensitivity of the film was low, and the exposure needed would probably be five to ten times as long as without the filter (factor, 5 or 10). It follows that a filter should only be used with films of good colour sensitivity.

Yellow filters are made in light, medium, and dark shades, but the light and medium ones are usually all that an amateur needs to have. A dark yellow filter is only needed for special purposes, as when it is desired to make an exactly correct reproduction of a painting.

Yellowish-green filters are also obtainable. Green is the complementary colour to red, so a yellowish-green filter will subdue red as well as blue, but will allow green to pass freely. Such filters are intended for use with films which are over-sensitive to red, as are some of the very fastest panchromatic films. The emulsions of slightly slower films are mostly ortho-panchromatic; that is to say, their relative sensitivity to different colours is correct, except that the excessive blue sensitivity remains, and with them only a plain yellow filter is therefore required.

When special " night " effects are desired it may be necessary to use a red filter to suppress *all* blue light from the sky. A red filter allows only red and some yellow light to pass, absorbing all green, violet and blue rays. The blue sky will then reproduce as black, while the clouds, the white light reflected by which contains red, will still affect the emulsion. Thus the clouds will print white against a nearly black background of sky. A panchromatic plate is, of course, needed, since one must use an emulsion sensitive to red. This filter is rarely necessary for artistic purposes, and the filter factors are rather high (5 to 15).

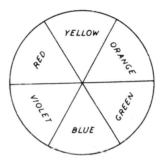

To see what colour of filter is needed refer to Fig. 151, the colour circle. In this diagram complementary colours are placed opposite one another. A yellow filter makes blue darker, a green filter does the same to red.

Fig. 151—The colour circle. Complementary colours are opposite one another

Filter Mounts

Filters can be fitted in various ways—by being screwed on to the lens, or fitted on to the lens with a bayonet catch, or slipped on and kept in place with a spring.

Screw-on filters are very convenient, and should be chosen whenever possible. Those with a bayonet fitting are equally good, but few cameras are equipped to take them. Slip-on filters (with a spring) are not so satisfactory, as they sometimes come off " in the heat of battle," and if recovered unbroken they at least have to be cleaned. Also they are easily lost, especially when photographing water scenes.

Filters of well-known make may be relied upon to be correct in colour and satisfactorily flat. This is important, for if the faces are not strictly plane, and strictly parallel, the definition given by the lens will be impaired.

There are two kinds of filters, namely those cut from glass coloured in the mass, and those made by cementing a piece of coloured gelatine between two pieces of glass. In theory the latter type is preferable, as the colour can be more precisely adjusted, but in practice the two types are equally satisfactory.

There is a great deal of blue and violet light by the beach and on the sea;

much more than in the woods, for example. The yellow filter in consequence absorbs much active light when in these " blue " surroundings. The effect of the filter on exposure is correspondingly greater, and the filter factor will be decidedly higher. Towards sunset the light will be yellow or even reddish, showing that it contains less blue, and is spontaneously giving the effect of a yellow filter. In yellow evening light the filter can be left unused.

Ultra-violet and Graduated Filters

In mountain photography at an altitude of about 6,000 ft or over there is a good deal of ultra-violet radiation. This gives rise to fogginess and loss of sharpness, and so has to be cut out by means of a colourless ultra-violet filter.

A graduated filter (sky filter) is of a dark yellow at the top, but this tint shades off progressively towards the bottom, where it is almost colourless. The intention is to absorb light from the sky without obstructing the light coming from a landscape. To obtain this effect, it is essential for the filter to be placed some distance—2 in at least—in front of the lens. It is evident that such a filter must be fairly large. A graduated filter used close against the lens has exactly the same effect as a filter of an even tint intermediate between the darkest and lightest tints of the filter used.

Very often the main charm of a subject in woods, meadows, or at sea lies in a slight haze that helps the impression of distance and gives depth to the picture. These atmospheric effects, especially when the sun is just breaking through the clouds, are among the most attractive of subjects. No branch of graphic art can reproduce atmospheric effects as well as photography. But for such subjects a yellow filter must never be used; haze is caused by the scattering of light by droplets of water, and the light so scattered is predominantly bluish.   If we eliminate it with a filter, nothing will remain of the hazy effect.

Polarizing Filters

These are special filters that are colourless, and yet absorb light. Normally light vibrates in all possible directions, but when it is reflected (for example by

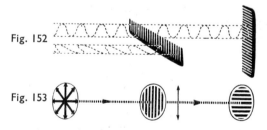

Fig. 152

Fig. 153

a sheet of glass) it vibrates chiefly in one plane. Such light is called polarized, and may be thought of as light that has passed through a comb. If a second comb is rotated in the path of this light (Fig. 152) a position will be found in which it will bar the passage of the light.

Polarizing filters do in fact behave in the way we have imagined for these combs. With a filter of this sort we can extinguish reflected light. If we look at a polished table top and rotate a polarizing filter before the eye, a position

Fig. 154—Ordinary photograph. Note reflections on table top; these often occur in technical or advertising photographs

Fig. 155—The reflections have been extinguished by using a polarizing filter set at the correct angle

can be found for the filter in which the reflected light is extinguished. This can be exceedingly helpful when photographing such objects as shop windows or still-life subjects. But reflections from metallic surfaces can *not* be extinguished in this way; notice the lighter in Figs. 154 and 155. As a polarizing filter absorbs some light, extra exposure must be given when using it; the filter factor is usually 2 or 3.

In passing, it is worth mentioning that it is possible, with the help of two such filters and two projectors, to project pictures stereoscopically. The spectators have to be equipped with glasses consisting of two polarizing filters, so adjusted that each eye sees its own picture.

Infra-red Filters

Infra-red filters absorb all visible light, and so appear to the eye to be completely opaque, but allow invisible infra-red light to pass. With an infra-red filter over the lens, it is possible to take photographs with invisible rays of longer wave-length than ordinary light. It is, of course, necessary to use plates or films that have been specially sensitized for these rays. Infra-red photography is used for criminal investigation, for the examination of old documents and letters, and also for haze penetration.

GRAIN AND OTHER TROUBLES

With the growing popularity of the miniature camera, whose small negatives have to be considerably enlarged in printing, the inevitable graininess of the photographic image has become important to all amateurs. This graininess of a negative depends on several factors, chief of which is the inherent graininess of the film used, but it can be modified to quite a considerable extent by suitable choice of developer and methods of development. In consequence, the question of fine grain was for some years one of the chief photographic topics among amateurs. Let us consider the origin of graininess.

Fig. 156 shows the appearance of a sensitive film as seen through the microscope; the crystals are sensitive silver bromide. On development the exposed crystals are converted to black silver, and they clump together in the process. It is the resulting groups of silver particles that give the negative a grainy structure. What this looks like in the enlarged print can be seen by studying the right-hand half of Fig. 157.

It will be noticed that in preparing the two negatives from which these two prints were made, two different films had to be used, one fast and one slow. This was made necessary because really fine grain can never be had with a high-speed film, no matter how carefully it is developed. Conversely, slow films give fine grain almost automatically, without any special care on the part of the user. There is no *exact* relationship between graininess and speed, but it may nevertheless be taken as a guiding rule that the faster the film the more grainy it is likely to be.

Besides making the print unpleasant to look at, graininess leads to the loss of fine detail; individual leaves on a tree, or individual hairs on the head in a portrait, run together into a common blur. For really sharp enlargements, a fine-grained negative is essential.

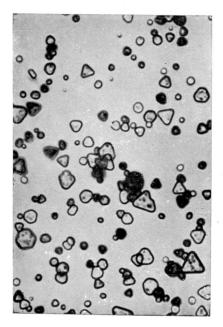

Fig. 156—Silver bromide crystals in a sensitive film. Enlarged 2,500 times. On development the grains turn black and clump together

Fig. 157—Small parts of two big enlargements (24 × 36 mm negative enlarged to 30 × 20 in). The left half was taken with a fine-grain film, the right half with a coarse-grained film of high speed

It must be clearly realized that the crystals of silver bromide in the unexposed emulsion (Fig. 156) form a structure many times finer than that of the finished negative. As already stated, it is the clumping together of the small particles of silver formed from the individual crystals during development that produces graininess—one " grain " in the negative may contain silver from many originally separate crystals. It is evident, therefore, that it is the clumping that has to be avoided, and to this end the film manufacturer can contribute most, in the making of the emulsion. The improvement in graininess that the user can bring about in development is small by comparison, but still a useful help.

The control of graininess that can be had in development is of two distinct kinds; by controlling degree of development and by choice of special developers. Often both methods are used together.

If development is interrupted before the grains are completely blackened—at the fourth or fifth stage of Fig. 158—we shall obviously get smaller grains. But, on the other hand, we obtain only a part of the density we should have had on full development.

This is felt most in the shadow regions, where the density even on full development would have been slight; with short development there may be no image at all. Nothing can be done to correct this at the time of development, but it can be prevented at the time of taking the photograph by giving a little extra exposure: *shortened development demands longer exposure.*

1. *EXPOSED GRAIN WITH DEVELOPABLE SPECK.......*

2. *WHICH BEGINS TO GROW..........*

3. *IN THE DEVELOPER.......*

4. *STILL FURTHER..........*

5. *AND FURTHER...*

6. *UNTIL THE WHOLE GRAIN IS BLACKENED.*

THE GRAIN IS DEVELOPED OUT.

Fig. 158

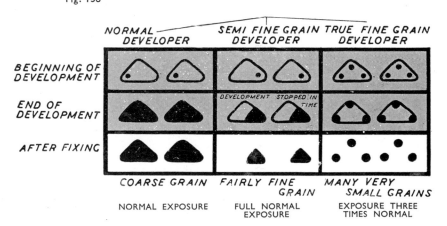

	NORMAL DEVELOPER	SEMI FINE GRAIN DEVELOPER	TRUE FINE GRAIN DEVELOPER
BEGINNING OF DEVELOPMENT			
END OF DEVELOPMENT		DEVELOPMENT STOPPED IN TIME	
AFTER FIXING	COARSE GRAIN	FAIRLY FINE GRAIN	MANY VERY SMALL GRAINS
	NORMAL EXPOSURE	FULL NORMAL EXPOSURE	EXPOSURE THREE TIMES NORMAL

Fig. 159—The three types of development

The second help towards fine grain is the choice of a special developing agent, of which paraphenylene diamine and Meritol are the best known. These have the property of starting the development of a grain at more than one point, so giving the image a finer structure. Fig. 159 tells the story more clearly than words could do.

Speed and Grain

In an emulsion of low sensitivity the grains are fairly equal in size. To obtain a more highly sensitive film the manufacturer lets the emulsion " ripen," and during this process the crystals grow, group together, and form larger aggregates. As the whole of a grain becomes developable when any part of it is affected by light, larger grains give more density for a given amount of light—hence a faster film. Though increase of grain-size is only one of the ways of increasing the sensitivity of a film, any emulsion can always be made faster by increasing the size of the grain. For the fastest films *all* methods of increasing speed have to be used, which explains why the grain of a fast film is always coarser than that of a slow one.

Bearing this in mind, it is evidently a sound plan to use a slow or medium-speed film whenever possible. When on the beach, for example, do not load your camera with an ultra-rapid film of 34° or 37° B.S., and give exposures of $\frac{1}{500}$ second at f/16. Choose instead a fine-grain film of about 26° to 28° B.S., and give $\frac{1}{100}$ second at f/11, or $\frac{1}{200}$ at f/8. You will get sharper pictures, for a film of lower speed will always record finer detail. This is particularly important when using a miniature; in fact, a film faster than about 27° B.S. should never be used in a small camera unless it is impossible to get the required pictures without it.

Even the best of fine-grain developers cannot give really fine-grained results on an ultra-fast film; at most it can only make the grain rather less bad than it would otherwise have been. So we repeat: miniature workers should *always* choose a fine-grain film unless highest sensitivity is absolutely essential.

With cameras of the larger sizes the question of grain is of less importance. The influence of enlarging on the visibility of grain is discussed on page 174.

Halation and Irradiation

Halation is a fault that is not often encountered nowadays, for practically every film made for amateur use embodies protection against it. Fig. 161 shows what halation looks like; the light from the window, which is many times brighter than any other object in the picture, has spread beyond its proper boundaries and enveloped nearly half the picture in a blur of fog.

This spreading of light is caused by reflection from the back of the film or plate, as shown in Fig. 160. This represents a cross-section through a plate, and a ray of light is represented as falling on a grain, or small area, of the emulsion. This illuminated grain or area reflects light in all directions into the layer, so that other grains close to it receive light that is not part of the picture formed by the lens. The effect on the picture is that a small bright dot or point is broadened into a circular patch.

This effect is sometimes called halation, but its correct name is *irradiation*. Its effect is to obscure fine detail whenever there is a sharp contrast between light and dark. The twigs of a tree seen against the sky often vanish in a photograph: they have been blotted out by the spreading of light from the sky part of the image.

Irradiation can never, in the nature of things, be completely prevented, but by making the emulsion thin and more transparent it can be greatly reduced. Greater transparency means less speed, for less light is absorbed, and a thinner emulsion necessarily has less latitude. Nevertheless the newer "thin-emulsion" films have proved very popular, especially among miniaturists, because of their higher "acutance," a term meaning simply that they can give much sharper pictures.

As indicated in Fig. 160, there is always some light not absorbed or reflected by the grains of the emulsion; this light passes through to the back of the glass or celluloid. If it were not scattered and deflected by the emulsion this would not much matter; it would either pass out of the back of the film or plate or else be reflected back to the spot it came from (vertical arrow). But an appreciable fraction of the light spreads outwards and reaches the back of the support at an angle. As the angle becomes flatter and flatter a smaller proportion of the light emerges from the back of the support and a larger proportion is reflected, until after a certain angle (the " critical angle " of the treatises on optics) it is *all* reflected. As Fig. 160 suggests, this gives a more or less sharp ring round the central point. The ring is small, closely surrounding the point, if the support is thin (celluloid) but is much larger on the thicker base of a glass plate. This effect is true halation.

There are two ways of preventing halation. One is to have a dark or coloured layer between the emulsion and the glass so that the light cannot penetrate.

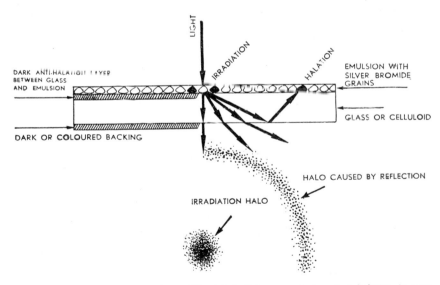

Fig. 160—Section through a plate. The left half is protected against halation in two ways (see text); the right half is unprotected. The section shows how irradiation and halation arise; the result is shown underneath. On the left, no halation; but irradiation remains

Fig. 161—Interior, taken with an un-backed plate. Halation has quite spoilt the picture. This is not a fault in the lens

Fig. 162—The same interior taken with a backed plate. All details, even those in the view from the window, are clearly seen

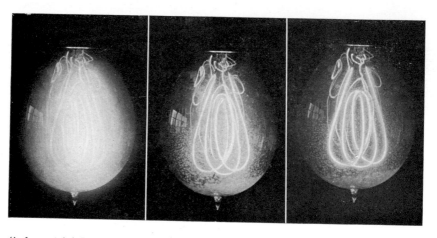

(Left to right) Fig. 163—Halation on a glass plate. The filament has almost vanished, and the white spots of paint put on the glass cannot be seen at all. Fig. 164—The same subject, taken on a backed plate. Fig. 165—The same, taken on 35 mm film. Here the filament is broadened by halation, the effects of which are limited to the immediate neighbourhood of the filament owing to the thinness of the celluloid

This is the method used in most amateur ciné films, and it completely prevents halation—though it gives no protection against irradiation. The second method is to use " backing," which is a coating of anti-halation dye or a kind of black varnish on the back of a plate. After exposure, the varnish is cleaned off with a bit of damp sponge and the dye becomes colourless in the developer. With films the back of the celluloid is coated with a coloured layer, which is immediately decolourized in the developer. If a little greenish colour should remain after washing, a bath of 5 per cent ammonia will remove it readily.

Modern miniature films are protected against halation by coating them on light grey celluloid. This grey tint should not be mistaken for fog.

In taking pictures of Christmas trees or other subjects in which it is desired to include candles, it is often preferred to use an unbacked plate, which will surround each candle flame with a bright halo. This gives a very acceptable suggestion of light radiating from the flame.

Solarization

Solarization is a fault, once not uncommon, that is almost unknown with modern films. We have already seen that the silver bromide on a plate or film is blackened by the effect of light followed by development, and that the effect is greater or less in proportion to the amount of light reaching the emulsion. In a portrait a white collar is shown black in the negative, whilst a dark suit remains transparent. If the exposure is made extremely long, the white collar will be so black that it cannot possibly turn blacker. If the exposure is made still longer the process is reversed, and the density decreases again. By giving a sufficiently long exposure, it is in consequence possible to obtain a positive, though a dense and foggy one, in place of a normal negative. As shown in Fig. 166, such a positive, when printed in the ordinary way, gives a negative print.

Solarization can give reversal—that is a positive where a negative would normally be expected, and vice versa —but the process is not practical, if only because of the immensely long exposures required. When reversal is desired, as in making amateur ciné films, a different process is employed. We shall not go into details, because this book does not set out to deal with cinematography, but in outline the procedure is as follows.

The film is coated with a layer of emulsion that is exceptionally thin and

Fig. 166—A good example of solarization (reversal) is seen in the view through the window, which was greatly over-exposed

Fig. 167—Negative showing genuine solar-ization. A spotlight was directed on a book and a floodlamp. The book is still black on the negative. Because the lamp was so much brighter, the emulsion there was over-exposed and became lighter than the book. This part of the " nega-tive " is a positive. This can only occur with a great amount of light

Fig. 168—Pseudo-solarization. The plate, lying flat in the developing dish, was showing the first traces of image when someone opened the darkroom door and let light in. The underlying silver bromide was exposed through the de-veloped image. Result, partial reversal. Part of the area is shown as a normal positive in this print, the rest is almost entirely a negative. This is not real solarization, for which there was not nearly enough exposure

exceedingly even. After exposure in the camera, it is developed to give a negative. But instead of dissolving away the unused silver bromide in the usual fixing bath, the black image is dissolved away, thus leaving the unused silver bromide still in the film. This bromide is thickest in the shadows, where little or no emulsion has been used up in making the negative, and thinnest in the highlights. All that is necessary, then, is to expose the film to light to render this remaining emulsion developable, and then to develop it in the usual way. The result is a positive, dense in the shadows and nearly transparent in the highlights.

By this process the actual film exposed in the camera can be used in the projector; obviously a great saving of film as compared with making a negative first and then printing from it on fresh film.

Pseudo-solarization

In the early stages of development only the highlights have darkened—for example the sky, a white collar, or a light jersey. If by mistake white light is switched on, or the lid of the developing tank gets loose and lets light reach the film, the parts that are still blank will receive the full light. In other parts, where there is already a faint image, the emulsion will be protected to some extent against the light. Put more simply, the negative already developed is printed on the emulsion beneath it. In this way a positive is unintentionally produced in place of a negative.

This is not solarization, though it resembles it. It is correctly called pseudo-solarization or, scientifically, the Sabatier effect. A good example is seen in Fig. 168. The most usual cause is a leaky or unsafe darkroom light.

Applied Solarization

A most unusual film has recently been put on the market under the name Controtipo Diretto (Ferrania). If this film is put into developer without being exposed, it turns completely black. But if it is exposed to light before development, it becomes less dense the more it is exposed. So if a negative is printed on this film, it develops up to give a negative. Hence the name, which means " direct duplicate."

This is a most useful material when more than one negative is needed. It makes it possible to obtain a second negative which, if correctly exposed and developed, will be equal to the first. It is even possible, by careful processing, to make the new negative a little more or less contrasty than the original if this is desirable. Further, miniature negatives can be enlarged to give, say, a 9×12 cm negative from which contact prints can conveniently be made, or which can be retouched and then used for making enlarged prints.

Direct duplicate film is slow, requiring ten to fifteen times the exposure of bromide paper. A test-strip is of course essential in practice to determine the precise exposure needed in any given case.

Keeping Films

On every film there is an expiry date, generally in the form " Develop before June, 19—." This need not be taken too literally, for it cannot be imagined that on May 31 the film would be in perfect condition, and that the next day it would be stale, spoilt, and useless. The deterioration of a film with age is a slow process, and the date means no more than that the makers anticipate that, with sensible storage, deterioration of the film would probably not be noticeable till about the date they state.

Note the words: " with sensible storage." A film that has got wet, or is kept in a very damp place, will deteriorate quite quickly; one kept in a really dry place, especially if it be cool as well, will keep much longer. Generally a film remains usable, and is often perfect, for a year or two after the expiry date.

As a film ages it loses speed and decreases in colour sensitivity; at a later stage it begins to become foggy, and eventually will show, on development, mottling from the backing paper with which it has been in contact so long. An out-of-date film should therefore be given a slightly generous exposure, especially if a filter is used, and should be developed in a developer containing extra bromide or other anti-foggant (see later in this book).

6 CHOOSING THE CORRECT EXPOSURE

CHOOSING the correct exposure time is an important matter when taking a photograph. The three possibilities here are (1) under-exposure, (2) correct exposure, or (3) over-exposure.

In taking a photograph, the photographer causes his lens to form a picture on the sensitive material in his camera. An unused film, on which no light has yet fallen, is called " unexposed." A film on which a picture has been impressed is called an " exposed " film, and the action of impressing the picture on the film, which is done by allowing the picture to fall on the film for a brief instant, is called " exposing," or " making the exposure."

Note that " exposure " can also mean " exposure time " or even " amount of light action on the film." We may say: " I have made two exposures this afternoon " (which means that two photographs have been taken), but we might also say " I hope I gave that one enough exposure." This would normally imply some doubt about the shutter having been open long enough (exposure time) but might equally be used if there was doubt about the lens aperture having been opened wide enough. A wider aperture, of course, would give more light action in a given time.

It is in this latter sense, of light action on the film, that correct exposure is essential. Too little light action, or too much, will infallibly lead to failure. This chapter is devoted to the means of finding correct exposure: and this makes it almost the most important chapter in the whole book.

FACTORS CONTROLLING EXPOSURE

The subject:	Latitude
	Time of year
	Time of day
	Weather
	Type of subject
Camera and film:	Stop
	Film speed
	Filter
	Development

These factors can all vary. The beginner must simplify the problem. The best way is to work for the time being with one type of film, with the same stop, and change the exposure time according to the brightness of the subject. It would be easy to say: " Go and buy a photo-electric exposure meter, determine your exposures with it, and in general you will be all right." But this would give the beginner no training in recognizing conditions of light, and this is most important for every amateur. So we must discuss the factors mentioned above in more detail.

Latitude, Weather and Time of Day

The height of the sun above the horizon is the chief factor determining the

120

amount of light it gives. At any one moment, this varies from equator to pole. Exposure tables must take this into account.

No exact tables or instructions can be given for weather, for the amount of light obstructed by a cloudy sky is a matter of guesswork. Only practice can help the beginner here, though exposure tables will at least tell him within what limits to place his guess.

It is obvious that the time of exposure cannot be the same at midday in summer and on a dull winter afternoon. For the less observant person the variation of light at different times of day will not be so apparent. One can still read the paper at 8 o'clock or even 9 o'clock on a summer evening, but the light is many times weaker than it was in the afternoon. Therefore the exposure needed in the afternoon will be much less than in the evening. The same applies to the time of the year. The change of light with the seasons can be measured with an exposure meter. At 12 o'clock on a clear December day it is nearly twice as dark as at midday in July.

Type of Subject

We have the widest variations of all in the type of subject. It makes a world of difference whether the subject is a fair girl on the beach or a child in a blue raincoat in a town garden; the latter will need at least ten times as much exposure as the former.

All these varying factors make exposure a question of experience, and this experience is best acquired by keeping a list of exposures made, so that when taking another photograph under similar conditions of light the records will show, at least approximately, how long to expose. The exposure tables in this book are based on this.

We have no control over the factors that determine the light. But we need not complicate matters still further by varying the factors we can control. So we repeat: keep to one film and learn to know it thoroughly. The use of one stop—we suggest f/6·3 or f/9 —will simplify matters still more. The use of one filter, increasing the exposure twice, and also the use of one kind of developer, all help to make things less complicated.

On the subject of the extra exposure needed when using fine-grain developers, see pages 119 and 153.

Fig. 169—Sixtomat exposure meter

Fig. 170—Weston exposure meter

Exposure Meters

There are three kinds of exposure meters: chemical, visual and photo-electric. The chemical meters, which measured the light by seeing how long a piece of sensitive paper took to darken to a standard tint, are no longer used; measuring took too long, especially in a poor light. Nevertheless, the indications given were completely reliable.

The majority of visual meters were made like small telescopes. The meter was pointed at the subject, and one saw a series of small areas of progressively increasing brightness. Usually a number was printed on each. After making sure which number was the dimmest that could be read, calculating scales gave the exposure.

An uncertain factor was the condition of the eyes. In a darkened room the eyes are highly sensitive, and the pupil is wide open; in brilliant surroundings the pupil closes and the retina becomes much less sensitive. This affects the reading of this type of meter. Later patterns of extinction meter have reduced this error by introducing means of allowing for the brilliance of the prevailing light. Such meters are serviceable, and on the whole give a reading that is not far out.

The photo-electric exposure meter contains a light-sensitive cell that converts the light falling on it into electrical energy. The electric current generated causes a small milliammeter to register, and the movement of the pointer is proportional to the amount of light.

All the factors just discussed (of time of day and year, the weather, etc.) now cease to interest us; the meter simply measures the amount of light present. The purchase of an expensive instrument such as this is by no means a luxury, but a wise investment, for its cost will soon be saved by the waste of film through incorrect exposure that it prevents. For colour

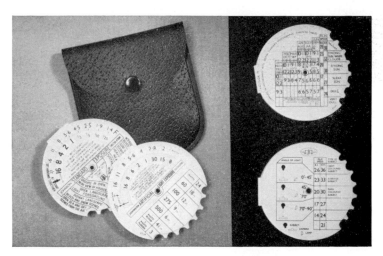

Fig. 171—The Johnson exposure calculator is a handy device for finding correct exposure in both daylight and artificial light conditions.

photography, where exact exposure is essential, an electric exposure meter is indispensable.

Your dealer will have various makes of meter. He knows all these well, so ask his advice. The good qualities of a meter are robustness, sensitivity, compactness and directional properties. As they are mutually exclusive, you must choose the one that gives the balance of advantages that you personally appreciate most.

When you have bought your meter, read the instructions carefully, use it

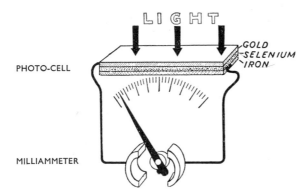

Fig. 172—Diagram of a photo-electric meter. At the top is the sensitive cell which transforms light into an electric current, the strength of which is indicated by the needle of the milliammeter

thoughtfully and act accordingly. Meters are to be had separately and also built into some cameras; we prefer a separate one as it can also be used for a ciné camera, if you happen to have one.

The best rule for using a meter is a simple one; measure with it the brightness of the most important part of the subject. A meter simply pointed at the subject as a whole will receive light from everything within its field of view, and its reading indicates the total amount of light it picks up. If everything is of about the same average brightness the exposure so indicated will be correct. But if the subject is a girl sitting on a sunlit beach in the shade of a parasol, most of the light reaching the meter will be from the sand, not from the girl sitting in the shade. Follow the meter reading blindly, and the photograph will reproduce the sand beautifully, but the girl will be just a silhouette. To measure the exposure needed for her, take the meter up close to her to take the reading.

When photographing against the light, if the shadows are the important part of the subject, measure the light in the shadows, protecting the meter from the direct light of the sun.

The electric exposure meter measures exposure for subjects of average contrast. Light and medium tones are then fully exposed, while the negative shows just enough detail in shadows of normal depth. If the subject is a very light one, such as a still life of eggs in a white bowl on a white tablecloth, there will be little or no shadow. This is a subject of low contrast. For

123

this the exposure need at most be half that indicated by the meter. If on the other hand the subject has unusually dark shadows, the meter should be directed into the shadows to measure the amount of light there, and the exposure should be based on the reading so obtained.

Practical understanding and experience are needed when using a photo-electric meter. Some American instruments have a separate scale for normal, strong and low contrast. This is a very accurate way of measuring and is referred to again in connection with " Colour Photography " on page 194.

Calibrating a Meter

It is a sound plan to calibrate a meter. This can be done as follows:

Measure the exposure for a subject of normal contrast, not including sky. Suppose the reading is f/8, $\frac{1}{50}$ second. Then expose three films, one at f/8 for $\frac{1}{25}$ second (double the time), one at f/8 for $\frac{1}{50}$ second (indicated time) and one at f/8 for $\frac{1}{100}$ second (half indicated time). After development the three negatives are compared, and by seeing which is most correctly exposed we know in future whether to expose for the exact time given by the meter, or whether a longer or shorter exposure is to be preferred.

Take great care of your exposure meter; it is a delicate and precise instrument. A handy way of carrying it is on a long cord in the pocket, so that it cannot reach the ground if it falls when taken out.

Keeping a Note-book

Experience concerning exposure times is worth preserving. It is therefore a good idea to get a note-book and rule it into columns of the kind shown below, and make the appropriate entries. In a year's time your notes will be a mine of information.

No.	Subject	Meter Reading	Stop	Filter	Exposure	Film	Developed in minutes	Result

7 MAKING A START

BEFORE we go on to development let us have a short outing with the camera. You are now familiar with your camera and film, you know what ortho and pan films are, you can find the correct exposure and use your stops to give the right depth of focus.

Remember that the choice of subject is the most important thing of all. The owner of a camera with a focusing screen, especially if it be a reflex (in which the picture is right side up), has the best equipment for choosing his subjects. From the multitude of possible subjects each photographer must choose those that appeal most to him personally, for if he restricts himself to the obvious ones he will succeed only in producing a series of picture post-cards. It is not always easy to isolate the subject from its surroundings without some assistance. The focusing screen of the reflex will do it, but if this is not available a " view meter," as shown in Fig. 173, is a great help. It consists simply of a little frame the shape of the negative, with a piece of light-blue celluloid in it to look through. With this one can isolate the subject, just as painters can.

What will you isolate? And in what shape; upright or oblong? You have to choose. The light-blue celluloid rather exaggerates contrasts, but it subdues colours so that they do not deceive you. In photography the contrasts are always a trifle excessive.

Is the subject pleasingly lit? Is it simple enough? A good photographer

Fig. 173—View meter in use   Fig. 174—A darkroom in a cupboard

once said, " A lens is always hungry," by which he meant that a photograph almost always includes too much. Remember always, the simpler the subject the more effective it is. Make sure the composition is good. The important thing is to learn to " see," and to this end the view meter is a great help.

In the long run, however, skill in taking photographs comes by experience, aided by reading a good photographic journal and by contact with other amateurs.

A word of advice: keep to one type of subject for your first trials. Do not take sports pictures one day, a church interior the next and a portrait by artificial light the third day. Choose one kind of subject and stick to it for a month or two; this will perfect your technique.

Get advice from good amateurs and, if you can, join a photographic society. Remember that simplicity in your methods of work is the first step to success. The same is true of accessories. Do not burden yourself with wide-angle and telephoto lenses, and with all kinds of filters. Learn the uses of just one filter; take a steady tripod with you and one exposure meter and master their use thoroughly. Never buy things until you really need them. The choice of a good subject is much more important than the possession of many accessories.

Now suppose you are in the country; what will you photograph? You see much around you, but no really good subject. Look through your view meter and at the focusing screen of your reflex. Take a simple subject, perhaps just one tree, and photograph it really well. The background must be well chosen. You are lucky, the clouds are lovely. If you use your yellow filter the background will be splendid. The horizon does not look right; it cuts through the tree, so place your camera lower down, almost on the ground. This brings the horizon down; the arrangement is pleasing now and the exposure can be made.

You will be proud of your picture of this fine old oak tree; indeed, it can be the first of a collection of beautiful trees in England. This is photography with an aim in view. Seek such subjects with seeing eyes and reproduce them with skilled technique.

8 DEVELOPING

THE DARKROOM

"ONE'S family and the sun are best avoided." This Mexican proverb certainly applies to the darkroom. Interruption is most undesirable and the room must be absolutely dark.

In modern houses it is often rather difficult to set a room apart for our hobby. Nevertheless we must try to find some place or other that no one else will enter, even if it is only a big cupboard that can be locked. A room in the attic is not suitable, as it will be too hot in summer and too cold in winter. Any private room, such as a study or dressing room, can be adapted; one essential is a storage cupboard for chemicals and equipment. A piece of linoleum over the table top will suffice to protect it.

A special darkroom is, of course, ideal, and in modern houses with central heating the amateur is often much better off than many a professional.

If space permits have two tables, one for wet and one for dry work. Or a single long table can be divided into wet and dry halves by an upright board. If the tables are definitely to be devoted to photography, it is a good plan to

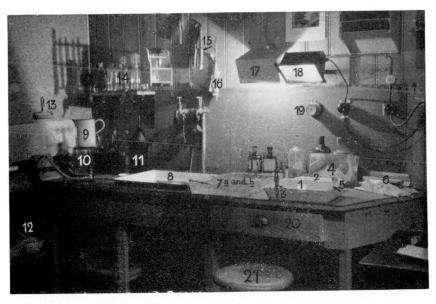

Fig. 175—Large amateur darkroom. (1) Developing dish. (2) Stop-bath. (3) Paper clip. (4) Pilot print. (5) Thermometer. (6) Towel and dish-cloth. (7a and b) First and second fixing baths. (8) Rinsing dish. (9) Measure. (10) Bunsen burner. (11) Four bottles of fixing bath (two for negatives, two for prints). (12) Mortar. (13) Squeegee. (14) Beakers and flasks. (15) Film wiper. (16) Wash leather. (17) Shaded white light. (18) Darkroom lamp. (19) Clock. (20) Drawer for developing clips, corks, filter paper. (21) Stool. On the right is a table for the enlarger

nail a piece of oilcloth on them to make them waterproof. Or a marble-topped washstand may be used; it makes an excellent workbench.

If a makeshift arrangement has to be accepted, the bathroom can be used. Chemicals and dishes must then be stowed away in a cupboard and some kind of wooden contraption over the bath will serve to take our things (see Fig. 176).

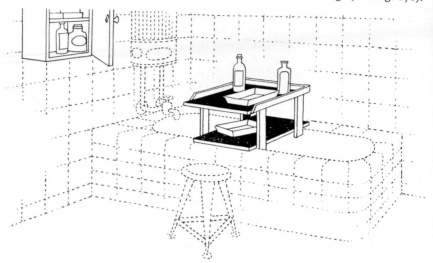

Fig. 176—A support over the bath is very convenient in a confined space

This support, which will also take the enlarger, is perfectly suitable for modern development, as we shall soon see.

No daylight at all may enter the darkroom. Curtains and strips of felt are no longer considered practical, as the room must be free from dust. So use shutters of thick cardboard or three-ply wood.

Running water is indispensable in a darkroom. If it cannot possibly be obtained we must do the best we can with a bucket of water, but for washing films and enlargements running water must be available, so they have to be carried into the kitchen.

Kitchen Darkroom

In the evening after dark, provided that there is a good blackout, the kitchen can serve as temporary darkroom. But here is some good advice: always put *all* photographic appliances and equipment back into their own cupboard after use.

Not the slightest chance of an accident can be permitted, and other members of the household must learn to regard all photographic gear as something that only the owner himself may touch. Special care is needed with chemicals, for some developers are poisonous.

In a darkroom where regular work is done everything—bottles, dishes and developing tanks—must have its own place. Always tidy everything up carefully after working. An amateur's character can be read from his darkroom; its tidiness or disorder shows at once how he works. The war on dust must be energetically fought out, and the strongest weapon is the vacuum cleaner. No papers should be left about; they must all be put away in the cupboard or drawer. Then the room can be cleaned up properly, and there will be no trouble from dust. For rubbish a kitchen dustbin with a lid opened by a pedal is the best choice. Above all, look out for spilt hypo or the results may be disastrous.

Heating and Lighting

In houses without central heating, warming the darkroom is sometimes difficult. The most convenient plan is to use an electric fire, turned out before developing films or plates. When printing or enlarging the fire can be left on, for its light will do no harm at all.

Another trouble is keeping the baths warm; this can conveniently be done with a hot-plate. Warm tiles, the temperature of which can be regulated, can be used, but they must be replaced as they cool.

A modern darkroom should not be gloomy, but well-lit. The best combination consists of:

(1) Indirect light for illuminating the room as a whole.

(2) Extra light over the work bench.

For (1), a lamp fitted with a 15-watt or 25-watt bulb, and having a suitable safelight at the top, is suitable. This gives light that is reflected from the ceiling, flooding the darkroom evenly. The walls should be painted white or a light colour, for if the lamp gives a safe light, only safe light can be reflected from them. Fig. 177 shows a commercial lamp of suitable type, and its

Fig. 177—Darkroom lamp to be hung from the ceiling, giving direct downward light, or upward light to be reflected from ceiling, or both. (Kodak)

Fig. 178—Darkroom lamp to be attached to wall over working bench. This type of lamp is generally much smaller than the hanging type of Fig. 177. (Ilford)

Fig. 179—Pull-on switches with different handles to prevent one making mistakes in the dark. Further, the switches cannot be touched with damp fingers

equivalent could easily be made at home from a biscuit tin and a safelight bulb.

For (2), the direct light over the bench, a lamp fixed to the wall (Fig. 178) is most convenient. It should be capable of taking interchangeable safelight screens for negative developing, enlarging, or printing. Standard sizes are 7 × 5 in and 10 × 8 in. Safelight screens should never be made at home (though the lamp itself may be) as the commercial screens are quite cheap and guaranteed effective. Home-made ones are usually either unsafe or darker than they need be—often they are both.

Development, and loading films into the tank, are done in darkness nowadays, as most modern films are sensitive to all visible light. But for ortho films, which are not red-sensitive, a dark red lamp can be used. For general use a white lamp above the bench will be needed.

All lamps must have independent switches. As one's hands are often damp in a darkroom, pull-on switches operated by cords are safest. To each cord should be attached a differently-shaped handle, easily distinguished in the dark. If possible darkroom lamps should be earthed by connecting them to a waterpipe, to remove all risk of danger from shocks.

Equipping the Darkroom

Some people hold the view that with modern developing tanks all development can quite well be done in a sitting room or kitchen. It is quite possible, of course, but not advisable. A separate darkroom, however small, is better and far more convenient. It is a pleasure in itself to work comfortably in one's own darkroom, where one can concentrate on obtaining the best results.

The equipment required for comfortable working in a darkroom depends very largely on the type and amount of work to be done. Type of work decides whether we shall want a tank for films, or dishes for developing plates. The amount of work will settle whether the outfit shall be simple or complete, for it must be emphasized that, once the necessary minimum of equipment has been acquired, extra items may offer additional convenience in working, but will do nothing actually to improve results.

The following list includes everything necessary for developing both films and plates with the maximum of convenience. By no means all the items are essential, even if every type of work is to be undertaken; those articles which the beginner wishing to develop roll films should not try to do without are marked with an asterisk. Most people will be able to provide Nos. 8, 13, 15, 18, 19 and 21 from existing household resources, leaving only Nos. 2, 3, 5, 8, 10 and 12 to buy, and even for some of these they may already have acceptable substitutes.

An Outfit for Developing

The following list is a complete one. Only the items marked * are strictly essential for developing films.

(1)	Cupboard or box with a lock	For keeping chemicals.
(2)	Scales or	For weighing chemicals (a letter scale
(2a)*	Packet of ready-weighed developer powders	will answer the purpose).
(3)*	Thermometer	(Tested). Need not go higher than 130° F.
(4)	Small mortar	For powdering chemicals.
(5)*	Large measure	500 c.c. or 20 oz glass or enamel. This size is handy for preparing developers.
(6)	Medium measure	About 250 c.c. or 8 oz.
(7)	Small measure	10 or 25 c.c., or 1 oz marked in drachms.
(8)*	Small glass or plastic funnel	For developers.
(9)	Large glass or plastic funnel	For fixing baths.
(10)*	Developing tank	See page 140.
(11)	Glass or china bowl ..	For fixing and washing. Should just comfortably take the reel of the tank.
(12)*	Box of darkroom pins ..	For pinning films up to dry.
(13)*	Towel and dishcloth.	
(14)	Overall or laboratory coat.	
(15)*	Large and small bottles ..	For developing and fixing baths, each clearly labelled.
(16)	Two developing dishes.	
(17)	Two fixing dishes.	
(18)*	Watch or clock	With seconds hand.
(19)*	Spring clips	For weighting film strip when hung up to dry.
(20)	Dropping bottle	For potassium bromide.
(21)*	Filter papers or cotton wool	For filtering solutions.

CHOOSING AND MIXING A DEVELOPER

The beginner who glances through a big photographic reference book will find that it contains literally dozens, if not scores, of developing formulae for plates and films. He may well be hopelessly perplexed about the choice of one to develop his first negatives. But the expert looking through such a book realizes that a big proportion of the formulae are not for general work at all, but for specialized purposes, that quite a number are old formulae now hardly ever used, and that the remainder, from which he has to choose for all ordinary work, fall into four groups.

Within each group, differences between one individual formula and another are so small that few experts, and no beginners, could find any difference between the negatives yielded. In this book we therefore give a selection of formulae from three of the groups; those of the fourth, the special fine-grain developers, are best chosen from the many proprietary developers, but we cannot give formulae because the makers do not divulge them. One or other of the developers mentioned will be the correct choice for any but very specialized work such as copying. The developers chosen are:—

(1) **Ordinary M.Q.** (metol-quinol, quinol being a synonym for hydroquinone). This is only included for those who require a single developer for negatives, contact prints, and enlargements. Although designed for contact papers, it can be used with fair satisfaction for negatives, but does not bring out the full speed of the film and gives rather coarse grain. Those who make negatives $2\frac{1}{4} \times 3\frac{1}{4}$ in or larger, but nevertheless are content with small enlargements, may be satisfied with it, but it cannot really be recommended for negative development, especially as development time has to be very accurately controlled.

(2a) **M-Q-borax.** This is a standard modern developer for all roll-film work, and for miniature films too when the finest grain is not essential. It brings out nearly the full film speed, and gives very acceptably fine grain.

(2b) **Leitz Two-bath.** Similar to M-Q-borax in most respects, it is also useful in subduing contrast in harshly-lit subjects without loss of detail in shadows or highlights. It is especially valuable for pictures taken by artificial light, but is quite often used as a general-purpose developer.

(3) **Fine-Grain Developers.** These fall into two sub-classes; those, like Microdol, which sacrifice a little film-speed in exchange for finer grain, and those, like Microphen and Promicrol, which give a little extra film-speed without coarsening the grain beyond the standard set by M-Q-borax. They give fine grain indirectly, by allowing a slightly slower, and hence more finely grained, film to be used in the camera without increase of exposure. These are all proprietary products for which no formula is available.

(4) **Beutler-type Metol-carbonate.** This is designed to give the absolute maximum of speed, together with the sharpest definition, with the slow or medium-speed thin emulsion films, whose natural grain is so fine that no fine-grain developer is needed even for miniature work. It will give terribly coarse grain with the faster films. Proprietary equivalents are the Neofin developers (Tetenal) and the Kodak High Definition developer.

A Developer for Plates

For developing a plate which is sufficiently large for grain not to matter, ordinary MQ is entirely satisfactory, and it is the best type to choose when development is to be done in a dish, progress being watched by the darkroom lamp. We give the Ilford I.D. 36 Universal formula:—

Metol	..	3 gm	26 gr
Sodium sulphite (cryst.)	..	100 gm	2 oz
Hydroquinone	..	12·5 gm	110 gr
Sodium carbonate (cryst.)	..	194 gm	1,700 gr
Potassium bromide ..	..	0·75 gm	$6\frac{1}{2}$ gr
Water up to	..	1,000 c.c.	20 oz

For dish development of plates (2 to 4 minutes) add 1 part to 3 parts of water. For tank development (4 to 8 minutes) add 1 part to 7 parts of water.

For contact papers add 1 part to 1 part of water; for enlarging papers add 1 part to 3 parts of water.

Weights are given in the metric system (grams, cubic centimetres) and in the British system (grains, ounces, fluid ounces). Unless the beginner is already familiar with the British system, he should buy gram weights for his scales and get measures marked in cubic centimetres (or millilitres, which are the same thing). The metric system is far easier to learn and use.

In making up a solution from any formula in this book, either the metric or the British system must be used *for every constituent in the formula*; 3 grams of metol is nearly twice as much as 26 grains, but as 1,000 c.c. is likewise nearly twice as much as 20 oz, the solutions obtained are identical in composition.

Making up the developer is easy. In a kettle, bring rather more than enough water to the boil, let it boil briskly for two or three minutes, then let it cool to about 130° F. With a fresh piece of paper on the scale pan each time, weigh out the prescribed amounts of the various chemicals, remembering to put a second identical piece of paper on the pan with the weights to ensure accurate balance. Put the five pieces of paper, each with its chemical, in a row on the table, being specially careful that metol and hydroquinone do not blow about, as if they do they will stain anything on which they may fall.

Measure out about 750 c.c. (or 15 oz) of the boiled water and put it in a jug. Put into it a pinch—about half a teaspoonful—of sulphite and stir till dissolved. Then dissolve the other chemicals in turn, *in the order in which they are given in the formula*, letting each dissolve before adding the next. Finally, enough of the boiled water is added to bring the solution up to 1,000 c.c. (or 20 oz).

The mixed developer is then placed in a bottle of such size that it is filled right up to the neck, and tightly corked with a rubber stopper or a cork that has been dipped in melted paraffin wax (candlewax) to render it completely air-proof. As developer in contact with the air in a half-filled bottle deteriorates fairly rapidly, it is even better to divide the solution between several small bottles that need not be opened until their contents are wanted for use.

Those who have no scales can purchase the chemicals for I.D. 36 in packets, ready-weighed; all that then has to be done is to dissolve them according to the instructions on the package and bottle the solution as described.

In either case the bottles should be clearly labelled " I.D. 36 Developer for Negatives: Stock Solution." The latter term implies that the solution is a concentrated one for storage, needing the addition of water before use.

Developing a Plate

Developing a film out of sight in a tank is a routine operation from which the beginner can learn little or nothing. But a very great deal can be learnt from watching a plate develop. We shall therefore describe in detail the development of an ortho plate of moderate speed, as seen by the red darkroom lamp. The beginner is urged to carry this out himself if he can, but if this should be impossible he should read and re-read this section till he has absorbed every detail of it. This knowledge will be of the greatest possible assistance later in detecting wrong exposure or wrong development in his tank-developed film negatives.

As an ortho plate is insensitive to red, it can be developed by the light from a darkroom lamp in which is placed the correct red filter, or safelight screen.

The latter must be designed specifically for use with orthochromatic emulsions.

On the developing bench place three dishes. In the first put (for a 9 × 12 cm or 3¼ × 4¼ in plate) 50 c.c. (2 oz) of developer made by taking one-third this amount of I.D. 36 stock solution and making up the total bulk with water. The second dish should contain about 100 c.c. (4 oz) of water, and the third about the same amount of acid fixer (see page 136). Turn out the white light, and wait until the eyes are accustomed to the much dimmer darkroom lamp.

At a respectful distance from the lamp, open the dark slide and remove the plate. One side is shiny glass, the other dull white with a faint sheen. This is the emulsion side, and must be uppermost in the dish. Tip the developing dish, slip the plate into it face up, and lower the dish to make the developer run evenly over the plate. Rock the dish gently and watch. In three-quarters of a minute or so the first traces of the image will appear; they will represent the brightest part of the subject—e.g., sky in a landscape (see Fig. 180a). As development continues, the half-tones, and then the shadows, will appear, until after about two minutes the negative will look like Fig. 180b.

At this stage, the red light, and the cream-coloured unused emulsion still underlying the image, conspire to make the picture seem far stronger than it really is. Continue rocking for a total time of some six minutes, or until the image appears decidedly too dark, and veiled over. The edges, protected from all light in the dark slide, will stand out sharply, pure white. Then rinse the plate quickly in the water in the second dish, and transfer it to the fixing bath in the third. After a minute or so in this, the white light may be turned up.

The four stages of development are shown in Fig. 180. But the experienced photographer judges when a plate is far enough developed by holding it between his eye and the red lamp, and looking *through* it. This the beginner must study for himself; it is impossible to reproduce satisfactorily on paper the appearance of a negative as seen in this way.

Continuous rocking of the developing dish is important, for if the developer is allowed to stand still, uneven development of the negative may result. For this there is no cure. Airbells sometimes occur, but can be avoided by flowing the developer evenly over the plate when it is first put in. If any airbells are seen, they can be broken by wiping the plate, in the developer, with cotton-wool or with the finger-tip.

Developing Panchromatic Plates

Pan plates are sensitive to all colours, including red. Hence development must be done in complete darkness. Usually the instructions given with the developer give the exact time needed, so for the expert there is no great difficulty. But the novice finds mistakes all too easy with no light at all.

Desensitizing

By bathing a plate or film in solutions of certain dyes, of which pinacryptol green is one of the best known, its sensitivity to light can be greatly diminished without harming the image. Desensitizers are supplied ready-prepared in powder or liquid form, complete with instructions. Usually two minutes' immersion in complete darkness is required, after which even a panchromatic plate can be developed by a bright green light. A special safelight screen for

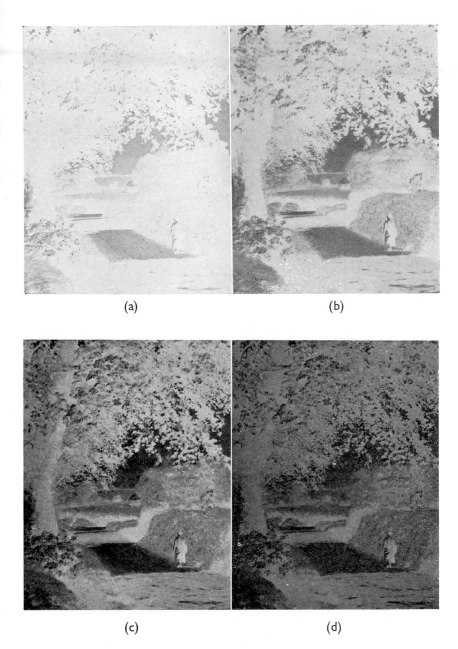

(a)   (b)

(c)   (d)

Fig. 180—Four stages of development: (a) One minute—the image appears. (b) After two minutes. Not nearly done yet. (c) Four minutes. Still not done, though this is what the plate will look like when fixed. (d) Six minutes—ready to fix. But if the plate looks like this AFTER fixing, it has been developed too long

Fig. 181—One cannot see through an incompletely fixed plate, owing to the creaminess of the unused emulsion

Fig. 182—When fully fixed the negative becomes much more transparent. Always hold a plate by the edges, as shown here

this can be bought. But as nearly all amateurs develop in a tank, except for occasional special purposes, desensitizers are not much used.

Fixing

Only part of the emulsion on the plate is used to produce the negative. Some silver bromide is left unexposed and undeveloped, and is still sensitive to light. This is converted into a soluble form in the fixing bath, and is washed out in this bath and in the early stages of the washing that has to follow.

The fixing bath consists of a strong solution of sodium thiosulphate, which is invariably known to photographers as hypo. This is an abbreviation of hyposulphite of soda, its name in a system of chemical nomenclature now long obsolete. A simple solution of hypo in water does not make a very satisfactory fixer, and an acid fixer is always used. A suitable formula is:

Hypo	.. .. ..	200 gm	4 oz
Potassium metabisulphite..		25 gm	$\frac{1}{2}$ oz
Water to	.. .. ..	1,000 c.c.	20 oz

Acid should be added to the fixing bath, in the form of potassium metabisulphite, to prevent the brown discoloration that occurs where a trace of developer has been left behind. Ready-mixed acid fixing salts, with instructions for dissolving, can be had from any dealer and save weighing.

In the fixing bath the cream-coloured layer quickly disappears. A plate or film should be left in the fixer for twice the time that is needed for the cream-coloured layer to disappear. This is necessary to ensure that fixation is complete; if it is not, the finished negative will in time develop stains and marks that will render it useless.

To ensure that fixing is complete it is a good plan to treat all negatives (and prints too) with two fixing baths in succession, the second being fresh and unused. When the first bath is exhausted it is replaced by the second, which in turn is replaced by a fresh one.

136

The fixing bath can be used several times, but after some time it begins to work more slowly, and then it is better to renew it. Fifty plates size 9 × 12 cm, fifteen 3¼ × 2¼ roll films, or fifteen 36-exposure miniature films can be fixed in each litre of hypo. In a fixing bath reserved for prints, at least 200 9 × 12 cm prints or an equal area of enlargements can be fixed. The same fixing bath should not be used for both negatives and prints, chiefly because it then becomes very difficult to know how long it may safely be kept in use.

Hardening Fixers

As the gelatine carrying the image on plates or films is easily damaged, a hardening fixer is always advisable for negatives, especially in warm weather. These include alum, or chrome alum, which tan gelatine. A standard formula is:

Hypo	240 gm	4¾ oz	
Sodium sulphite (cryst.) ..	30 gm	260 gr	
Acetic acid (glacial) ..	64 c.c.	1¼ oz	HARDENING
Alum	7½ gm	65 gr	FIXING BATH
Boric acid	15 gm	130 gr	
Water to	1,000 c.c.	20 oz	

Hardening fixing salts can be obtained ready weighed, requiring only to be dissolved in water. The beginner should buy them in preference to mixing his own, as these baths require to be compounded with skill and accuracy.

Fig. 183—Washing plates in a special washing tank. They should be allowed one hour in running water

Fig. 184—Plates drying in a rack. Choose a dust-free place, out of the sun and not near a stove

137

Washing and Drying

When it is fixed the plate is taken out of the hypo and held under the tap to wash off the hypo on the surface. Then it must be washed in running water for an hour to remove all traces of hypo, which, if allowed to remain, will crystallize out on the negative as soon as it dries if present in quantity, and will cause eventual fading if present in smaller amounts. If running water is not available, washing can be done by changing the water eight times in an hour. When washed, the plate is placed on a rack to dry.

When drying more than one plate in a rack, see that the glass sides are turned towards each other, and that the emulsion sides are sufficiently wide apart to allow free circulation of air. Put the rack in a dust-free place, in *still* air, and they will dry in a few hours. Never carry half-dried plates from room to room, because this produces variations in density that show as drying marks. Do not dry plates in direct sunlight, or near a stove, or the gelatine may melt. Do not touch the surface till the plates are fully dry.

An Instructive Experiment

In order to get acquainted with the commonest negative faults, it is a good plan to make some bad negatives on purpose. On a subject such as the still-life of Fig. 125, make three sets of exposures. The first three should be under-exposed (1, 2 and 3), the next three correctly exposed (4, 5 and 6) and the last three over-exposed (7, 8 and 9), all on identical plates or films. Develop 1, 4 and 7 for too short a time, 2, 5 and 8 develop normally, and develop 3, 6 and 9 for too long a time.

The results of this experiment are shown opposite (Fig. 185).

1 is under-exposed and under-developed, and so is very thin.

4 is correctly exposed but under-developed, so that the lights show good detail and gradation, but the shadows are not nearly dense enough. The negative as a whole is too thin.

7 is over-exposed and under-developed, and is grey all over and too thin. Still, it is usable.

2 is correctly developed but under-exposed, so that the light parts are well rendered, but the shadows are missing.

5 being correctly exposed and developed is a good negative.

8 is over-exposed and very dense, but shows good gradation and can be used for both prints and enlargement.

3 was under-exposed so that detail in the shadows is missing, and, being over-developed, what has been recorded is too dense. The negative is therefore hard and unusable. The tone contrasts are harsh.

6 was correctly exposed but over-developed, so that the gradation has become harsh. But fairly good prints can be made on soft printing-paper.

9 has become so dense through over-exposure and over-development that it must be reduced before trying to print from it.

Compare your own negatives with these examples and try to make them like 5.

Tank Development

Though the technique of development is best learnt by handling plates, modern cameras nearly all use roll films. These are best developed in a tank.

138

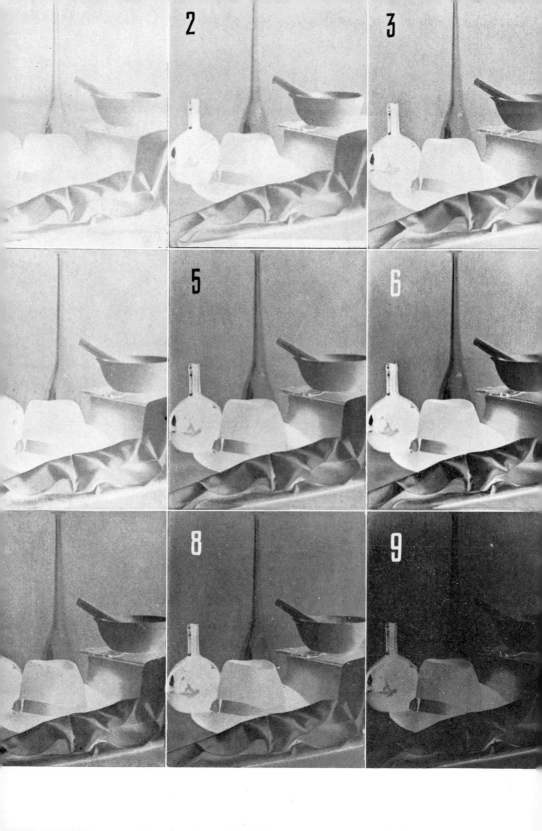

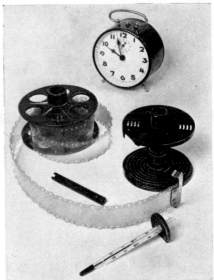

Fig. 186—Daylight-loading developing tank for 35 mm film. Note the built-in thermometer. Developing can be done anywhere, even when travelling

Fig. 187—Left, spool of Correx tank, with apron. Right, spool of spiral-groove tank; the film is held by its edges in a groove cut in the inside of the flanges. Note clock and thermometer; tank development requires both

There are two kinds of tank: those in which the film is held in a spiral and the Correx tank in which a celluloid " apron " with raised dimples along its edges is wound on to the spool with the film. The raised dimples keep the film away from the apron, thus allowing the developer free access to the film. The two types are shown side by side in Fig. 187. You will need both a clock and thermometer for tank development.

Both types have their drawbacks, for with the spiral-groove tanks there is sometimes a little difficulty in inserting the film, while with the Correx tank the dimples on the apron produce tiny dots on the edges of the film that lose us a few millimetres of the picture. For 35 mm film the Correx tank is entirely satisfactory, as the film is held by its perforated edges, and the picture space is not encroached upon.

Ease in loading the tank can be acquired by practising, in daylight, with a length of old film. With a spiral tank it is a good plan to round off the corners of the leading edge and take the curve out of it by flattening it. The film then slides in more smoothly.

Development takes place in complete darkness, as the lid of the tank is light-trapped; but the work is done in a fully-lit room. Developer and hypo are poured in through a light-trapped aperture in the lid, and there is a spout at the side of the tank for emptying it,

Fig. 188—Tank development: 1, 6, 7, 9, and 11 are stages in the " step by step " outline (see page 142). 10 shows one stage in the improved second method

Development Step by Step

(1) Separate the parts of the tank; body, lid, reel, knob.

(2) Prepare the developer.

(3) Bring the developer to the right temperature. Prepare the fixing bath and bring it to the same temperature.

(4) Check the developer temperature; it should be 65–68° F.

(5) Look up development time for the developer *and film* being used.

TURN OUT THE LIGHT.

(6) Unroll the film and slide it into the spool. Discard the paper. Do not touch the surface of the film; handle it by the edges.

(7) Put the loaded spool into the tank.

(8) Put the lid on.

LIGHTS UP.

(9) Pour developer in carefully.

(10) Lift the tank and tap it gently on the table. This gets rid of any airbells.

(11) Put in the knob and turn. Continue to turn regularly.

(12) Half a minute before the developing time is up, pour off developer into a basin. Keep the tank closed.

(13) Pour in water, temperature 65° F, and immediately pour it off again.

(14) Pour in the hypo. Turn now and again.

(15) After a quarter of an hour the tank may be opened.

(16) Pour off fixer.

(17) Wash for an hour in running water.

(18) Remove film from the spool.

(19) Hang it up, and wipe off adhering moisture.

(20) Rinse the spool and put it to dry.

One end of the film is pinned to a shelf with a darkroom pin so that it hangs freely; the bottom end is weighted with a clip.

The photographs of Fig. 188 show clearly how this method works. No darkroom is needed, and in a well-blacked-out sittingroom or bathroom the light need only be out for a few minutes while the film is loaded into the tank. This can equally well be done in a cupboard, or even under blankets. All the rest can be done in daylight.

Of course, there may be occasional failures. The progress of development cannot be watched in a tank and sometimes, however much care has been taken, the film turns out too thin or too dense, usually the first. If exposure has been correct, the most usual cause of this is exhausted developer.

Drying Films

To ensure that the film dries evenly, it should be wiped down with a well-washed wash-leather kept for the purpose and stored in a Bakelite box to keep it clean and free from dust. The wash-leather is well wetted, then wrung out and rolled up so that there are no folds in it. Pull the film taut with the left hand, first making sure it is firmly pinned at the top, then wipe down first one side and then the other with the leather. A useful arrangement for drying is shown in Fig. 191, which explains itself.

After wiping down, inspect the whole film to see that no loose specks of gelatine from the edges have found their way on to any of the negatives. At

Fig. 189—Winding a miniature film on to the spool in company with a Correx band. This is hung on a hook to keep it off the floor

Fig. 190—When washed, the film is hung in a dust-free and not over-warm place to dry. A darkroom pin secures the top, and a weighted clip on the bottom keeps it straight

this stage any such particles can easily be removed with a corner of the damp wash-leather, but once the film is dry they cannot be removed.

A careful worker, whether beginner or expert, will keep a small notebook in which, for every film developed, he will make a note of the make and name of film, developer used, temperature, time of development, and the result obtained. It will not be long before he regards the book as indispensable (see page 124).

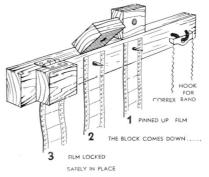

Fig. 191—A convenient way of drying films

Perfected Tank Development

Pouring in the developer takes time, and so does pouring it out again. It is impossible to know *exactly* how long the developer is acting on the film. Where the development time is short this may be important.

Here is a method of working that allows of precise timing. In addition to the developing tank, two basins that will take the spool, or two extra tank bodies, are needed. The tank is used for development, then the spool is

143

rinsed in the first basin and transferred to the second for fixing. Successive steps in the procedure are then as follows:

(1) Separate the parts of the tank—body, lid, reel and knob.
(2) Put the two basins beside the tank. Prepare the developer, bring it to the right temperature and fill the tank before the film goes in.
(3) Prepare the fixing bath, and fill basin 2 with it. Fill basin 1 with stop-bath at the right temperature. Formula—

Chrome alum	..	..	15 gm	260 gr	
Water	..	..	500 c.c.	20 oz	STOP-BATH

This both stops development at once and hardens the film.

Note. It is more convenient to keep this as a strong solution to be diluted with water for use. Put 150 gm (6 oz) of chrome alum in a litre (quart) bottle and fill up with *cold* water. It will dissolve very slowly: invert the bottle occasionally till all or most has dissolved. This will take a week or so. Take one part of this and four parts of water for the actual stop-bath, and use once only.

(4) Check the temperature. Developer and stop-bath must be at 65–68° F.
(5) Look up development time.
(6) LIGHTS OUT.
(7) Load film into spool. Start the darkroom clock (it should have a seconds hand), and put film into developer. Put the lid on the tank.
(8) Switch on light. Rotate the spool evenly and continuously to avoid uneven development.
(9) Half a minute before developing time is up: **lights out.** Count seconds until development time is up, then lift the spool out of the tank and drop it into the stop-bath, where development will stop immediately and the film will be hardened. After five minutes or so in this it goes into basin 2 to be fixed. Since the basins have no lids, all this has to be done in the dark, but as the exact time in the stop-bath does not in the least matter, and the later stages of fixing can be done in full light, this is no handicap.

When the Film is Dry

The wet film should not be handled more than necessary, no matter how anxious we may be to see the results. But a careful examination of it when dry will reveal any mistakes we may have made. These are much more likely to be mistakes of exposure than of development.

Probably most of the negatives on the strip will be dense enough, but some may be too thin. This indicates under-exposure. No developer, or change in development time, could have helped much here (see Fig. 185—the series of pictures opposite page 138), and if any improvement could have been made it would only have been at the cost of spoiling the correctly exposed negatives. *Good negatives can ONLY be made by correct exposure.*

If, when we are taking a photograph, we are not sure of the exposure, we can make two exposures instead of one, giving one about four times the exposure of the other. One at least will give a usable negative, especially as an exposure more than the minimum is usually harmless, while one less than the minimum always lead to failure.

Comparing the negatives with Fig. 185, the wrongly-exposed ones will easily be recognized. There may be one or two fully-exposed ones that might have been developed longer, but all negatives on one roll have to be developed together, and one cannot spoil the successes to patch up the partial failures, which again emphasizes the importance of correct exposure.

Watch the Temperature

In the instructions already given for developing, the temperature of the solutions has been prominently mentioned each time. Development is a chemical process and, like all other chemical processes, it proceeds more rapidly at a high temperature than at a low one. *Development time means nothing unless temperature is fixed.*

If the correct development time is 10 minutes at 65°, then if 10 minutes is given in a developer at 58° the negative will be thin and flat—under-developed, in fact. At that temperature the time needed would probably be 13 or 14 minutes. Similarly, if developed for 10 minutes at 72°, the negative will be dense and harsh; at this high temperature only 7 or 8 minutes would be needed for correct development. We advise that development be always carried out at a temperature of 65° to 68° F. At higher temperatures the gelatine may get too soft; at lower temperatures development is inconveniently slow and the gradation of the negative may suffer.

Not only the developer, but all other solutions—hypo, stop-bath, *and* rinse-water—must be at the same temperature, or the sudden change from one to another may cause the gelatine to crinkle into a network of fine lines— the dreaded " reticulation." But once the film is hardened, either in a chrome alum stop-bath or in a hardening fixer, no further attention need be paid to temperature.

Choice of Developer: Formulae for Plates, Roll Films, and Miniature Negatives

As we said earlier in this chapter, we are restricting ourselves to a few picked developer formulae. All are popular and well-tried, and all can be purchased ready-made or ready-weighed.

On the whole, the best developers to choose are as follows:

For plates and roll films (6 × 6 cm, VP size, or larger) Ilford I.D. 36 may be used (formula on page 130) but MQ borax (Kodak D76 or Ilford I.D. 11) is much to be preferred.

35 mm films (and roll films smaller than VP size). With moderately fine-grain films, or where the biggest enlargements are not contemplated, D76 or I.D. 11 is perfectly satisfactory. With faster films, or for the finest grain, Kodak Microdol can be recommended, but some slight increase in exposure is needed. Alternatively, change to a slightly slower film and use Promicrol or Microphen: these allow a slight *decrease* of exposure as compared with D76. Thus a film of speed 34° developed in Microdol needs about the same exposure as one of speed 31° developed in Microphen or Promicrol, and it depends on the particular films chosen which combination gives the finer grain.

145

When using the slower thin-emulsion films, such as Kodak Panatomic-X, Ilford Pan F, Agfa Isopan FF, or Adox KB 14 or KB 17, the Beutler metol-carbonate developer should be chosen. It does not give fine grain—the natural fine-grain characteristics of these films is relied upon for that—but it does give the highest resolution (image-sharpness) that the film can record. With this developer, films of this type should be exposed as though they had double their officially rated speed.

None of these developers should be used for negatives of sizes smaller than that for which they are recommended above, or there may be rather too much grain. But there is no harm in using a small-negative developer for bigger pictures. In particular, D76 (or ID. 11; the formulae are identical) is generally accepted as a standard tank developer for negatives of all sizes.

Roll-film Developer: Kodak D76 and Ilford ID. 11

This developer gives moderately fine grain without involving any loss in film speed; indeed, films to be developed in it may safely be given a trifle less exposure than if they were to be developed in the plate developer I.D. 36 (speed difference, 1 to 2 B.S. degrees). The formula is as follows:

Metol	..	..	..	2 gm	17½ gr	
Sodium sulphite (cryst.)	..	200 gm	4 oz	D76 or
Hydroquinone	..	..	5 gm	44 gr	ID. 11
Borax	..	..	..	2 gm	17½ gr	
Water to	..	..	.. 1,000 c.c.	20 oz	

Dissolve a pinch of the sulphite, followed by the metol, in about one-fifth of the water at 125° F. In a second fifth at about 160° dissolve about one-quarter of the sulphite and the hydroquinone; when dissolved, add to the metol solution. In about two-fifths of the water, at about 160°, dissolve the rest of the sulphite and the borax, mix with the rest of the solution, and make up to full bulk with cold water.

Store in bottles as described under I.D. 36 (page 133) and label clearly.

This developer is used undiluted, and the average development time is about 10 minutes at 65° F. The exact time to give depends on the film being developed; for it, refer to table on page 149.

Each half-litre (17½ oz) of D76 will develop three lengths of film, and it can be re-bottled after use to await the next film. The second film should be given 10 per cent and the third 25 per cent longer development time than the first.

Do not keep unused D76 in store (in solution) for too long; a bottleful that has been standing for several months tends to give harsh and over-developed negatives. It may be modified   D76d to prevent this by increasing the borax to 8 gm (70 grains) and adding 8 gm (70 grains) of boric acid. But in this form it is rather more quickly exhausted by use, and may give slight fog. The modified formula is known as D76d, and is not obtainable in packets ready prepared.

Leitz Two-bath Developer

A two-bath developer is designed to give rather more development to the shadow parts of a negative than to the highlights, which has the effect of

146

keeping excessive subject-contrast under control and tends also to enhance the speed of the film. The method used is to develop to a greater or less extent in a developer of low alkalinity, and then to transfer the film, without washing, to a solution of an alkali. This vigorously energizes the developer retained in the gelatine of the film; in the denser parts, where development is rapid, the developer carried over is exhausted almost at once; in the shadows, where little development takes place, it remains active for several minutes.

If the solutions are so compounded that nearly all the development takes place in the second bath, contrast is heavily controlled but the highlights tend to be badly flattened, especially if the exposure given was in excess of the necessary minimum. If, on the other hand, most of the development takes place in the first bath, there is very little preferential development for the shadows, and the resulting negative hardly differs from one developed in a normal single bath. The Leitz two-bath developer, due to Stoeckler, occupies a place midway between these extremes.

The formula is:—

A.	Metol	..	..	..	5 gm	44 gr
	Sodium sulphite	..		..	100 gm	2 oz
	Water to	..	..	.. 1,000 c.c.	20 oz
B.	Borax..	..	..	..	10 gm	90 gr
	Water	..	..	.. 1,000 c.c.	20 oz

At 68° F, a slow film should be developed for 3 to 4 minutes, or a fast one for 5 to 6 minutes, in A, and then transferred, *without* washing, to B for 3 minutes. Exact times are best found by experiment, as the thickness of the gelatine, which necessarily controls the amount of A carried over into B, exercises at least as much control over the degree of development attained as do the characteristics of the emulsion itself, and in consequence relative times in this developer do not necessarily follow the film-classification on page 149.

Fine-grain Developers for Miniature Films

Although innumerable formulae for special fine-grain developers have been published since the miniature was first introduced, of late years they have all dropped out of sight. Films are so much less grainy than they once were that for most ordinary purposes M-Q-borax is perfectly satisfactory, and those who do want to improve upon it nowadays rely on proprietary preparations, of which the formulae are not published.

For the faster miniature films we have already suggested (p. 145) Microdol, Microphen, and Promicrol, but it must be understood that these three are only a few of the proprietary developers available. They were chosen for mention solely because they are well-established, popular, and sponsored by important and responsible films, but we have no doubt there are others as good.

Beutler Metol-carbonate

For finest definition with thin-emulsion films of speed 27° B.S. or lower, this developer, or one of its commercial equivalents, is very strongly recommended. Remember that films to be developed in it should be given half the normal exposure for their rated speed. Care *must* be taken over correctness of exposure, for thin-emulsion films have little latitude.

The two solutions needed are:—

Solution A			
Metol	10 gm	90 gr
Sodium sulphite (anhydr.) ..	50 gm	1 oz
Water to	1,000 c.c.	20 oz
Solution B			
Sodium carbonate (anhydr.)	50 gm	1 oz
Water to	1,000 c.c.	20 oz

Solution A is made up as already described; with boiled water, dissolving a little of the sulphite first, then the metol, and lastly the rest of the sulphite. It keeps well for long periods in a full and tightly-corked bottle. No precautions are needed in making up solution B, and it will keep almost indefinitely. But it *must* be made up, and measured out, with accuracy.

For use, 1 part of A and 1 part of B are added to 10 parts water. The mixed developer will not keep for more than an hour or so, and must be used once only. Development times at 65° F are from 7 to 10 minutes with films of the type suggested. The slower films require the shorter times.

Proprietary equivalents of the Beutler metol-carbonate are the Tetenal Neofin developers and the Kodak High Definition developer. Equally good results can be had using Rodinal, Azol, Kodinol, or Certinal, all of which are concentrated developers needing only to be diluted with water, but when using any of these the film should be exposed at its rated speed.

Developing Times for Different Films

The correct developing time to give will obviously depend on the developer chosen. It also depends very greatly on the particular make and type of film used, on the grade of paper on which the negatives are to be printed, and on the contrast of the subject photographed. It is not possible to allow precisely for all these factors, so tables of development times can only be a guide for first trials.

All we can hope to do is to give a development time that will ensure that a correctly-exposed film, no matter whether exposed on a flat or a contrasty subject, will give a negative that will print well on paper of one or other of the several grades of contrast.

If first trials give negatives of too much contrast, give shorter development next time.

If first trials give negatives of too little contrast, develop longer next time.

On the strict understanding, then, that the times we give are no more than guides, and not inflexible rules, we will go on to actual figures of development times.

In general, the faster films develop more slowly, and so require longer developing times than the slower ones, but there is no *exact* correspondence between development time and speed. So instead of taking the speed-number as a guide to development time, we divide films into the five groups as shown below. All the films in any one group require approximately the same time of development. But of course the characteristics of any of these films may have been altered by the makers since the book was printed.

Group 1 35 *mm films:* **Adox** K.B.14, K.B.17; **Agfa** Isopan F.F.; **Ferrania** Pancromatica F.2; **Super-Pancro** P.3; **Ilford** Pan F.; **Perutz** Pergrano.

          Roll films: **Adox** R.14, R.17; **Agfa** Isopan F.F.

Group 2 35 *mm films:* **Adox** K.B.21; **Agfa** Isopan F.

          Roll films: **Adox** R.21; **Gevaert** Gevapan 27.

Group 3 35 *mm films:* **Ilford** F.P.3; **Kodak** Panatomic X.; **Perutz** Peromnia, Perpantic.

          Roll films: **Agfa** Isopan 17; **Crumiere** Super Aviachrom; **Gevaert** Gevapan 27; **Ilford** F.P.3; **Kodak** Panatomic X; **Perutz** Peromnica and Perpantic.

Group 4 35 *mm films:* **Agfa** Isopan I.S.S. and Ultra; **Gevaert** Gevapan 30, 33, 36; **Ilford** H.P.3; **Kodak** Plus X.

          Roll films: **Agfa** Isopan I.S.S. and Ultra; **Gevaert** Gevachrome, Gevapan 30, 33, 36; **Ilford** H.P.3, Selochrome Pan; **Kodak** Verichrome Pan; all **Bauchet** and **Lumière** films.

Group 5 35 *mm films:* **Ilford** H.P.S., **Kodak** Tri X.

          Roll films: **Crumiere** Aviapan; **Ilford** H.P.S.; **Kodak** Tri X.

Development Times

The following table gives suggested developing times, in the four developers of which formulae have been given, for all the films listed above:

Development times in minutes at 68° F			
Film Group	I.D. 36 Dish strength	I.D. 36 Tank strength	D76
1	2	4	6
2	$2\frac{1}{2}$	$4\frac{3}{4}$	7
3	$2\frac{3}{4}$	$5\frac{1}{2}$	8
4	$3\frac{1}{2}$	7	10
5	4	8	12

Super-speed Developers

There are one or two proprietary developers on the market for which it is claimed that with their use a film may be exposed as though it had a fantastically high speed-number—*i.e.*, it may be grossly underexposed by normal standards,

149

but nevertheless will yield a satisfactory negative if developed in one of these " super-speed " developers.

The position is this: with almost any developer the thinness and lack of contrast typical of underexposure can be compensated for, up to a point, by prolonging development—or, what comes to the same thing, using a more concentrated developer than usual or developing at a higher temperature. But if, on the film so treated, there are any normal exposures, they will necessarily be grossly overdeveloped—that is, they will be far too dense and contrasty, and terribly grainy. Briefly, the amount of extra development has to be carefully adjusted to suit the particular film and its exact degree of underexposure.

This, evidently, is not practical in general photography, where exposures on different subjects are bound to vary a little, but for special purposes like photography at the circus, this technique is entirely successful, particularly when a preliminary trial exposure or two can be made. The proprietary superspeed developers are not, in fact, appreciably better or worse for this work than any standard developer like D76, but nevertheless their use, when needed, is strongly advised—simply because the originators supply, with the developer, full details of the best development times for several degrees of underexposure for each of many different films. Such information could only be worked out by the amateur at the cost of many hours of experimenting and a good many feet of film.

Faults in Developing

Accidents of many kinds can happen during development if the worker is careless, but the amateur who uses chemicals in good condition, and follows instructions exactly, rarely meets with faults or failures. Any that he may encounter are usually easy to diagnose if he has a clear mental picture of what goes on in the tank. The results of incorrect exposure and development are shown in Fig. 185 (opposite page 138); the results of using old film are described on page 119. Dark streaks are nearly always due to light leaking into the camera, while general fog may be due to an insufficiently dark darkroom or to an unsafe darkroom lamp.

Some unusual faults are shown in Fig. 192.

RETOUCHING

Our aim, let us remember, is a perfect negative, which alone will give a perfect enlargement.

The commonest imperfection in negatives is tiny clear spots, caused by specks of dust on the film at the time of exposure, or airbells in the developer. With 9 × 12 cm and 6 × 6 cm negatives these spots, with care, can be touched out. For this a fine sable paint brush, No. 1 or No. 0, will be needed, together with a little brown or black water-colour paint. Touch the point of the damp brush on the paint and fill up, very lightly, every pin-hole in the negative. *The brush must be almost dry.*

Retouching is best done on a retouching desk, as shown in Fig. 193. After a little practice, retouching will be found quite simple. Miniature negatives are too small to retouch, so great care must be taken to avoid dust in the camera

Fig. 192—SOME UNUSUAL FAULTS

Top left: blurred circular patches of light (indicated by arrows). Cause: internal reflections in the lens, and not halation or a fault in development. Usually due to forgetting the lens hood. Top right: reticulation (enlarged). Due to sudden shrinkage of the gelatine on transferring it, while soft, from a warm solution to a cooler one, or to the use of cold tap water for rinsing after development. There is no cure. Bottom left: these are not trees, but fog due to electric discharges on the celluloid of the film. This may occur when the film is too dry, especially if it was unrolled rapidly before development. Bottom right: the lamp is drawn out to the right as a result of winding on the film with the shutter still open

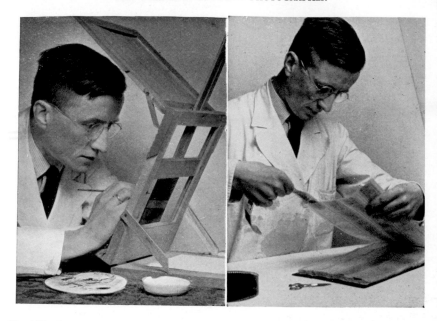

Fig. 193—Retouching desk in use. Bright, well-diffused light is needed for easy working

Fig. 194—For storage, miniature films are cut into strips and slipped into a wallet or negative album. All sharp corners are first rounded off

or in the developer. Specks of dust that settle on the negative during drying are less harmful; they cause white spots, not black ones, on the enlargement, so the retouching can be done on the print. For any elaborate retouching an enlarged negative must be made, but it is less trouble in the end to take such care throughout that the original negative is flawless, and so needs no retouching.

REDUCTION AND INTENSIFICATION OF NEGATIVES

These processes are far less necessary nowadays than they used to be. Gaslight and bromide papers, for contact printing and enlarging, can be had in so many grades of contrast, ranging from extra-soft to ultra-hard, that for every variety of negative there is a paper that will give a good print.

Reduction depends on dissolving away part of the silver of which the image on a negative is composed, so reducing its density. This process is useful if the negative is " fogged," with a grey veil over the whole image. The usual cause of this is unwanted light, an old film, or over-long development.

Fog can be removed by a weak solution of Farmer's reducer, which consists of a mixture of hypo with a little ferricyanide. Acid hypo, or a prepared acid fixer, must *not* be used; the reducer must be prepared from crystals of plain hypo. The formula is:

Solution A					
Hypo ..	..	..	..	10 gm	1 oz
Water to	..	..	..	100 c.c.	10 oz
Solution B					
Potassium ferricyanide		..		10 gm	1 oz
Water to	..	..	..	100 c.c.	10 oz

Potassium ferricyanide consists of light red crystals dissolving to give a yellow solution. This solution must be stored in a dark bottle. Note that potassium ferrocyanide (bright yellow crystals) is useless.

For use, 10 c.c. of B is added to 90 c.c. of A. The negative, which must have been fully fixed and well washed, is soaked in water and put into the reducer. In this it remains until the reduction has gone very nearly far enough. Then it is rinsed under the tap, washed for half an hour and dried.

Farmer's reducer first affects the least dense parts of the image, so that heavily veiled shadows can be cleared; the contrasts then become greater.

It is characteristic of Farmer's reducer that it first attacks and dissolves the weakest deposits of silver. A negative with little detail in the shadows should *not* be reduced with Farmer's, or the details will be completely lost, but it is invaluable for over-dense or foggy negatives. Once mixed, the bath quickly loses its ability to reduce.

Fig. 195—(Left) Fogged negative, of which half has been treated with Farmer's reducer. The fog is gone and the shadows cleared. (Right) An over-hard negative, half of which has been treated with ammonium persulphate. The reducer has chiefly attacked the dense parts and made the negative much softer

Reducing Contrast with Persulphate

Sometimes, through over-development, a negative may be a little too hard. Such a negative will be too dense in the lights and with plenty of detail in the shadows, so that even with the softest of papers it will not give a good enlargement. Farmer's would be no help here, since it attacks the shadows first. For a negative such as this ammonium persulphate should be chosen. This reducer has the special characteristic of acting first on the densest parts, leaving the shadows untouched for a time.

Ammonium persulphate should be bought in a sealed bottle, for much depends on its condition. It attracts water and, if there is any liquid among the crystals at the bottom of the bottle, some at least of the contents have decomposed and are unusable. The crystals must be dry.

To make the reducer dissolve 2 grams ammonium persulphate in 100 c.c. water, or 26 grains in 3 ounces. Distilled water is absolutely necessary for this. The crystals make a curious crackling sound when dissolving. Then add 2 c.c. (or 30 minims) of concentrated sulphuric acid. This solution must be made up at the last moment and can only be used once.

The negative to be reduced must have been thoroughly fixed and properly washed, and should be dry when immersed in the solution. A whole length of film can be treated at once in a developing tank. The densest parts are most quickly and vigorously attacked, with the result that the contrasts of the negative are reduced.

Reduction must be stopped just before the desired result is attained. The action is checked by transferring the film to a 5 per cent solution of sodium sulphite crystals. Then fix for a short time and wash in the normal way. If the stop-bath of sodium sulphite is not used, the reducing action will continue and the film will be reduced further than intended. Before putting a whole length of film into the reducer it is best to try the effect on one of the less important negatives, carefully noting the time necessary for reduction.

By the addition of 30 drops of 1 per cent solution of potassium permanganate to 100 c.c. (3 oz) of the solution of ammonium persulphate the reduction can be made more regular. The brown stain that results on the film is easily removed if the stop-bath of sodium sulphite is replaced by a 5 per cent solution of potassium metabisulphite.

Intensification

If a film or plate is not dense enough, then by adding something to the negative image its density can be increased. This, however, involves coarsening the grain.

It is essential to note that intensification can only take place where there is already some density. If, through under-exposure, the shadows are completely blank, intensification will not produce detail in them.

The traditional mercury intensifier coarsens the grain too much for the small negatives made by the modern amateur; for this reason we will not discuss it further. For larger negative sizes the uranium intensifier will be found valuable.

The formula of this is as follows:

A	Uranium nitrate	..	..	12 gm	100 gr	
	Water to make	..	..	500 c.c.	10 oz	URANIUM
B	Potassium ferricyanide	..		12 gm	100 gr	INTENSIFIER
	Water to make	..	..	500 c.c.	10 oz	

For use take 4 parts of A: 4 parts of B; and 1 part of glacial acetic acid. After intensification, wash in several changes of still water till the yellow stain has gone.

For miniature negatives, and indeed for most amateur work, the chromium intensifier is best. Prepare the following solution:

Potassium bichromate	..	20 gm	175 gr	
Potassium bromide ..	..	20 gm	175 gr	CHROMIUM
Hydrochloric acid (25%)	..	20 c.c.	2½ drachms	INTENSIFIER
Water to	.. ..	.. 1,000 c.c.	20 oz	

The plate or film must have been properly fixed and well washed. In the above solution the negative is bleached as far as it will go, after which it is washed until all yellow colour disappears. In the bleaching the silver in the negative is converted into silver bromide, and at the same time chromium is precipitated on it, which produces the intensification. The negative must next be exposed to bright light—for example, for one minute to diffused daylight—and then redeveloped. For this a fine-grain developer must on no account be used; of the developing formulae we have given the *only* permissible one is ID. 2. But a developer as used for printing papers is equally suitable. Redevelopment must be thorough; there is no danger of overdoing it, as at the most all that can be developed is the original image plus the additional material from the intensifier.

The chromium intensifier serves very well when only the shadow-details need intensifying. For this one part of the above bleacher is diluted with four parts of water, and in this the negative is left only long enough to bleach the thinnest parts of the image. The negative is then washed and redeveloped as before. Considerable improvement usually results.

Dye Intensification

Intensification by dyes involves no coarsening of grain, and can in consequence be specially recommended for miniature work. The silver of the image is converted into a substance that will readily absorb dyes, which can give density enough to provide very considerable intensification.

Copper sulphate	..	..	20 gm	350 gr
Potassium citrate, neutral	..		125 gm	5 oz
Acetic acid (glacial)..	..		15 c.c.	5 drachms
Ammonium thiocyanate	..		12 gm	210 gr
Water to make	..	..	500 c.c.	20 oz

Dissolve the first three chemicals in 400 c.c. (16 oz) of water. Dissolve the thiocyanate separately in 50 c.c. (2 oz) of water and add to the first solution. Dilute to volume. Then wash, and immerse the negative with the help of a plate-clip for one minute in:

Victoria green	.. ..	0·14 gm	1¼ gr
Safranin	.. .. ..	0·28 gm	2½ gr
Acetic acid (glacial)	..	6·5 c.c.	64 minims
Water to	.. ..	800 c.c.	16 oz

Finally wash for five minutes.

STORING NEGATIVES

This is very important. There are a hundred and one methods of doing it, and almost any is better than just leaving them lying about.

Miniature films should never be rolled up for storage, as successive turns rub against each other and produce scratches. The film should be cut into strips of four, six, or nine negatives, and kept flat in a negative wallet or album. In this they are protected from greasy or damp fingers, dust and so forth. (See Fig. 194, page 152.)

Each film should be numbered; preferably the numbers should correspond with those in the development notebook. In an album there is generally an index, in which we can record the film by subject and date.

If the films are inserted in the envelopes in chronological order, they are quickly found when wanted. Mark the number in ink on the perforated edge so that when a negative has been taken out for making enlargements it can easily be replaced in its proper place. To prevent damage the sharp corners should be rounded off with scissors.

A similar scheme should be adopted with 6 × 6 cm negatives, which may also be stored in separate negative envelopes kept in a box with an index. Glass plates are kept in their original boxes with a label showing subjects and dates. Orderliness in this respect will save hours of time otherwise lost in searching in the wrong places!

9 THE POSITIVE PRINT

EVERY good photographer must be able to make perfect prints from his negatives. Next to the exposure, this is the most important part of photography. The whole effect of the pictures depends on correct printing technique. Expose the print too long, and a sunny landscape can be made to look as though taken in a thunderstorm. Care is very necessary when printing.

The old printing papers that slowly darkened when exposed to daylight are entirely obsolete. The modern amateur uses contact papers which are worked like a film. They are first exposed and then developed. Printing paper, however, is much less sensitive than films. The emulsion of a film consists of silver bromide while that of the paper consists of silver chloride. As this is only sensitive to violet and blue light, it can be handled and developed in bright yellow light. Printing can even be done in a corner of the sitting room, where it is warm and we have someone to talk to, but in this case you must pick the darkest corner of the room, and arrange a bright yellow light to work by. Sit there with your back turned to any other light there may be in the room (it must not be daylight).

For exposing the prints a desk light with a switch in its base (Fig. 196) is ideal.

In a negative the tone values are reversed compared with those of the subject.

Fig. 196—Printing in the sitting room with a desk lamp

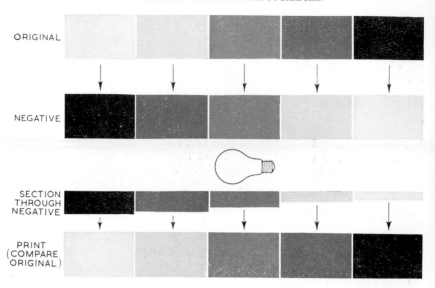

ORIGINAL

NEGATIVE

SECTION
THROUGH
NEGATIVE

PRINT
(COMPARE
ORIGINAL)

Fig. 197—Negative and print: photographing the original subject gives a negative in which the tone values are inverted. In making a print from this negative the tones are again inverted, giving a positive having the tone values of the subject

The sky is dark, a house light; a face dark and a dark suit transparent in the negative.

In printing we expose the paper to light *through the negative*. When the negative is transparent much light reaches the paper, so that it goes very dark in the developer. The half-tones of the negative pass less light, so here the paper only turns grey. Very little light can pass through the densest parts, so that hardly any effect is produced on the paper. The effect of this, as Fig. 197 shows, is to produce a positive.

For holding negative and paper in close contact while printing, a printing frame is required. The negative is laid in the open frame with the dull (emulsion) side uppermost. On this, emulsion side down, is placed a sheet of printing paper, and the frame is closed. Next it is exposed for a few seconds to artificial light and the paper is taken out and put into the developer. The image speedily appears and is completely developed in a minute or less. The print is then transferred to an acid stop-bath, in which development is abruptly checked. After this it goes into the fixing bath, to dissolve the unused parts of the sensitive emulsion and so make the picture permanent. The print is then washed and hung to dry, when it is ready for the album.

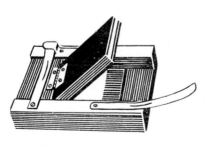

Fig. 198—A printing frame

This is an outline of printing; now we will discuss it in detail.

For ease in printing it is a good plan to sort the negatives to be printed into piles of similar type. An obvious plan is to put them in three piles: thin, normal and dense. Since a piece of paper exposed under a thin negative will need less exposure-time than one exposed under a dense negative, this will make it easier to give correct exposure to each of a batch of prints.

But this is not the only consideration; negatives can vary in contrast as well as density. In practice it is even more helpful to group negatives as soft, medium and hard, for each set will require paper from a different packet.

Printing Papers

Photographic manufacturers produce different kinds of paper to suit different negatives. A normal paper is used for negatives of normal contrast, but for negatives that are too hard and contrasty we can buy a soft-working paper that, while giving too soft and grey a print from a normal negative, will give excellent prints from a hard one. The principle is simple; if there is too much contrast in the negative, make up for it by using a paper lacking in contrast. Between them, negative and paper have to supply the amount of contrast needed, but it does not much matter how much each provides so long as the total is right. If 1 stands for normal contrast, whether in negative, paper-characteristics, or final print, we can use a normal negative on normal paper and get normal contrast: $1 \times 1 = 1$. But if the contrast of the negative is over 1, say $4/3$, then we use a soft paper, of contrast characteristics $3/4$, and still get a normal print: $4/3 \times 3/4 = 1$.

With soft paper, evidently, much change in the amount of light reaching it through the negative makes little difference to the depth of tint produced on development.

Contrasty paper is just the opposite; small differences in the light reaching it make big differences in the depth of tint produced when it is developed. Such paper will in consequence give a good print from a negative with very little contrast.

Fig. 199 shows all this clearly, and shows how important it is to be able to judge the contrast of negatives and to become familiar with the various grades of paper needed.

There are several grades of contact paper. In all makes and surfaces three grades—usually called soft, medium and hard—can be had, while in some makes four or even more grades are offered, especially in paper with a glossy surface, which is the most popular. And we must learn to use them all. The right paper must be carefully chosen for each negative.

Choice of the correct grade of paper to suit the negative brings us exactly half-way to making a good print. There is a second essential: correct exposure.

Investigation has shown that it is chiefly the tone-rendering in the highlights that determines the technical excellence of a print. This means that in a good print the texture of the material of a white dress should be visible; that a bath towel must not be just a white patch on the print, but must look as rough as it would feel. A hand in a portrait must not be just chalky white, but must show the fine detail of veins and wrinkles. Though a dark suit

NEGATIVE

PRINT

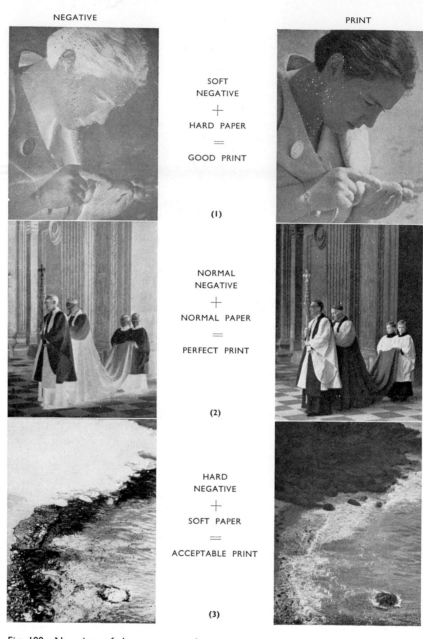

SOFT
NEGATIVE
+
HARD PAPER
=
GOOD PRINT

(1)

NORMAL
NEGATIVE
+
NORMAL PAPER
=
PERFECT PRINT

(2)

HARD
NEGATIVE
+
SOFT PAPER
=
ACCEPTABLE PRINT

(3)

Fig. 199—Negatives of three types, each printed on a correctly chosen paper, all give good prints. (1) " What on earth is this ? " (2) The Archbishop of Canterbury leaving St. Paul's Cathedral. (3) Breakers on the Devonshire coast

should not be shown as solid black, it is even more important to show all gradations of light and dark in the sitter's face. In all cases gradation in highlights is much more important than in the shadows, though it must of course be present there too.

These considerations lead to the following rule:

(1) *Correct highlight rendering depends on correct exposure*

In Fig. 201 this is shown very clearly. The left-hand top print is under-exposed, so the light parts are blank white, a most unpleasant effect. The right-hand top print has been correctly exposed and has beautiful detail in the highlights. Print 3 was badly over-exposed, so that the lights are too dark and grey. Comparison of these three shows how important it is to expose so as to bring highlights to just the right depth.

Number 4 is a complete failure. It was under-exposed and then over-developed in an attempt to bring up detail. As a result it is fogged. It is only fit for the waste-paper basket.

The second rule for printing is no less important than the first:

(2) *The depth of the shadows depends on choosing the right grade of paper*

If these two rules are faithfully followed success can be guaranteed.

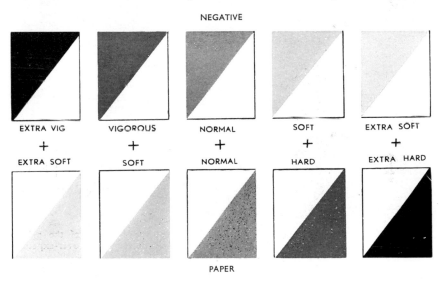

NEGATIVE

EXTRA VIG	VIGOROUS	NORMAL	SOFT	EXTRA SOFT
+	+	+	+	+
EXTRA SOFT	SOFT	NORMAL	HARD	EXTRA HARD

PAPER

Fig. 200—Prints of normal contrast are given by any of the above combinations of negative and paper. Nevertheless, normal negatives give the best prints

161

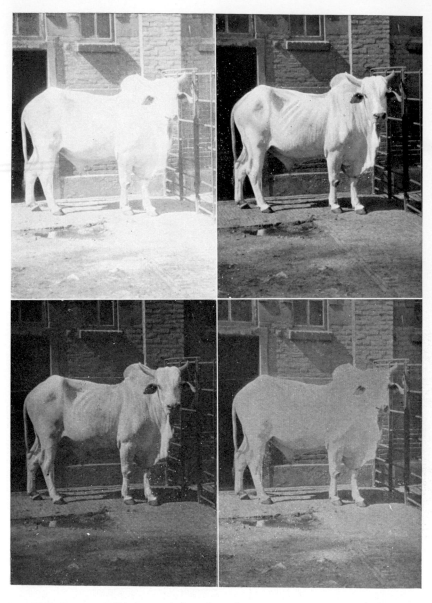

Fig. 201—Correct highlight rendering depends on correct exposure of the print: Top left: under-exposed. Top right: correctly exposed. Bottom left: over-exposed. Bottom right: under-exposed, and then fogged

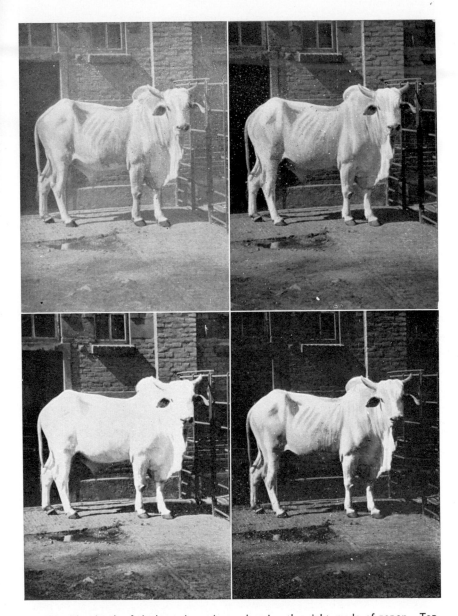

Fig. 202—The depth of shadows depends on choosing the right grade of paper. Top left: printed on too soft a paper. Top right: perfect print. Bottom left: a layman would call this nice and sharp, but it is too hard and has no detail in the highlights. Bottom right: exposed longer than the last in trying to get detail in lights, but now the shadows are far too dark, for the paper was too hard

Let us imagine that we take a negative and make a print from it that shows good detail in the highlights but has shadows which are only grey instead of rich and deep. Then the paper chosen was too soft. So we try again, this time with a harder paper, and again expose so that the highlights are of the correct depth. The shadows will now be stronger, owing to the greater contrast of the paper.

By keeping to these two rules anyone can become an expert printer.

Determining Correct Exposure

Exposure is found by making a test strip. The negative is put into the printing frame and a piece of contact paper is laid on it, sensitive side down. The frame is closed, turned over, and put under the lamp. Suppose we have decided to try six different exposures. We place the frame 18in from the lamp, and switch on. After 5 seconds we cover the first strip with a piece of cardboard without interrupting the exposure of the rest of the negative. After another 5 seconds the card is moved on to cover the second strip. The first strip has then been exposed for 5 seconds and the second for 10 seconds. So we continue, moving the card up every 5 seconds to cover yet another strip, until finally after 30 seconds the whole frame is covered. The paper is then developed, and will show a result like that of Fig. 203.

Fig. 203 shows that the fourth strip is correctly exposed. As this had 20 seconds, we take a fresh sheet of paper and expose the whole negative for this

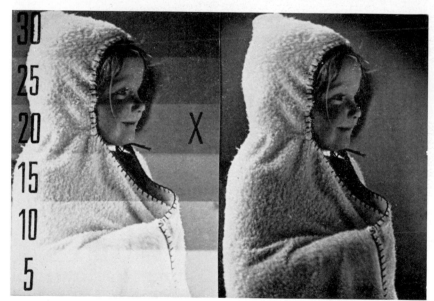

Fig. 203—The test strip. The test strip was exposed for 5, 10, 15, 20, 25 and 30 seconds. The 20-second exposure is correct

Fig. 204—The correctly exposed print: 20 seconds. On a second sheet of paper, the whole picture is exposed for 20 seconds, giving an excellent print

time, being careful to have the frame at *exactly* the same distance from the bulb as for the test strip.

When examining a test strip, choose the section that gives the best rendering of the highlights. If in this section the shadows are too grey, a harder paper must be used: if they are too black and heavy a softer paper is required. In general it is better to make the print too soft than too hard, as a print that is even a little too hard will show either blank highlights or solid shadows without detail.

An Instructive Test

Lay two strips, one of soft paper and the other of extra-hard, face down on the glass of the frame, without using a negative. Give a total exposure of 128 seconds, sliding a card progressively over the frame after 1, 1·4, 2, 2·8, 4, etc., seconds as shown in Fig. 205. The exposure is then doubled at every second step.

When developed the steps will look something like Fig. 205. On the soft paper the first step is light grey with an exposure of one

Fig. 205

second, and only really black after an exposure of 64 seconds. But the hard paper gives quite a different result. On this 4 seconds exposure is needed to produce a faint grey, and full black is produced by 32 seconds. The range of exposure times on hard paper is 4 : 32 or 1 : 8, and on soft paper 1 : 64. So that with a soft negative, showing only small differences in density, we can still get a print of high contrast. From hard negatives that show differences in opacity of 1 to 64 (the shadows pass 64 times as much light as the highlights) we can still produce a well-graded print on soft paper.

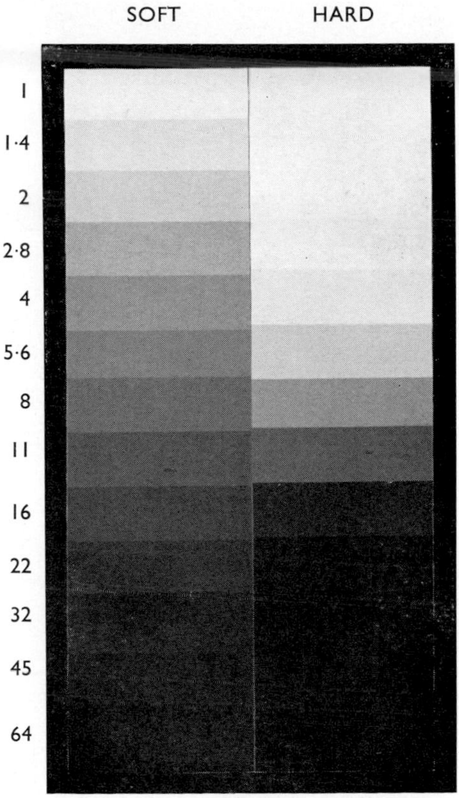

If the exposure is chosen to give well-graded highlights, it is not always necessary to use the deepest black that the paper can give. This depends very much upon the nature of the subject and on the impression we wish to convey. A portrait of a fair-haired girl, or of a baby (Fig. 207), is more than dark enough when the shadows are printed a good grey. Strong blacks would be out of place in this sort of work. Pictures of this kind are said to be in a high key.

In documentary photographs it is generally preferred to have as much contrast as possible, but over-heavy shadows without detail should be avoided as they give a gloomy impression and rob the picture of its brilliance.

Fig. 206—Printing box in use

Fig. 207—" FAST ASLEEP "

Printing Boxes

A printing box is a convenience used by professionals who have to make prints in quantity. Though printing boxes for professional use are often quite complicated, a simple one can easily be made at home. The printing light is contained in a box on the upper side of which is a hole over which a printing frame is screwed. A yellow light which is permanently on so that one can see to adjust the paper in relation to the negative, and a switch on the outside of the box to control the printing light, provide all the essentials. The great advantage of a printing box is that a print may be exposed without flooding the room with light; one person can then expose prints in rapid succession and pass them to a second person for development.

The chief disadvantage is that, as the negative faces inwards into the box, it is not possible to " print up " denser parts of a negative (usually the sky) by giving a little extra exposure while covering the less dense (landscape) parts of the negative with a card.

Developer and Development Time

There is only one *best* developer for contact paper; the formula depends on the make of paper, and will be found in the packet you buy. That is the developer you should make up if you mix your own. In many cases, this same developer is sold in ready-prepared form by the maker of the paper, but there are also excellent general-purpose contact paper developers on the market.

The time of development will be given in the instructions accompanying the paper, and will be correct so long as the maker's developer is used at the temperature mentioned in the instructions. Times vary from one make of paper to another; some require 20 to 30 seconds, others a minute or more.

When the exposed paper is put in the developer the image will come up quite quickly, get rapidly darker, and then quite suddenly cease to darken any more. This marks the end of development; allow the print another few seconds to make sure the end has really been reached and then fix it. Longer development will give stains or fog; with shorter development the print colour will be poor and the tones muddy-looking. Errors in exposure (except the slightest) *cannot* be corrected by longer or shorter development; development must *always* be complete but not unduly prolonged.

When the print is fully developed, it must at once be taken out of the developer and dropped into an acid stop-bath, which will immediately check the developing action. A 2 per cent solution of acetic acid or potassium metabisulphite serves well as a stop-bath. After one minute in this the print is transferred to the fixer.

Fixing Bath

The fixing bath for which the formula is given on page 136 is just as suitable for prints as for films, but two separate supplies of it should be kept, one for prints and enlargements and the other for negatives.

Again two fixing baths should be used in succession. When first put into bath 1, turn the print over and over several times, and at intervals during the fixing time of ten minutes move the prints about, separating them from one another so as to ensure that hypo has free access to every part of every print.

To ensure complete fixation, which is necessary if prints are not to fade, fix for another five minutes in bath 2. When bath 1 is exhausted, bath 2 is promoted to its place and a new bath 2 of fresh hypo is taken into use.

For thorough washing it is advisable to put the prints into a 2 per cent solution of ordinary washing soda for one minute; this neutralizes the acid and allows the time of washing to be halved.

Washing, Drying and Trimming and Glazing

Fill a dish with water, preferably at about 65° F, and after rinsing each print separately under the tap to remove hypo from its surface, put it into the dish. After 10 minutes fill a second dish, and transfer to it the prints, one by one, draining each thoroughly as it is lifted out of the first dish. After another 10 minutes empty both dishes, fill them up with fresh water, and transfer the prints as before. Do this six times at intervals of 10 minutes and the prints will be thoroughly freed from hypo.

The prints are free from hypo if a little of the wash water does not decolourize a very pale pink solution of potassium permanganate. If it does decolourize it, the washing must continue. The permanence of a print depends on proper fixing and thorough washing.

When the prints are washed they are laid face down in a little pile on a piece of thick plate glass. The water between them is then pressed out with a towel or a folded piece of blotting paper. This gets rid of a good deal of water. Now lay them out to dry, face upwards, on blotting paper or a towel. (They can be pinned to corks threaded on a string, but as the pins make holes, laying out is, perhaps, the better method.)

After drying, the prints will probably curl. Carefully flatten them out by drawing them face up over the edge of a table, damp them very slightly at the back with a moist sponge, and place them under a thick book. In 24 hours they will be absolutely flat. With a small trimmer cut the edges square.

A brilliant glaze can be given to prints on glossy paper. Here are two points that assure success:

(1) The prints should first be thoroughly dried, then soaked in water for 5 to 10 minutes. Next they are squeegeed face down to spotlessly clean plate glass using a rubber-covered roller called a squeegee. It is not necessary to harden the prints beforehand, as prints that have been thoroughly dried do not stick to the glass when they dry again.

(2) The glass must be very carefully cleaned before using. Scrub it more than once with a brush and soap. The first prints will stick, so for first trials use spoilt prints or enlargements.

The plate glass is cleaned with a rag soaked in spirit and a little French chalk. When the plate is clean bend the print backwards into a gentle curve, and press it down on the glass, beginning with one end. In this way water and any airbells there may be are expelled. Superfluous water is worked out with a squeegee or a wash-leather, which also forces the print into close contact with the glass. Do not dry near the fire, but in dry air. If glazing is done in the evening, the next morning the prints will be found lying beside the glass with a beautiful glaze. If they are still on the glass, a corner lifted with the edge of a knife is enough to bring the whole print away.

A high gloss is particularly desirable for prints that are to be reproduced.

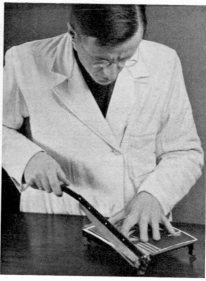

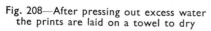

Fig. 208—After pressing out excess water the prints are laid on a towel to dry

Fig. 209—Using a trimmer. For big prints a knife and straight-edge is generally used

10 ENLARGING

MODERN small negatives require to be enlarged. This is simple, pleasant work that is well repaid: instead of small contact prints we make big pictures over which we have full control, for the photographer himself chooses the right part of the negative to enlarge, and settles how large the picture shall be.

If there is any difficulty in understanding how an enlarger works, think of a magic lantern. The principle is the same. A small picture on glass (the slide) is put into the lantern and gives a big picture on the screen. If the screen were replaced by a sheet of sensitive paper, the projected pictures could be captured permanently. Fig. 210 tells the story more clearly than words.

Enlargers

Nowadays vertical enlargers, with the sensitive paper laid horizontally, are almost exclusively used. The requirements for a good enlarger are these:

(1) A first-class lens capable of giving the finest definition. Its maximum aperture need not be wider than f/4·5, and it will usually be stopped down to f/5·6 for greater sharpness.

(2) It is of the greatest importance that the negative should be evenly illuminated.

(3) A well-finished negative carrier that holds the negative flat, and is free from sharp points or rough edges that could damage the film.

(4) The whole apparatus must be solidly built to avoid lack of sharpness due to vibration.

THE MAN HIMSELF

Fig. 210—In taking a photograph a reduced image of the subject is produced on the film. Reversing the direction of the rays of light can give an enlargement as the final print

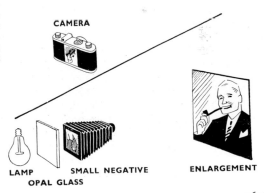

CAMERA

LAMP SMALL NEGATIVE ENLARGEMENT
OPAL GLASS

169

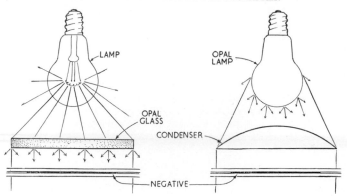

Fig. 211—Two ways of providing diffused light. (Left) A clear bulb with flashed opal glass. (Right) An opal lamp with a single or double condenser. A clear bulb with a condenser gives hard pictures

It is sometimes thought that a specially-designed lens is needed for enlarging. Though this is true if a very wide aperture is used, at all medium stops most camera lenses will give equally fine results.

The best lens to choose is one having the same characteristics as the one in the camera—the camera lens itself should be used if it can be detached from the camera or otherwise adapted to the enlarger. In any case, the lens used in the enlarger should have the focal length normal for the size of negative; a 5 cm lens for a miniature enlarger, a 7·5 cm lens for a 6 × 6 cm enlarger, a 10·5 cm lens for a 3¼ × 2¼ enlarger, and a 13·5 or 15 cm lens for an enlarger for quarter-plates or 9 × 12 cm negatives.

A lens of shorter focal length will not " cover " the negative, but will cut off the corners, while a lens of longer focal length will necessitate inconveniently long distances between lens and bromide paper, and with many enlargers will limit the size of picture obtainable.

Even illumination of the negative can be obtained in two ways. One is by diffusing the light from the lamp by a sheet of flashed opal glass above the negative. It is important to obtain genuine *flashed* opal, which can be distinguished from true opal glass by looking at the cut edge. Flashed opal is transparent glass with a thin layer of milky glass on one side; true opal is milky throughout, and obstructs far too much light.

Fig. 212—The Valoy enlarger made for the Leica, with masking frame. This enlarger, which uses an opal lamp and a single condenser, is suitable for miniature negatives only

The second way of obtaining even illumination is with an opal lamp and a condenser. This is a crude lens a trifle bigger than the negative, and may consist of either one or two glasses. The condenser collects light from the lamp and directs it through every part of the negative towards the lens.

For amateur work it is best to use either an enlarger with a diffuser of flashed opal, or else the combination of condenser and opal lamp. In the latter case the lamp chosen should have a *large* bulb, for a clear lamp with a small filament will give rise to the Callier effect, which results in strong over-accentuation of contrasts. Hard enlargements then result. A single condenser gives this effect just as much as a double one. The Callier effect does not depend on the type of condenser, but solely on whether the light is focused by it. With a large bulb of opal glass the light is too diffused for this to be possible.

Accessories

Four dishes, big enough to take the largest prints likely to be made.

Four smaller dishes, if the first four are too big for general work.

Focusing aid (mirror, ground glass, and lens) or a focusing negative (dense negative or fogged film with a few cuts in the emulsion). Both the mirror device and focusing negatives with a geometric pattern can be bought quite cheaply.

Tongs (tweezers, forceps) for handling the prints—these keep the fingers out of developer and hypo.

A bromide-paper safelight for the darkroom lamp. A red light, though it is safe, should *not* be used, for it is dim and makes the prints look more contrasty than they are. This is a prolific cause of spoilt prints and wasted paper. A proper bromide-paper safelight is brighter, easier to work by, and much more restful to the eyes.

Choice of Negatives

Good enlargement can only be made from good negatives. Choose those that are full of sharp detail and moderately soft, not too contrasty, and free from the clear shadows that indicate under-exposure. But above all, they must be *sharp*.

When a negative is enlarged, any faults it may have are enlarged too.

Paper for Enlargements

The chloride paper used for contact prints is far too slow for enlarging; exposures would run into many minutes, and sometimes even

Fig. 213—The Agfa Varioscop, an automatic enlarger for $2\frac{1}{4} \times 3\frac{1}{4}$ in down to miniature negatives. As the head is raised or lowered for a larger or smaller picture, the image is automatically re-focused.

into hours. The fastest is bromide paper, which gives a neutral black image. The newer types of chlorobromide paper (Plastika, Bromesko, Bromega, Prestona) are but little slower, and give pictures of a slightly warm black with better gradation than bromide paper.

For first attempts choose a white glossy paper and learn to enlarge on this. The criterion for a technically good print is that the paper base shall remain white and that the image should have a good tone. Later on all sorts of tints and surfaces can be tried.

Paper can be had with a white, ivory or cream base. These again are made with different surfaces; glossy, semi-matt and rough. Glossy white is best for documentary work. Ivory semi-matt is better for child portraits and sunny landscapes. Personal taste must be the guide in this. Gevaert Gevaluxe is a special paper with a very beautiful soft velvety texture specially suitable for large prints. Its particular attraction is the great richness of the blacks.

Enlarging paper, like the gaslight paper used for contact prints, is made in several different grades. The ideal plan is to choose a good make of paper and buy two or three packets of different contrast grades. Do not expect them all to be of the same speed, for they are not likely to be; even different batches nominally identical may require different exposures. Once you have got to know one type of paper, keep to it.

The rules for printing given on page 161 apply with equal force to enlarging. So we repeat:

(1) *Correct highlight rendering depends on correct exposure.*

(2) *The depth of the shadows depends on choosing the right grade of paper.*

Follow these rules implicitly, and technically faultless prints can be guaranteed.

Developers for Enlargements

As for contact papers, the best formula to make up is that in the instructions for the paper you use. In most cases the makers of the paper supply it in packets or bottles. But a general-purpose formula for bromide papers is not noticeably less satisfactory. If circumstances compel the use of papers of mixed makes, the following will be found to work well with all:

Metol	2·6 gm	24 gr		
Sodium sulphite (anhydrous) ..	46 gm	400 gr		
Hydroquinone	9 gm	80 gr	M.Q. FOR
Sodium carbonate (anhydrous) ..	37 gm	320 gr	ENLARGING
Potassium bromide	1·5 gm	13 gr	PAPERS
Water to .. .. 1,000 c.c.	20 oz		
For use, dilute with an equal quantity of water.				

In addition, ready-weighed general-purpose bromide-paper developers are offered by several makers.

Note that the development time required for enlarging papers is much longer than for contact papers: usually $1\frac{1}{2}$ to $2\frac{1}{2}$ minutes at 68° F, but a few papers need longer.

Fig. 214

Determining Exposure

When the projected picture on the baseboard of the enlarger has been brought to the required size and sharply focused, a test strip is made in exactly the way previously described. The whole story is told in Fig. 214.

It is best to arrange that the exposure time required is ten seconds or more, so as to allow for shading. In doing this any part of the picture that we wish to keep light is shaded for part of the exposure by, say, a piece of cardboard, the edge of a piece of black wrapping paper from the packet of printing paper, or by the hand. It is surprising how flexible the hands are, and how many shapes their shadow can be made to fit. The shadow should be kept in gentle movement during the exposure in order that no visible edge should be left on the finished print. In this way it is easy, for example, to darken the foreground.

If this shading is well done, it gives many an opportunity of improving the tone values of the picture.

Grain

We know that the image of a negative is composed of grains of silver of varying size, which can be seen quite clearly with a strong pocket magnifier. When a negative is enlarged the grains are enlarged too, and if they show too clearly they will spoil the print.

This is particularly likely to happen if the grains have grouped together in clumps.

Both theoretical investigations and practical experience show that in a miniature negative grain is just on the verge of becoming obtrusive. Many miniature workers are not capable of producing a whole-plate print that is perfectly free of grain, even when using a film not faster than 27° Sch. Many miniature enlargements are blurred and granular in the even tones as a result of grain. This is most noticeable in the lighter half-tones, such as the face of a portrait, rather than in the highlights or shadows. This fault occurs when a wrong type of film (one that is too fast) has been chosen, or through wrong development.

Intensive research is enabling the manufacturers to produce films of finer and finer grain. Some day we may expect to have films of high speed with so fine a grain that this trouble will disappear. Still, there are limits. No matter what advances are made, it will probably always be necessary to use large negatives and contact prints for work demanding the highest technical perfection, such as advertisement pictures of textiles and similar subjects. In these larger sizes, even with highly sensitive emulsions, grain gives no trouble at all.

It is self-evident that paper contrast affects grain. If a negative is looked at through a lens, we can see grains with transparent spaces between them. If printing is done on a hard paper, the contrasts are exaggerated not only between the shadows and highlights of the negative, but also between the grains and the intervening spaces. A hard paper gives coarser grain; soft paper gives less grain.

If care is taken to produce negatives that require to be enlarged on soft paper, graininess will be less troublesome. But beware of making negatives that are *too* hard. They should be moderately dense, even in the shadows, if they are to enlarge really well.

Newton's Rings

If a miniature negative is placed between two pieces of glass, it is often possible to see coloured rings that are reminiscent of spots of oil on a wet road. In both cases they are due to a phenomenon called interference that occurs when

Fig. 215—Part of a print showing Newton's rings

two surfaces are separated by an exceedingly small distance. These more or less circular figures were first observed by Newton, and are called Newton's rings. They sometimes arise in enlarging a miniature negative when the negative carrier is one in which glass comes into contact with the celluloid side of the film; in the print, where they are devoid of colour, they look like Fig. 215. They can be avoided by slipping a mask between negative and glass, or by using a glassless negative carrier.

Practical Enlarging

The negatives to be enlarged are first arranged in groups of similar contrast. (This only applies with large negatives, as 35 mm film is handled in the strip.) The developer is mixed, and the print tweezers put ready. The stop-bath (see page 144) and two fixing-baths are prepared just as for making contact prints. The negative carrier is cleaned to remove any spots of dust, and the negative inserted, emulsion side towards the lens. The yellow-green light is switched on, and the white light is extinguished.

On the baseboard of the enlarger, lay a piece of white paper cut to the size of the printing paper to be used. On this, focus the image, including only the desired part of the negative. This is a very important moment, for it is the time when an exhibition print can begin to take shape.

The exposure is determined with a test strip (see Fig. 214). This strip is developed to finality; that is, it is developed until the dark parts cease to go darker. The strip is taken out of the developer with the tweezers and dropped into the stop-bath. If the tweezers touch the stop-bath, which is acid, they must be washed under the tap before putting them back in the developer. After a minute in the stop-bath the strip is transferred to the hypo. After another minute the white light may be switched on and the strip examined to find the right exposure and to check that the right grade of paper has been chosen, allowing for the fact that prints usually go a little darker in drying.

It is a good plan to have a pilot print beside the developing dish. In the darkroom light a print may seem dark enough and yet turn out to be too light when seen in full light after fixing. If we have a good print beside the dish, we can judge the right depth by comparison.

Now that the exposure is decided, put a full sheet of bromide paper on the baseboard of the enlarger and expose. After developing it for the same time as the test strip, transfer it to the stop-bath, and then give 10 minutes in the first hypo and another 5 minutes in the second. Rinse it next for one minute in the soda bath, then wash in the way described for contact prints. Check that the print is free from hypo and then dry. Flatten and trim the print as already described.

Mounting and Finishing

If the print is a really good one it should be mounted on a piece of good white mounting board. The title is written in pencil under the left of the print and under the right of it is put the author's signature. Nothing should be written on the print itself.

A good-sized trimmer is, in general, too expensive for amateur use. A glass or zinc plate, a trimming knife and a steel rule, with a set-square to give true corners, do the same work in a cheaper way. By placing over the print two L-shaped pieces of cardboard, it is easy to find the best composition and cut away what is unnecessary. But it is more economical to leave out what is not wanted when making the enlargement. Remember also that a horizon must be horizontal.

With the help of a large set-square, mark out in pencil the rectangle decided upon as the final shape of the print, lay the ruler along each line in turn and trim with a slow firm pressure of the knife. For professional work a large trimmer is a necessity.

For Whom Are Your Pictures Meant?

Surely this is a question worthy of an answer. What is the aim of your photography? You photograph for your own pleasure, but who looks at the prints? Nobody has any use for negatives that never get beyond the darkroom. They must be printed and enlarged.

And then who looks at them? You in the first place, and with, it is hoped, keenly critical eyes. And who enjoys them? Your wife? Does she just stick them in an album that is occasionally shown to friends and acquaintances? Is this a worthy fate for prints that have been made with such care from negatives taken with so expensive a camera? If that is all, you are not getting full value from your camera.

In case you agree, we suggest you make, and keep, these three resolutions.

(1) All negatives that are still waiting " to be finished some day " will *now* be enlarged—or at least printed.

(2) Every print will be technically perfect. These prints will be put in an album in correct order of dates, for it is every photographer's duty to keep a family history in chronological order. The best negatives are put on one side for enlarging.

(3) The best of these enlargements are mounted and kept in a portfolio.

From among these you select the best for criticism at your local camera club or for entry in competitions. When you have had some success in these, try sending them to exhibitions. Do not try for the big London exhibitions at first; there are plenty of smaller ones where competition is not so keen.

Hang your prints on the wall; let them be seen. A picture gives no one any pleasure while it remains in an album or portfolio. It must be seen by many to fulfil its purpose.

176

Fig. 215a—" SUMMER MAID "   Raymond P. Smith
This delightful photograph was placed first in the " Daily Mail " Summer Photo
Contest. Vivid contrast of light and shade evoke the brilliance of summer sunlight.
The photograph was taken with a Microcord camera; a green filter was used.

11 MAKING LANTERN SLIDES

EVERYONE will remember the magic lantern of his childhood. It is quite easy for any amateur to make lantern slides from his negatives, and every photographer should possess a projection lantern with the aid of which he can show his own pictures to family and friends. Owing to the greater range between lightest and darkest tones, a picture thrown on a screen from a good lantern slide is far more effective than a print from the same negative can ever be. Three things are needed:

(1) Projector and screen.
(2) A darkened room.
(3) Good slides, in black and white or colour.

There are three accepted sizes for slides, and although there is no rule about it, they are generally used for different purposes. The oldest standard size is $3\frac{1}{4} \times 3\frac{1}{4}$ in overall, and most slides of this size are made by printing from monochrome negatives. The most popular nowadays is the slide measuring 5×5 cm, or 2×2 in overall—the size of a mounted colour transparency 24×36 mm, taken with a miniature camera. More recently a slide $2\frac{3}{4} \times 2\frac{3}{4}$ in overall has been introduced; this is mainly used for colour transparencies taken with a 6×6 cm ($2\frac{1}{4}$ in sq) camera.

Larger negatives, including 6×6 cm and $2\frac{1}{4} \times 3\frac{1}{4}$ in, can be printed directly on $3\frac{1}{4}$ in sq slides, while quarterplate and 9×12 cm negatives are printed by reduction. Equally, all larger negatives can be reduced to the 5×5 cm size. This is done by placing the negative in front of a sheet of opal glass illuminated from behind, and photographing it with a miniature camera, using a suitable supplementary lens or extension tube to ensure sharp focus at the close distance involved.

Slides by Contact

There are three types of lantern plate. These are as follows: the ordinary black-tone plate, which has about the speed of bromide paper; the warm-tone

Fig. 216—Aldis projector for miniature slides   Fig. 217—Rollable glass-beaded screen

ACCEPTED
15th Intern. Focus Fotosalon
AMSTERDAM 1955

(Left) Fig. 218—A 5 × 5 cm miniature slide, actual size

(Below) Fig. 219—Leitz Eldia printer for contact prints from miniature negatives on paper or positive film

plate, much like chloro-bromide paper; and the gaslight plate, again chiefly for black tones.

For making a slide by contact the negative is placed, face up, in a printing frame, with the lantern plate face down on it, exactly as when making a print on the paper. For a black-tone (bromide) plate an exposure of only a few seconds is needed, at a distance of about 2 ft from a 25-watt lamp. For gaslight slides the exposure may be about ten seconds at about 6 in from the same lamp. The correct exposure is found with a test plate exposed in steps, exactly as is done when printing. Do not forget that slides, like bromide prints, must be developed fairly fully. An under-developed slide never gives the brilliance and delicate gradations that a lantern slide is really capable of showing.

Correct exposure and full development are thus essential. Again, great attention must be paid to the detail in the highlights, which is as important here as when printing on paper. Contrast is largely controlled by development, and longer development gives greater contrast, as in negative making.

Lantern plates of different contrast grades often have very different speeds. Hard plates often need five times, and extra-hard ones as much as a hundred times, longer exposure than normal ones. Always use tweezers, just as in developing plate negatives.

Fixing and washing are done in exactly the same way as with plates. After fixing, the slides are hardened, or a hardening fixing-bath can be used. The best developer is that given by the makers of the lantern plates used, and the instructions with the box of lantern plates should be most carefully studied.

Halation on Lantern Slides

This fault often occurs in glass lantern slides. In this case it is the *shadows* that spread, not the lights, as in negative making. Some makes of lantern plates can be obtained with an anti-halation backing, but ordinary plates can be " backed " by brushing them over on the glass side with a thick mixture of burnt sienna and dextrine. This is sponged off again before development. The improvement obtained is considerable.

The charm of the lantern slide lies in the greater wealth of tones that it can reproduce. The deepest black on bromide paper is 100 times darker than

179

the brightest white. This is a very limited range if we recall that in nature there are contrasts of 1 to 500, or even 1 to 1,000. On glossy white bromide paper this scale is reduced to 1 to 100 at most. It is even further reduced on cream matt papers, where it may be no more than 1 to 20. Lantern slides give a much longer scale of tones, especially in such subjects as those showing light falling through an archway, interiors, and all contrasty subjects. These are rendered with far more brilliance and sparkle than they can ever be on paper. This is the special charm of the lantern slide.

When the slide is dry, it is masked to show only the required part of the image. This is often done by laying strips of gummed paper on the gelatine, or by means of special masking papers ruled in squares to enable an exactly rectangular opening to be cut easily. For miniature slides a ready-made aluminium mask is often used if it is desired to project the full picture size. Then a cover glass is laid over the masked slide to protect it, and is bound in place with strips of black paper round the edges.

The whole procedure must be done with painstaking care, and the operation is a continuous struggle against dust, particularly with miniature slides.

Slides by Enlargement

When it is desired to make a slide that is larger than the negative, or to fill a slide the same size as the negative with a part only of the subject, printing

Fig. 220—Binding miniature slides. (1) White tablecloth, which makes it easier to see. (2) A negative album for flattening the film. (3) Aluminium masks. (4) 5 × 5 cm cover glasses. (5) Scissors. (6) Strips of film. (7) Single frame cut from strip. (8) Tweezers for handling the film. (9 and 10) Dusting brushes. (11) Binding frame. (12) Wash-leather for cleaning the glasses. (13) Binding strips (Cellophane). (14) Viewer. (15) Box for finished slides

is done through the enlarger. This is particularly useful when a few additional slides for a $3\frac{1}{4}$ in sq set are needed, and the only negatives available are of miniature size. The procedure is perfectly straightforward; the exposure is made exactly as in enlarging on paper, and the exposed lantern-plate is developed in the way described in the preceding paragraphs.

Two points, however, need attention. First, the image must be focused on a piece of white paper pasted to a glass the thickness of the lantern-plate instead of on the baseboard of the enlarger; when the lantern-plate replaces the paper-covered glass for the exposure one is then sure that the projected image is in sharp focus on the sensitive emulsion. And second, the lantern-plate must be laid on black paper and not directly on the white baseboard.

Slides on Film

With the aid of special equipment, miniature negatives can be printed on a continuous strip of film instead of on glass. As it is very difficult to ensure the correct exposure for each of a number of different negatives, this method is only suitable for experts. Further, these strips soon get damaged from being wound through the projector. Another disadvantage is that the order of the slides cannot be changed.

For the miniature worker it is often convenient, and certainly very inexpensive, to make lantern-slides on 35 mm positive film, which can be bought in uncut lengths very cheaply. This film can be thought of as a bromide-paper emulsion coated on a clear celluloid base; except that it often needs longer development, it can be handled exactly like bromide paper. To make a slide, a piece about 2 in long is cut off, put in a printing frame with the negative as in making a glass slide by contact, exposed and developed. As with lantern-plates, longer development gives greater contrast, and of course calls for a slightly shortened exposure to prevent it from becoming too dense. Development is usually best done in a cylindrical measure (or a tea-cup) rather than in a dish. When dry, the transparency is trimmed with scissors and bound up between glasses.

Monochrome Negatives from Colour Transparencies

It is not difficult to make excellent black-and-white enlargements from colour transparencies. The transparency is put in the enlarger with its emulsion side away from the lens, and focused to give an image of size, say, 9×12 cm.

Instead of bromide paper, panchromatic film is used, giving a black-and-white negative. Soft-working panchromatic flat film is very suitable; or, if only a little red is present in the transparency, orthochromatic film (see page 105) can be used. Films are so much more sensitive than bromide paper that a very short exposure is needed; to prevent its becoming too short, it is usually best to stop down to f/11 or f/16. Do not let the film get fogged by white light from the lamphouse. A black cloth over this latter is a useful safeguard.

The correct exposure is found by means of a test strip, and development is carefully carried out to obtain a well-graded negative. Desensitizing is strongly advised (see page 134). Contact prints or enlargements can be made from this 9×12 cm negative. The advantage of this method is that, if need be, the negative can be retouched.

The second method is by making a negative by contact on 35 mm panchromatic film in a miniature printer (see page 179). A slow panchromatic film is very suitable for this. Development of the film should be controlled to give a soft and well-graded negative. This is then enlarged in the ordinary way, and will show no grain.

Excellent results can be had by either method. The second one is particularly suitable when reproducing a number of slides, while the first is best when only one or two are to be copied in black and white.

Monochrome Slides Direct

It is possible to produce slides for projection on the film actually exposed in the camera, by developing this to a positive instead of a negative. This is specially interesting to the man who makes mostly colour transparencies, but wishes to use black-and-white film sometimes either for economy or for subjects needing something faster than colour film. One film—Gevaert Dia-Direct—is specially made for this purpose, but Ilford publish reversal processing details for their own films. Write to them for Data Sheet T203.

Projection Screens

The choice of the screen on which to project the slides is important. For home projection a sheet is often used. This reflects comparatively little light. A white visiting card held in the middle of the projected picture will at once show the difference. For home use there is nothing better than a sheet of really opaque white paper, which should be rolled up like a map on two broomsticks, to prevent its tearing.

Screens specially made for projection can be bought in several forms: plain white, glass-beaded and silver. These can also be used with an amateur ciné projector.

12 COPYING

THE camera is invaluable for making copies of written or printed matter of all kinds. Etchings, drawings, paintings, maps, accounts, music—all these can be copied. There are also methods of copying without a camera, and we will discuss these first.

If we have a piece of music, printed in black and white on one side only of the paper, it can easily be printed on contrasty gaslight paper.

The printed side of the music is placed face downwards against the sensitive side of the paper, and a sheet of glass laid on the whole to keep it flat. Holding a lamp at a known distance above the glass, a test strip is made in the usual way and developed fully. When the correct exposure is found, the whole sheet is printed. This gives white notes on a black ground, and a print made in the same way from this negative will give a positive again.

Papers are also made for music or other matter printed on both sides, and these papers make use of reflected light. Fig. 221 shows how they work. With

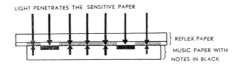

LIGHT PENETRATES THE SENSITIVE PAPER

} REFLEX PAPER

MUSIC PAPER WITH NOTES IN BLACK

Fig. 221—The principle of reflex copying

the two papers in contact, the back of the printing paper is exposed to light, and some of this light penetrates it. It is reflected by the white music-paper, while the black notes and lines absorb it. If the exposure is correct, this difference is enough to give strong contrast on the very contrasty paper used. The result is, of course, a negative reversed as in a mirror, but by reproducing this in its turn, using the same method, as many copies as desired can be made.

The other method of copying is by photographing with the camera.

Types of Original

It is by their contrast that subjects to be copied are classed. A greyish pencil sketch has very little contrast between dark and light. A woodcut has more contrast, a photograph less. In all these subjects the contrast is weak; though a woodcut appears strong, a landscape has far more contrast. The plates or films used for ordinary photography in consequence give poor results.

The plates and films used for copying are often described as having photo-mechanical (or " process ") emulsions, and the type of emulsion to be used, whether hard or extra-hard, depends on the characteristics of the original. A woodcut, for example, shows only black and white, without intermediate tones. It is therefore called a " line " subject, in contrast to a " half-tone " subject, which does contain intermediate tones. A photograph, for example, is a half-tone subject.

A 9 × 12 cm plate camera is particularly suitable for copying, for it is easy to adjust it to give a sharp reproduction of the right size.

The first condition for the production of good copies is to have the plane of the ground glass parallel to that of the object, and the lens exactly opposite the middle of the original being copied.

For larger objects, such as paintings or architectural drawings, the best way of proceeding is first to adjust the camera until the right size is obtained. Then, to make sure that the four corners of the object are at an equal distance from the lens, take a piece of string, hold it against the lens and make a knot at the exact distance of one corner of the object. Now adjust the original until the knot will just reach all four corners. Then stop down far enough to give complete sharpness over the whole picture. The most frequently used stops are f/18 to f/36.

The lighting of the subject being copied must be as even as possible. Two lamps are usually enough for small work, but for larger objects four lamps may be needed. When focusing on a screen, reflections from the surface are easily detected. Care must be taken not to allow light to shine into the lens. Use a good lens hood.

Filters

Filters are not necessary for black-and-white work if the original is free from coloured stains. For coloured objects a colour-sensitive plate or film must of course be used; if the original contains red, panchromatic material will be needed.

Positive film is often useful in miniature cameras, but for the finest detail, and for all subjects containing colours, a panchromatic micro-copying film should be used. Ilford Micro-Neg and Kodak Microfile are among the best known of these. Contrast can be increased or decreased by longer or shorter development.

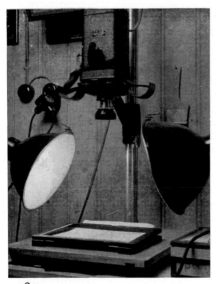

(Left) Fig. 222—Enlarger in use as a copying camera

(Below) Fig. 223—Leica focusing bellows with reflex housing

Fig. 224—Fragment of a drawing by Rembrandt: Jesus gives sight to a blind man. Copy of a photograph

Fig. 225—Copy of an old Dutch painting, made with panchromatic film and a deep yellow filter

Copying with the Enlarger

If a piece of sensitive material is placed in the negative carrier in place of a negative, and the original to be copied is put into the masking frame, all we have to do is to illuminate the original evenly and expose. The construction of the enlarger ensures that the original shall be parallel to the film. Focusing is simple, as it is done exactly as when enlarging. A negative is sharply focused to the size of the original to be copied; it is then replaced by the copying film, and the exposure made. Nothing could be simpler. To prevent stray light from reaching the film, the negative carrier, and perhaps the lamphouse, must be covered over with a dark cloth. In this way it is easy to make a good negative that can be enlarged to any desired size. For the modern miniature cameras special copying equipment can be had; this enables many valuable records to be made, including copies of accounts, of ledgers, card indexes, architectural drawings, etc.

Books can be copied page by page, and reproductions of drawings and other records can be quickly and cheaply made. Such reproductions are easily kept safe from fire, are easy to carry about, and can be reproduced when desired by enlargement or projection.

The things we copy are sometimes the property of others. For personal use (lectures, etc.) the right to copy is seldom disputed, though strictly speaking such reproduction is often an infringement of copyright. On no account should such copies ever be used for any but the most strictly personal and private uses.

13 STEREOSCOPIC PHOTOGRAPHY

STEREOSCOPY is one of the most beautiful branches of photography. It reproduces the *depth* of a subject. In looking at a view we see it with both eyes, and each eye sees from a slightly different standpoint, so that in fact each eye sees a slightly different version of the same subject. It is this that enables us to judge distances, and to see the space between near and far objects.

A stereoscopic camera consists, in effect, of two identical cameras side by side. The distance between the two lenses is about $2\frac{1}{2}$ in, which is the same as the average distance between the eyes. The negative size is usually 6×13 cm, giving two pictures each 6×6 cm ($2\frac{1}{4}$ in square). A smaller standard size is 45×107 mm for plates, and there is a 35 mm stereo camera for pictures 24×30 mm or 24×24 mm in size.

In a stereoscopic pair the pictures have slight differences, since the exposures are not made from exactly the same point. When we look at these two pictures, mounted side by side, with a special viewer, so designed that the right eye sees only the picture taken by the right-hand lens and the left eye only that taken by the left-hand lens, the two images are seen as one. By this procedure we have presented to each eye separately what it would have seen when looking at the original subject; in consequence the picture gives full relief and solidity. Near objects stand right out from those behind them, and everything seems most convincingly real. Subjects with a prominent foreground are the best to choose, as the effect depends largely on this.

Stereoscopic pictures of stationary objects can be made with an ordinary single-lens camera, using it on a stand and moving it about $2\frac{1}{2}$ in sideways between the two exposures. Stereo slides can be bought to make this moving of the camera easy.

Until recently stereo pictures could only be enjoyed by one person at a

Fig. 226—Iloca stereoscopic camera for 35 mm film. This gives two pictures each 23×24 mm, which are shown in a separate viewer. (But see also Fig. 229)

Fig. 227—Stereoscopic camera for roll film: the Rolleidoscope. There are two taking lenses; the middle lens is that of the finder

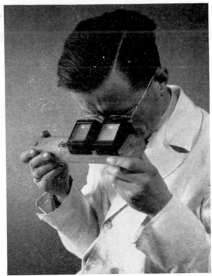

Fig. 228—Stereo viewer for 6 × 13 cm. A typical slide for such a viewer is reproduced in Fig. 230 below

Fig. 229—Two miniature viewers mounted on a pencilbox for miniature stereos in colour. An inexpensive and practical scheme

time, as only one person could look through the viewer. But it is now possible to project stereoscopic pictures; a separate projector is used for each, and polarizing filters are placed over the projector lenses. The pictures are then separated at the eye of the viewer, who wears a pair of polarizing spectacles.

Fig. 230—Stereoscopic pair, made up of two photographs, each 6 cm × 6 cm, which fuse in a stereo viewer to give one three-dimensional picture

14 HOME MOVIES

Super-miniature Photography on a Moving Film

CINEMATOGRAPHY involves the making of a continuous series of tiny negatives in rapid succession on a long strip of film. Each picture is slightly different from the last. Like the pictures of Fig. 69, they show successive steps of an action, but as sixteen exposures are made each second, all the gaps are filled in. The projector throws each in turn on the screen for an instant, and the eye links them up, since the retina holds the image for a little longer than it is actually seen. Thus the impression of movement is given to the observer.

The pictures are taken on very fine-grained "reversal" film, the original negative of which is reversed in processing to give a positive. This is best done by the film manufacturers, and with most amateur ciné films the cost of processing is included in the price of the film.

It is a mistake to think that interesting films can be made by photographing all kinds of moving subjects one after another. The result will be most disappointing. *A film must tell a story.* To make a film interesting there must be a connection between successive scenes. Once this idea is really grasped, it is not difficult to make good films. You can tell your audience, by way of the film, all about your travels, your home life, and the lives of your children. Even film plays can be successfully produced if the relationship between successive scenes is sufficient.

There are three sizes of films for amateurs: 16 mm, 9·5 mm and 8 mm. Those taking up cinematography seriously will choose the 16 mm size, which offers the widest choice of high-grade apparatus. Even sound films can be made in this size, and the pictures on the film are big enough to stand projection in quite large halls. The much smaller picture on 8 mm film restricts its use to smaller screens, but it is by far the most popular size for home use.

Fig. 231 — An 8 mm Kodak projector for amateur use

Fig. 232—The Sportster, a small 8 mm ciné camera by Bell & Howell

15 COLOUR PHOTOGRAPHY

THE world is full of colour. As ordinary photographs show only grey, black, and white, colour photography has been the object of much research all over the world. Thousands of patents concerning it have been granted, but only a few of the proposed systems have proved practical.

It is impossible to tell the whole story of colour photography in a single chapter. All that we attempt in the following pages is to explain the principles and give some advice, applicable to all types of films, for the actual taking of colour pictures.

Underlying Principles

Many years ago it was found by Young and Helmholtz that the human eye possesses three colour-sensitive organs. Each organ is sensitive to one primary colour: red, green or blue-violet. Every possible colour can be imitated to perfection by mixing these three.

This is the starting point for all colour processes. In principle, the steps involved are shown in Fig. 233. On three panchromatic plates, sensitive to all colours, a still-life consisting of a red tomato, a yellow banana and a blue bunch of grapes is photographed. First, the red parts of the subject are picked out and recorded on the first plate. This is done by exposing through a red filter. The second negative is made in the same way, but using a green filter, so that it records only the green and yellow tints of the subject. Finally, the blue and violet tints are recorded on a third plate exposed through a blue-violet filter.

In this way the colours of the still-life are analysed into the three primary colours. We have " separated " the colours, and the three plates are called " three-colour separation negatives." They are, of course, not coloured, but they have recorded, in their black-and-white tones, the amounts of red, green and blue respectively that the still-life subject shows.

If three positives on glass are now made by printing from these negatives, and if the images are respectively toned cyan-blue, magenta-red, and yellow, as in Fig. 233, it only remains to place them on top of one another, in register (that is, in exactly the right position), to give a composite print that shows the natural colours of the original subject.

It must be pointed out that there are two ways of mixing colours, and they must be clearly distinguished before the different colour processes can be understood. We can mix coloured paints on a palette, or we can mix light of different colours. The results of these two methods are entirely different.

We have seen that a spectrum is formed when a pencil of white light is analysed. If three projectors are placed side by side, as in Fig. 236, and the first one is made to project red only, by putting a red filter over the lens, the second green, and the third blue, then if these three beams of light are all directed to the same point on the screen, they combine to give a white spot.

Thus white light can be built up from colours, this being the reverse of decomposing it to give colours. This is the basis of the *additive colour processes*. A convincing experiment can be made by painting a top red, green, and bright blue in three sectors. When it is spinning, it appears a light neutral grey if the colours are correctly balanced.

But if red, green, and blue paints are mixed on a palette with a paint brush, the result is not white. The mixture is black (see Fig. 237). On first trying the experiment, the result is quite likely to be dark brown, but with the correct quantities of each of the three paints it is black. This necessarily happens because blue absorbs red and green from the white light falling on the paints, green absorbs blue and red, and red absorbs blue and green. Thus by one paint or another of the three, light of *all* colours is absorbed, and none is reflected. This is the basis of the *subtractive colour processes*.

The first method is used in what is called the screen-plate method, of which the Lumière Autochrome plate and Dufaycolor film are the best-known types. If a white cloud or a white dress on a Dufaycolor transparency is examined with a strong magnifying glass, red, green and blue squares or lines will be seen. These lines are too fine to be seen individually by the unaided eye, so all that is seen is their united effect—which is white, just as in the experiment with the three projectors. The other colour processes, Kodachrome, Gevacolor, Anscocolor, Ferraniacolor, Agfacolor, and the Ilford process, together with all methods of making colour prints on paper, are *subtractive*. Instead of being put side by side, the colours are superimposed. A mixture of all three colours thus gives black.

The principle is applied in this way. Instead of three separate plates on which to make the colour separation negatives, Kodachrome, Anscocolor and similar material, consist of three superimposed emulsion layers. The top layer is sensitive only to blue, the second sensitive only to green, and the third to red only. Between the first layer and the second there is a yellow filter that absorbs all blue light.

In the first layer, the light action at every point indicates the amount of blue there. In the second layer, the light action records the amount of green, and in the third the amount of red.

Next, all three layers of the film are developed, giving three negatives of black silver. In each emulsion the unused silver bromide that corresponds with the positive image is still present. This is *not* fixed out. This remaining silver bromide is now blackened by exposure to light followed by development. It is at this stage that the colours are formed. For this second development a colour developer is used. This has the property of producing an image in transparent dye at the same time as it develops the silver image, the amount of dye produced being proportional to the amount of silver bromide reduced. The action is so controlled that in the upper (blue-sensitive) layer, the image formed is in yellow dye; in the second (green-sensitive) layer the dye image is red, and in the third (red-sensitive) layer the dye image formed is blue.

In each of the three layers there are now two silver images, the negative and the positive, making the film completely opaque. If these are dissolved out in a suitable bath (a reducer: see Chapter 8) the three dye images remain, giving a positive in full colour.*

* The print " Symbol of Christmas " (Fig. 234, page 198) by M. Woldringh was made from an Agfacolor transparency.
" Haul Away " (Fig. 235, page 199) was made from a Kodak Ektachrome transparency taken by the author.

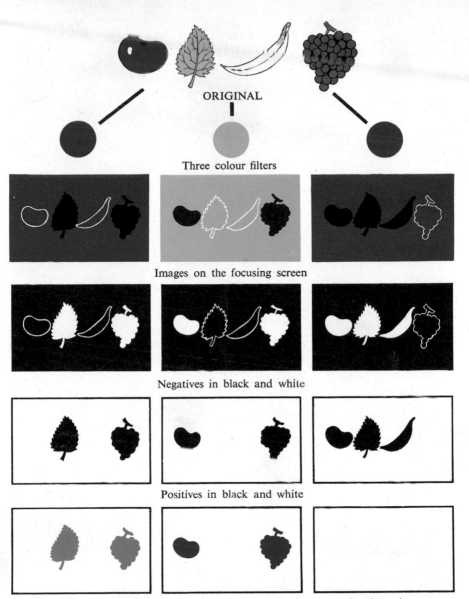

ORIGINAL

Three colour filters

Images on the focusing screen

Negatives in black and white

Positives in black and white

Positives in complementary colours, when printed over each other, give:

THE ORIGINAL IN COLOURS

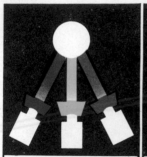

Mixing
coloured lights
Result: white

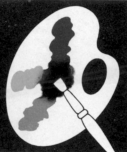

Mixing
coloured paints
Result: black

Lattice of
coloured lines on
Spicer-Dufay film

6×6 complementary colour
negative (slightly reduced)

Enlargement from part
of adjacent negative

Cine negative
in complementary colours

Colour positive printed
from negative on left

REVERSAL COLOUR FILM

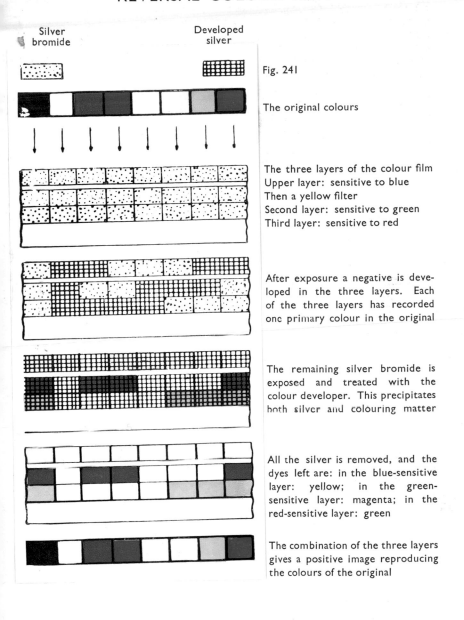

Silver bromide

Developed silver

Fig. 241

The original colours

The three layers of the colour film
Upper layer: sensitive to blue
Then a yellow filter
Second layer: sensitive to green
Third layer: sensitive to red

After exposure a negative is developed in the three layers. Each of the three layers has recorded one primary colour in the original

The remaining silver bromide is exposed and treated with the colour developer. This precipitates both silver and colouring matter

All the silver is removed, and the dyes left are: in the blue-sensitive layer: yellow; in the green-sensitive layer: magenta; in the red-sensitive layer: green

The combination of the three layers gives a positive image reproducing the colours of the original

195

Correct Exposure: Checking the Exposure Meter

The very thin emulsions used on colour films respond to deviation from correct exposure by a change in colour-rendering. Since the eye is much more sensitive to a slight change in colour than to a slight variation in density, errors in exposure are instantly noticeable. Accurate exposure is in consequence essential. Only a photo-electric exposure meter is accurate enough, and even this must be carefully tested. The first colour film used should be devoted to this test. Choose a normal subject with little contrast, such as a girl in a bright dress on a terrace against a neutral background. The meter is set at 22° B.S. or at whatever speed the film in use is rated by its makers. Suppose the pointer of the meter indicates $\frac{1}{50}$ second at f/5·6. Make five exposures, each at a different stop.

(1) $\frac{1}{50}$ at f/4	Double meter time
(2) $\frac{1}{50}$ between f/4 and f/5·6..	$1\frac{1}{2}$ × meter time
(3) $\frac{1}{50}$ at f/5·6	Meter time
(4) $\frac{1}{50}$ between f/5·6 and f/8 ..	$\frac{3}{4}$ meter time
(5) $\frac{1}{50}$ at f/8	$\frac{1}{2}$ meter time

When the processed film comes back, it is perhaps found that (3) is very good. In that case (1) and (2) will be rather thinner, and the colours rather pastel-tinted: (4) and (5) will be a little darker and warmer in colour. This clearly proves that the meter-setting chosen was correct for this subject. It might equally well be found that (1) is the best and all the rest too dark. This indicates that future exposures must be twice as long as indicated by the meter, or that the meter should be set to a speed-number three units lower.

For colour photography, and in all reversal work, the aim is to have the highlights of the finished transparency nearly, but not quite, free from image, leaving the shadows to be dark or light according to their tone in the actual subject. This means that exposure must be based on the brightest part of the subject, instead of on the shadows as in ordinary negative-making.

This is most easily done by making use of an artificial highlight, which can take the form of a piece of ivory-white cardboard about 6 in square. This must be held in the most important part of the subject and turned towards the camera. Now the meter is pointed at it from a distance of 6 in. The exposure found in this way is multiplied by three for subjects with bright colours, and by four for those with dark colours. This is a most successful method that ensures even exposure from picture to picture.

An outdoor subject is illuminated by light from two sources, the sun and the blue sky. The warm white of sunlight reaches part of the subject, but most of the light reaching the shadows comes from the blue sky. This gives them a bluish tint which the eye does not notice, but which is often very evident on a colour transparency. This tint is strictly correct, even though it may be unfamiliar.

The colour of daylight is warmer in the early morning and in the late evening just before sunset, when it contains more orange and red. The deep blue of the sky is then paler, and contains more white. The blue tinge in the shadows does not occur in colour photographs taken at these times, making them the best for colour photography. Days with many white clouds are also good; a soft layer of fleecy white clouds with sunshine is ideal for colour photography.

Colour-Temperature

If you switch on an electric bulb in daylight its light looks very yellow, yet after dark the same bulb looks white, and a white ceiling illuminated by it looks white too, for the eye has adapted itself to the yellow colour. But a film cannot do this, and any photograph taken by electric light on a colour film meant for normal use in daylight will have a strong yellow, or even reddish, cast. For colour photography by artificial light it is therefore necessary to have a special film made for the purpose. But that is only half the story; a photoflood bulb gives a much whiter, as well as stronger, light than an ordinary bulb, so a film that gives correct colours with one will yield yellowish, or bluish, transparencies with the other. The film has to be balanced, either in manufacture or by the use of a filter over the lens, to the exact colour of the light in use.

To do this necessitates some way of expressing the exact tint of the light, and this is done by giving its colour-temperature. Everybody knows that if a poker is put into a fire it becomes first dull red-hot, then bright red, then yellow-hot, and finally, if the fire is burning fiercely enough, even white-hot. Each shade of colour could be specified by the temperature of the poker at the time; that is colour-temperature. Direct sunlight has a colour-temperature of about 5,800 degrees, and a daylight colour film is balanced for that. Light from a blue sky, being bluer, has a higher colour-temperature; it may reach 8,000 or 10,000 degrees, and a colour transparency taken by such light (in shade on a brilliantly clear day) will be decidedly too blue. The yellowish light of an electric bulb has a colour-temperature of about 3,000 degrees, a photoflood 3,400 degrees, and artificial light films are generally balanced for 3,200 degrees, the figure for studio lighting. Some, however, are balanced for clear flashbulbs (3,800 degrees).

One make of exposure-meter (Gossen) has a " colour finder," which gives a rough idea of the colour-temperature of the light falling on it, but for accurate work a colour-temperature meter is needed. This, however, is for professionals rather than amateurs.

Remember always that colour photography has difficulty in reproducing contrasty subjects. One with soft lighting and little contrast is best, for the exposure cannot be exactly right both for bright highlights and deep shadows. In choosing a subject for colour, therefore, look more for pleasing combinations of colour than for the strong effects of light and shade that are so essential in black-and-white pictures.

Just as a blue sky reflects blue light, a red wall will reflect red light, or green trees green light. The eye makes allowance for the prevailing colour of the light, but the colour film does not. If we photograph a rosy-cheeked girl under a green tree, she will look like a corpse. The prevailing green light contains very little red. We know that the girl has red cheeks and consequently ignore the green. But a colour film has no experience of complexions; it just reproduces what it sees. The result is very often not what was expected.

Be wary, therefore, of surroundings that may affect the colour of the light that reaches the main subject.

A grey car, for example, is one colour when standing in the shade and receiving only light from the blue sky, and quite another when standing in late evening sunlight which is much warmer in tint. In both cases *we* call the car grey, but the film sees two very different shades of grey, neither of which would match that of the car itself in mid-day sunlight. So if colours on a slide sometimes look a little unexpected or wrong, try to recall the light at the time the exposure was made, and allow for this before you blame the film. And don't photograph your girl-friend standing between a sunlit brick wall and a bush; you may find she has one green cheek and one red one!

On the whole, close-up subjects are more successful than widespread landscapes. Avoid hard colours. No geranium beds! Mixed colours, such as brown, green-brown, light blue or soft red reproduce best. Still-life pictures of flowers in neutral surroundings, and with a neutral background, can be unexpectedly beautiful. Children playing on the sands, our friends in their leisure hours, and sports subjects will all make good colour pictures.

A lens-hood must always be used when photographing in colour. Interiors in picture galleries, artistically furnished houses, particularly by artificial light, are among the most effective subjects. But be careful of stained-glass windows; they can upset colours badly.

Colour transparencies are best seen by projection and, if much colour photography is done, a projector should certainly be acquired. A viewer, though much better than nothing, is only second-best.

In projection, a small bright image is always better than a large but dimly-lit one. A good way of getting an interesting collection of slides is by exchanging with friends abroad.

A sensitive feeling for colour and colour combinations can be cultivated by careful study at exhibitions and picture galleries.

Colour Prints on Paper

Paper prints in colour can be made from colour negatives, for which a special colour-negative film is used. This can be had as miniature film, roll film, or as cut film for plate cameras, and instead of being processed to give a positive transparency, it is developed as a negative. In this the colours, as well as the tones, are reversed, so that a blue sky is orange, grass is red, and a red frock is green. (See Fig. 239.) From this is made a print that reproduces the original colours by a second reversal. These prints can be good, but they cannot have the rich charm and high contrasts of a transparency. The developing of the negative and the making of prints can be done at home by the amateur, but is more usually done by the trade. It is a good plan to get contact prints made first from all the satisfactory negatives, and then to have enlargements made from one or two of the best of them.

When ordering an enlargement, it is best to send the contact print, as well as the colour negative, with the order. The processing firm can then match the colours of the enlargement to those of the contact print, which is done by correct choice of filters in enlarging. In advertisement or industrial work, where exact colour-rendering may be vital, it is quite usual to send a sample of the actual colour to be matched—for example, a snippet of the material from which a gown is made.

Colour-negative film is not made in two types, for daylight and artificial light, but in one type only which can be used in any kind of light. There is no need for two films, for any incorrect colour-balance can be rectified in making the print.

From a colour negative one can make, in addition to colour prints and enlargements, transparencies in colour; or prints, enlargements, or slides in black and white. Further, colour prints can be made by several different methods. All in all, the colour negative is by far the most universal type of negative it is possible to have.

The best colour prints are those of subjects with bold masses of colour rather than those broken up by a mass of fine detail in different colours. Correct exposure is very important; colour films must never be under-exposed, or negatives will be poor and the prints poorer. But quite good black-and-white prints can often be made from colour negatives of which the exposure was not quite right. For the best results, calibration of the exposure-meter is very necessary.

It is not altogether advisable to frame colour prints and hang them where bright daylight, or even sunlight, can reach them all day long. They may fade. But if pasted into an album they may be expected to last a good many years.

Colour negatives should be stored carefully in envelopes, for they are rather easily scratched. It is a good plan to write the emulsion number in ink on each negative; this will help the processing firm to make prints of good colour balance at a later date.

Colour Prints from Transparencies

Several firms, including Kodak and Ilford, will make colour prints, usually in about post-card size, from transparencies. The result depends very much on the character of the original transparency, which *must* be of good quality if it is not to yield rather a poor print. The best transparencies are those without too much contrast, and with plenty of detail in the lighter parts. If they are just a trifle denser than would be ideal for projection they should make good prints. When ordering, send a number of transparencies at once; the cost of each print is then less.

The View Meter

In finding good subjects for colour the view meter (Fig. 173) is a very great help. A ground-glass screen, as in a reflex, is much better in this respect than a viewfinder. With either screen or view meter an unsuitable background is much more easily noticed.

The Photographer at Work

16 LANDSCAPES

IN Part Two of this book we discuss landscapes, portraits, interiors and other types of subject, each of which has its own special technical difficulties and its own artistic possibilities. We shall start by considering landscape photography.

Landscape work is one of the most interesting branches of photography. It brings us into close contact with nature, which is always new and always refreshing, and teaches us to see and admire the beauty of the countryside. Photography provides an incentive to explore new places in our own country. Beginning in our own neighbourhood, we learn to see with our own eyes and develop our feeling for beauty.

A good landscape picture clearly shows the *character* of the landscape, which is something the photographer must find for himself. The picture should be kept as simple as possible. Learn to see in terms of lines and planes. Grasp the simplicity of large things, and the importance of small ones. Open expanses of country, however attractive to the eye, are always disappointing when reduced to a small size on a print. An open view from a famous vantage-point is seldom worth a film. A gate in the snow will usually make a much better picture.

The view meter (page 125) is very valuable in selecting subjects, and the screen of a reflex camera is at least as helpful.

Weather, Season and Time

" Real holiday weather " is not the best for landscape photography. The end of a passing storm, with patches of sunlight and dark clouds, will provide far more fruitful possibilities. This alternation of sunshine and shadow gives lovely effects of light.

The season is less important, for good pictures can be found at any time of the year, but perhaps summer is the least suitable, while early spring, autumn and winter generally offer more opportunities for pictures.

As regards times of day, early morning and late afternoon are usually the best, when the shadows are long and the lighting throws every object into relief. The midday hours are less suitable, as then the shadows are short and the light hard.

Direction of Lighting

A side lighting is usually best for a landscape subject, but many fine pictures have been made by exposing against the light. Water scenes taken against the light are often very good indeed.

Never forget that black-and-white photography does not reproduce colour,

Fig. 242—" SAILING "   J. Th. Hakkeling

In a landscape, concentration of light is very helpful, and is most easily obtained by
using a dark foreground as a frame.   Here the dark leaves and branches contrast with
the reflections on the water, and the pattern of their silhouette is very pleasing.   This
is a real landscape photograph, taken at the right time of day from a carefully chosen
viewpoint, giving a truly artistic picture

Fig. 243—" POEM IN SHADOWS "   J. M. Moerkerk

A beautiful landscape, taken from a high viewpoint. Entry to the International
Focus Salon of Amsterdam

and that the tints that make an autumn landscape so lovely to the eye will be lost in the print. Learn to see colours in terms of their relative brightness only.

Seeing in Lines and Planes

A " line " may be an upright tree, the horizon, a door-step, or a lane over the heath (Fig. 244). The course and direction of such lines is of the greatest importance to the composition of a picture; they should never carry the eye to the edge of the frame, but always to some point of significance—to the *centre of interest*.

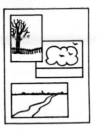

Fig. 244

Choice of Film and Filters

An orthochromatic film will suffice for many subjects, but the panchromatic film is usually more successful in capturing the mood of the picture. Where there are reds or browns panchromatic material should be chosen, and when used with a filter it is faster than an ortho emulsion of the same speed, because the filter factor is lower. But an ortho film with a medium filter gives an excellent rendering both of clouds and of green fields or trees.

However colour-sensitive the film may be, so much blue light is radiated from a blue sky that a filter is needed to keep it back. Quite a pale filter (factor 2) is usually enough, but a deeper one sometimes improves the effect.

A tripod is often needed when a small stop has to be used to give enough depth of focus. With a small stop and a filter, exposures of $\frac{1}{10}$ to $\frac{1}{2}$ second may be needed. In such cases a tripod is necessary to avoid risk of blur from camera shake.

Subjects can be selected with the greatest certainty on the focusing screen of a reflex. Though a large camera is best for landscapes, the miniature is a good second, but only when used with a thin-emulsion film, which necessitates very accurate determination of exposures. When in doubt, it is a sound plan to make two exposures, the second three times as long as the first. With these slow films a heavy tripod is desirable to prevent vibration during the exposure, especially when using a long-focus lens.

The three most important matters in landscape work are getting the light where it is wanted, ensuring that the lines of the subject are well arranged, and choosing a suitable foreground. The choice between upright and oblong must be made for each subject individually. Any foreground figures, whether people or animals, must be fittingly chosen.

Learning to reproduce the moods of nature is the photographer's greatest achievement. It demands a complete command of technique, a keen eye for beauty, and a sensitive nature. So do all other branches of pictorial photography.

17 PICTURES OF PEOPLE

AS a rule, it is people that interest us most. It is therefore not surprising that the majority of snapshots include persons—children, relations, or friends. To make such pictures interesting, the stereotyped group picture, of half a dozen people standing to be photographed, must be entirely avoided. Modern genre photography, by which is meant pictures of people at their work, their play, or their hobbies, is entirely different. It means the taking of scenes in ordinary life, showing people as they really are, and in their characteristic surroundings. This type of work is quite distinct from real portraiture; we do not reach that till the next chapter.

Every camera owner should keep a chronicle, in pictures, of the doings of his own family, especially if it includes children. Snapshots of their daily doings, though they may arouse but little interest at the time, are real family history, and gain in value with the years. A print that seems quite common-place now will be greeted with cries of delight, and will recall many forgotten incidents, when it is looked at in ten years' time. A trip to the sea-side, a day at the zoo, a visit to the country—any incident out of the ordinary will afford good material for the family history. So also will such occasions as Christmas, birthdays or parties, for these special days tend to remain in the memory, and especially in the memories of children. But to succeed in their object, such pictures must show the surroundings and something of the occasion, not just the people concerned staring at the camera.

The family chronicle, however, is but one branch of genre photography, though perhaps the most universal. In all work of this type, good composition, a well-chosen background, and the inclusion of the right accessory detail plays a great part. In all such work the miniature camera is at its best. Its lightness and convenience, its quickness in action, and the large number of exposures that can be made without re-loading are all important advantages, as is the great depth of focus of its short-focus lens.

Sports of all kinds—tennis, rowing, sailing, swimming—offer wonderful opportunities. Often they pass quickly; the best moment for exposure must be seized without hesitation. Do not stop to think too long; it is better to waste a little film than to miss a good picture. But you will get better pictures if you think a little in advance.

Men at their accustomed work—and women too—can also make splendid pictures that may later be of real historic value. In such pictures it is essential to show clearly what the worker is doing. The background and surroundings are therefore of great importance, but they must add reality and meaning, not confusion, to the picture.

Fig. 245—" THE NEW BROTHER "   B. Ph. Baron van Harinxma thoe Slooten

An unusually good family history picture. The boys' attitude, of mixed wonder and affection, is rendered in masterly fashion. The lighting is restful and well thought out: the main light was on the left, and there was an auxiliary light from the right, close to the camera

Fig. 246—" THE CHESSBOARD " C. Verloop
An effective little group. To the left there was a strong light or the sun, to the right
a weaker lamp to lighten the shadows. The intent concentration of the further player
is excellently rendered—notice the hands. Though neither face is fully shown, is not
more of the players' characters shown here than if they were just staring into the lens ?

Fig. 247—" THE DANCING CLASS "   L. A. Selleger

Instead of the stereotyped group of sitting and kneeling children with the teacher,
we have here a fine action picture taken with a miniature. The instant of exposure
was chosen to give an effective group, which demands close attention in this type of
work.

For success, complete familiarity with the camera is essential; it must be handled
unostentatiously but with instant decision. The photographer must have an eye for
lighting and for the contrast of each figure against the background. In outdoor work,
the soft light of morning or evening is far more suitable than the hard bright light of
midday. High shutter speeds are usually needed, especially in photographing children.
This means a high-speed film, even if the result is a little grainy.

An unusual viewpoint often gives an unusual picture; climb on something or lie
flat on the ground. In all genre work the same principle holds. Your subjects must
be doing something—playing chess, fishing, dancing, reading, or anything else that
makes them forget the camera. That is essential.

Remember, too, that action is best reproduced by exposing at a moment of rest
in the movement, for photography, by its very nature, can show a position more
effectively than an action. For that reason two people playing chess will always make
a much more hopeful subject than a diver. For him a ciné camera is really needed

E VEN an omnibus becomes a studio for those who have learnt to see people. Behind the mask of every face is hidden a history that should be sought for. Making life-like portraits is a difficult and unrewarding task if it is done to order, but a most interesting pursuit for those who can seek out their own models. It is no task for beginners, though they often attempt it, but is work requiring the skill of the expert who has full mastery of technique.

Begin with children, who are not made self-conscious by a camera and whose faces do not stiffen into a set expression at the thought of a portrait. Study light falling on the head and the strong contrasts it produces. Without a reflector or some additional light, the shadows are usually too dark and lacking in detail. Next learn to see which is the best aspect of a head; left or right, full face or profile. The background of a portrait is of great importance; it may be light, dark, or graduated in tone. It is often advisable to have the background darker than the lightest part, but lighter than the shadow side of the head.

Shall the portrait show the head only, or shall it include more—even the whole figure? This depends entirely on the sitter. What suits one may be quite unsuitable for another. The point can only be settled by personal taste, which can be developed by visiting exhibitions and picture galleries and by reading good books on art. Every photographer is recommended to study on these lines, for the older arts have much to teach our newer one.

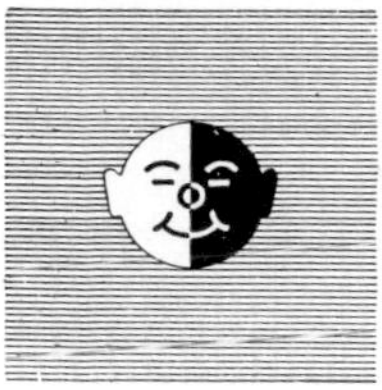

Fig. 248

Choose a camera with which a long-focus lens can be used. This gives a head large on the negative and makes it possible to keep the camera well away from the sitter, making it easier to work and giving much better perspective. The reflex is ideal for arranging the composition, but when using one of the 6 × 6 cm models with 7·5 cm lens, the camera should be kept at least eight feet from the sitter. Only the head, or head and shoulders, which will be small on the negative, should be included in the enlargement (see page 72).

For a miniature camera the 9 cm or 13·5 cm lenses (with a good finder) are particularly suitable, while with larger cameras of quarter-plate or 9 × 12 cm size, lenses of 25 to 30 cm (10 to 12 in) are used. They should be fast, so as to allow of short exposures. Experience plays a great part in this work, so that if you are far enough advanced for portraits, it is a good plan to do no other type of photography for a month or two. This makes for rapid progress. A photographer must have tact when dealing with his sitters. The making of a good portrait can be an event.

Daylight or Artificial Light

Direct sunlight is ideal, but only if there is available a good reflector—which may be a white wall, a large sheet, or a sail. It is often difficult to find a good background out of doors. Trees and bushes are quite unsuitable; they are much too spotty. A dark doorway, such as that of a shed, is far better. Out-

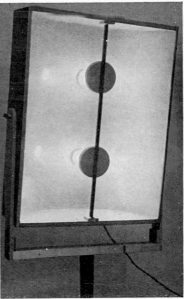

Fig. 249—A matt concave reflector, which gives soft indirect light

Fig. 250—Home-made indirect-lighting stand. Here, a large white-painted sheet of pressed fibre reflects the light of photofloods

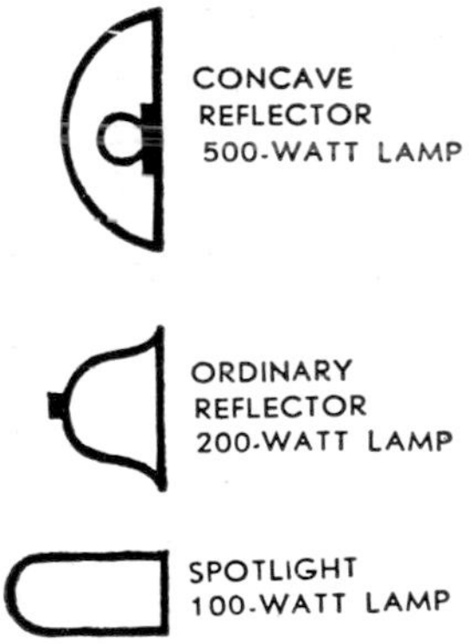

CONCAVE
REFLECTOR
500-WATT LAMP

ORDINARY
REFLECTOR
200-WATT LAMP

SPOTLIGHT
100-WATT LAMP

Fig. 251 (See also Fig. 256)

door lighting with sunshine is always contrasty, calling for ample exposure and soft development.

Artificial light has the great advantage of being easily controllable, and above all, constant. It can be arranged exactly as the photographer desires. The lamps most often used are not really suitable for portraiture: they give concentrated beams of strong light forming hard shadows. In particular the overrun lamps with a self-contained mirror reflector (Fig. 253) are to be avoided for general use. It is far better to use lamps giving only indirect lighting from a big white reflector (Fig. 249). The light-source itself is hidden by a cap, but its light is reflected from a large, curved reflector. This gives a beautifully soft light, ideal for portraits.

A handyman can easily make himself an accessory of this kind from a stand and a strong but light sheet of fibre painted matt white (see Fig. 250).

A lamp with a mirror reflector is sometimes useful as an additional light for special emphasis. For top light on hair, use a lamp on a high stand.

Special attention must be paid to reflecting surfaces when working with

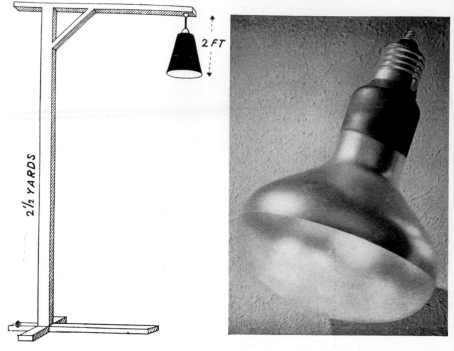

2½ YARDS

2 FT

Fig. 252—Home-made lamp for top-lighting in portrait work

Fig. 253—Lamp with mirror reflector—excellent as a spotlight

artificial light. A room with light wallpaper is far better than a large dark interior where furniture and curtains absorb all the light. An attic with a sloping roof is unsatisfactory, because too much light is reflected downwards. This can be corrected by hanging up some sheets.

Much care must be given to the placing of the lamps. The pictures of the shop-window figure in Fig. 256 tell the whole story.

Try taking some similar photographs for practice: with front light only, side light only, side light with reflector, and back lighting with reflector.

Soft Focus

Soft-focus portraits are often very effective. The matter-of-fact record given by an anastigmat, which registers every hair, is replaced by a softer rendering of curves and planes.

Special soft-focus lenses are beyond most people's means but a soft-focus attachment is a very useful substitute. These attachments consist of a plane glass with raised rings moulded on its surface; the glass is so mounted that it can be slipped on to the front of the lens. By refracting the light the attachments produce a halo round the lighter parts of the portrait, which can give a very sunny effect. For portraits of fair-haired children and girls taken by sunlight or strong artificial light this is well worth trying.

A soft-focus attachment should be used on the camera, not on the enlarger, where it will cause spreading of the shadows instead of the lights. This gives a gloomy effect which is usually displeasing, though it can sometimes be turned to account.

Fig. 254—A special soft-focus lens (Rodenstock Imagon) with perforated stops that allow marginal rays to reach the film even when using a small aperture

Fig. 255—(Left) " Listen ! It's ticking ! "—a good sharp portrait. (Right) A soft-focus portrait taken with a Wollensak Verito lens

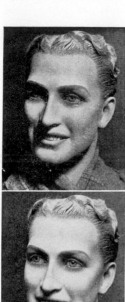

(A) HARD LIGHT from one lamp without reflector. Notice the hard, sharply outlined shadows under the nose and chin

(B) SOFT LIGHT Much more pleasing lighting from the surface of a matt reflector

(C) WRONG Cross-lighting. Two beams from opposite sides over-light cheeks and ears, and cause deep shadows round the mouth, nose and eyes. This, the worst possible lighting, is quite commonly used by beginners

(D) WRONG AGAIN. Moving the lights farther back exaggerates the faults of C

Fig. 256

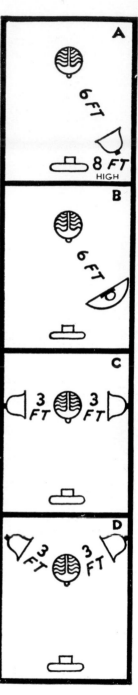

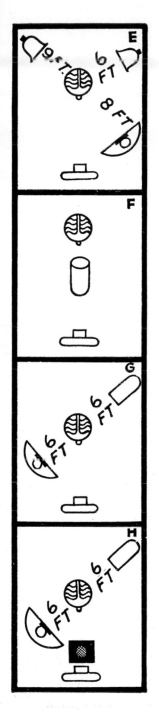

(E) PLASTIC LIGHT-ING round the whole head. Note that cross-lighting ceases to be wrong if a strong front light is also used. Here the modulation is better than in B

(F) EFFECT LIGHT-ING, coming from below only. It does not look bad with this dummy, but the likeness is entirely lost. With living models this lighting generally makes them look like stage villains

(G) SOFT + HARD. The reflector gave soft frontal lighting, while the modelling lamp produced a strong glancing light from behind the model.

(Cinema lighting)

(H) SOFT + HARD IN SOFT FOCUS. Cinema lighting used with a soft-focus attachment on the lens is often excellent

Fig. 256 (contd.)

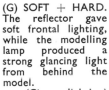

Fig. 257—" DUTCH SKIPPER   As Bonebakker

Taken with a miniature camera and long-focus lens. The head is very sharp, the
background blurred. Use of semi-back lighting has made the profile stand out
strongly. The presence of plenty of reflected light has given full detail on the
shadow side of the face. Probably the negative contained more than is shown here,
and this fine composition was picked out when making the enlargement

Fig. 258—" THE LETTER "   B. Ph. Baron van Harinxma thoe Slooten

A first-rate genre portrait with excellent lighting. Taken by artificial light using two lamps: a modelling lamp on the left, fairly close, with the second lamp near the camera for general lighting. Contrast has been kept under control by careful develop-ment, and reflection of light from the letter has been used to brighten the face. An excellent amateur portrait

19 ARCHITECTURE

A FINE building can have its own special appeal: the slender spire of a church rises upwards, leading the eye heavenwards; the new bank, square and strong, is a symbol of security. Only those people who have learnt to see know the joy of good architecture. And who should appreciate it better than the photographer? Look for an original viewpoint; better still, record the chosen building in the many moods evoked by varying lighting and the changing seasons.

Do you really know the buildings in your own town? Why not make a special portfolio of really good pictures of them, both outside and in?

Type of Camera

For architectural photography the large camera, of hand-or-stand type, is the one to choose, though many excellent pictures can be taken with a miniature or a 6 × 6 cm reflex. But these cameras have neither swing back nor rising front, both of which are very desirable for this work.

If the camera is tipped upwards to include the whole of a tower on the negative, then in the print the entire building will look as though it were falling over backwards. This effect is produced because with a camera in

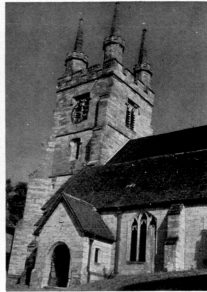

Fig. 259—When the camera is tilted upwards the building appears in the photograph as though it were falling over. This can be corrected in enlarging

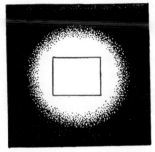

Fig. 260—If the circular field of view of the lens is big enough, an extensive rising front can be used

Fig. 261—A stand camera with the front raised (and swung). Note that the focusing screen remains upright

this position the edge of the roof is farther away than the ground, so that the top of the building is reproduced on a smaller scale. To prevent this the camera back, carrying the plate or film, is swung forward to bring it upright, parallel to the front wall of the building, while leaving the camera pointing upwards to include the top of it. This can be done with some large cameras, but not with the miniature or the small reflex.

The second method is to move the lens upwards. This again can be done with large cameras—most of which have a rising front—but not with a miniature or reflex. The effect of moving the lens is shown in Fig. 260, where the circle indicates the usable field of the lens, and the rectangle shows the part of this field actually used. When the lens is moved upwards it carries the circle, and the picture within it, upwards too, and if the circle is big enough, and the image within it sharp enough, the upper part of the building will move on to the focusing screen. The old double anastigmats, such as the Dagor, have a large field with good corrections, and can be specially recommended. It is evident that if the circular field of illumination is not large enough, the corners of the picture will be dark.

Wide-angle Lenses

A wide-angle lens is one with a relatively short focal length, so that objects are reproduced on a small scale, and a wide field of view is included. It should only be used when there is no alternative. We have already seen that these lenses exaggerate the size of objects in the foreground as compared with those in the distance (see page 75). Wide-angle lenses are too often unnecessarily used for photographing buildings; they give unnatural perspective because they are used from a viewpoint too near the subject. For instance, ordinary rooms are shown as large halls (see also Figs. 105 and 106, page 77). Only when a near viewpoint is the only possible one should a wide-angle lens be used.

Exterior Subjects

The lighting of an architectural subject is of the utmost importance. Under good lighting a building comes alive. An uninteresting grey facade can sparkle in a strong side light, and can look delightful in the glancing rays of low sunlight. Some buildings have to be photographed in the early morning, as only then is the sun in the right place. In the absence of sun, mist can be very helpful; by simplifying shapes it often provides a picture where normally there is none.

The combination of daylight and artificial light is also worth considering. At twilight, when the lamps are already shining through the windows but there is still daylight out of doors, unusual architectural pictures can be made.

Individual details of a building, such as statues, carvings, or details of walls or gables, will often make a picture. Remembering that the simpler subjects usually make the best pictures, it would be expected that a porch would often be a much more promising subject than a whole building.

With miniature cameras, long-focus and telephoto lenses are very valuable for such subjects as statues set high up in a church, which would be very small on the negative if taken with a lens of normal focus. The miniature is especially suited to this type of work, when it admirably supplements the large camera.

Interior Subjects

Delightful pictures can often be made of artistically furnished homes, using either daylight or artificial light, or sometimes both. Churches and public buildings also offer good opportunities for interior pictures.

It is a very interesting photographic undertaking to make a portfolio of pictures of the churches, public halls, libraries, and old buildings of one's own town. Carrying out such a project, which may take a month or two, will provide a training in technique difficult to obtain in any other way, and will impart a quick eye for the choice of subjects and of lighting.

Much that has been said about photographing the outsides of buildings applies just as much to interiors. A wide-angle lens should only be used when there is no alternative, namely when it is essential to include some part of the subject that would otherwise have to be left out. A wide-angle picture very often creates an entirely wrong impression, making an ordinary room look like a large hall. So keep to the lens of normal focus whenever possible.

Interior subjects always require a tripod, with careful focusing and a small stop. Never forget the lens hood. Where there is a choice, select a lens as free as possible from internal reflections; the old type of double anastigmat (Dagor, Collinear, etc.) is particularly suitable, and a coated lens is very desirable.

Sometimes the contrasts of the subjects are so great that shadow-detail can only be obtained by illuminating them with an auxiliary light. A flash directed towards the ceiling is particularly helpful, for the light reflected is so well diffused that it gives no impression of artificial light, but just lightens the room. A portable lamp, with a reflector and a long cable, is also helpful; keeping it always on the move during the exposure, it is directed into all the darker parts of the subjects one after another. The back of the reflector must be kept turned to the lens throughout, so that the camera can at no time see the bulb itself.

For determining exposures a useful rule is to take a meter reading, from the middle of the room, of the light coming through the window; then expose thirty times as long as the meter indicates. This rule, used by professionals, leads to good negatives of dark interiors.

Interior work is best begun at home, and when a good picture has been made of every room, the beginner will be qualified to go farther afield.

The presence of snow makes a big difference to interiors. So much sunlight is reflected up to the ceiling that even in a room normally dark and difficult to photograph there is no need for additional lighting.

A well-chosen foreground is always important, but doubly so in interior pictures. It must be in sharp focus, which is not always easy. Try photographing a church interior through the choir screen, or a garden through an iron-work gate.

The tripod can easily slip on a polished floor; this can be prevented by a loop of string round the points of the legs, or by fitting rubber feet. Never

Fig. 262—Snow on the ground makes for much better-lit interiors

walk about during the exposure, or the vibration may cause unexpected blur. Carefully note the position of the sun, and work out at what time it will shine through the window.

Choosing the time of best lighting makes all the difference to an interior. The success of the picture depends as much on lighting in this work as in any other.

Films and Plates

The plates or films for this work should preferably be panchromatic, and plates must always be backed. Orthochromatic material will serve for some subjects, but brown furniture generally calls for a panchromatic film, and even with this a yellow filter may be needed.

Exposures must be accurate, as these subjects generally show high contrast—for instance, many interior subjects include windows. Unless care is taken, the light parts will be fully exposed but the shadows will be under-exposed. One often sees dark-looking interior pictures with no detail in the shadows; this unmistakably shows under-exposure. In this kind of work always remember the old maxim: *Expose for the shadows and the highlights will take care of themselves.*

The implication is that development must be shortened to keep the negative soft and to prevent the highlights from becoming too dense. This result is most easily obtained by using soft-working (fast) emulsions and exposing generously.

15

Fig. 263—" EVENING "   P. Zwaal

An unusually sensitive rendering of the atmosphere of a quiet evening. The exposure
was made when there was still just enough daylight left to give good detail in the
shadows. Anyone could make a series like this about his own town. Panchromatic
film and a tripod should be used, with the lens stopped down enough to ensure
sharpness. The exposure needed will be a minute or two with the shutter at T.
The lens can be covered with the hand if a car or bicycle light comes into the field of view.
Pedestrians will do no harm so long as they do not linger. Develop for a soft negative

Fig. 264—" OLD AMERSFOORT "   A. Pastoor

Old towns provide lovely subjects, especially beautiful when taken against the light
on a misty day.   Notice the way the corners of the picture are filled, and the glancing
lighting that gives life to the house.   Foreground figures are quite unnecessary here.
Early rising is needed for these subjects: this would hardly have been worth a film
at midday

Fig. 265—" CHURCH INTERIOR "   J. Stoelman

The pervading lightness of the church is excellently reproduced. This is a carefully
made stand-camera picture, taken with rising front. The lighting is exactly right at
this time of day: earlier or later it would have been less pleasing. A filter was used
to cut out the scattered blue light, and a time exposure was given with a small stop

222

Fig. 266—" THE SUNNY WINDOW "   W. Heuveling

Here is a charming setting with an appropriate little figure looking out to the sunlit
garden.   The light pattern behind her, with its shadows of well-placed articles on the
wall, continues the luminosity of the ornamental windows and creates a good foil to the
strong outward gaze of the girl

STILL-LIFE subjects provide an inexhaustible field of work. The still beauty of flowers, the glowing texture of satin, the beauty of a dish of fruit, the dance of light through a crystal vase; all these offer subjects for the camera. Still-life work is an excellent test of good taste. Surround yourself with well-designed and well-made things, and they will of themselves suggest still-life subjects. The simpler they are the better.

As a base on which to photograph them, wood, glass, white paper, corrugated cardboard, and some wallpapers are worth experimenting with. The background is also important; it may be light, dark, plain, or varied in tint. It is often helpful to use a long strip of paper, beginning under the subject and curving upwards behind it as in Fig. 267, pinning it to the wall or other support. This gives a base that is continuous with the background, with no dividing line. Lighting should be soft and well diffused, and care must be taken to avoid unwanted shadows. Texture rendering is everything in this work, so that fine definition is essential. At these short distances depth of focus is small, so a small stop, such as f/22, is often needed. Nevertheless, an advanced worker can sometimes make good use of a soft-focus attachment.

Perfect rendering of texture is only possible, with most subjects, by the use of fully colour-sensitive films. Plates should be backed, and a yellow filter is generally advisable. As in any case a time exposure must be given, a fairly deep filter, of factor 3 to 4, can well be used for daylight work. Still-life subjects can also be photographed at night by ordinary room lighting.

For flower subjects lighting is of great importance, and can be arranged as desired. Side, frontal, and back lighting should all be tried in turn to see which best suits each different kind of flower. A combination of frontal and semi-back lighting usually gives the best results.

Fig. 267—A large sheet of paper, bent in a curve, serves both as base and background, so eliminating any dividing line between the two

The choice of viewpoint (as always) needs thought. Should the camera be on the same level as the subject? Or should it be raised and pointed down? Both possibilities should be tried before the exposure is made.

It is clear that a camera with a focusing screen has advantages over one with a viewfinder. For this work even the miniature camera user goes back to a focusing screen, making use of an accessory designed for copying.

If the camera will not extend far enough to focus these near objects, either a supplementary lens or an extension tube, or both, can be used.

Fig. 269—Table top photograph by
J. Nanninga.   Such pictures are best
taken from a tripod.   Focus accurately
with a small stop to secure sufficient
depth of field

Fig. 268—A miniature becomes a reflex.
Novoflex mirror reflex attachment with
double focusing movement

A lens of long focal length is to be preferred for the most natural rendering
of still-life subjects, as it does not render near objects disproportionately large in
comparison with those farther away.   A short-focus lens is unsuitable for
close-up work (see page 72).

With dolls, carvings, glass figures and similar material, pictures on a table
top can be constructed.   Fig. 269, of two toy mice and a piece of cheese, is
an example.   Imagination and good taste are the chief requirements for this
branch of work, which affords an inexhaustible fund of subjects.   Soft well-
diffused artificial light is best, and the lamps may be small as there is nothing
against a long exposure.   Again a small stop will be needed to give sufficient
depth of focus.   Colour pictures of table-top subjects are surprisingly charming.

Still-life Pictures Out of Doors

Out of doors, too, small subjects can be effective—as much so as a wide
landscape.   Often they have an arresting and intimate beauty.   Dew-spangled
cobwebs and flowers, insects, butterflies and other small creatures are instances
from what is an unlimited field of work.

The technique for it, however, is difficult.   A tripod is generally needed;
a strong and very short wooden one is best.   The background is of importance,
and the lens must usually be well stopped down, since at the very short
distances involved in this work there is exceedingly little depth of focus.

The wind can be most annoying; flowers sway to and fro, making a very
short exposure necessary, although the small stop calls for a long one.   Sometimes a screen, such as a raincoat held out by an assistant, will keep the wind
away.   The lighting of these outdoor still-life subjects needs close attention.
Experience should be gained in monochrome work before trying a colour film.

For colour film, mushrooms, a rockery, butterflies on flowers, strange exotic
flowers in a greenhouse, are all excellent subjects.   In fact, small subjects
are really far more suitable than landscapes.

In this kind of work, one should always have a sheet of white paper handy
for reflecting light into the shadows.

225

Fig. 270—" STILL LIFE "   K. G. Bijlstra

A tall vase, and a small round one with flowers—material enough for a photographer
with good taste. Still-life pictures must look natural. Unusual things are not
essential; one can do better with everyday objects harmoniously arranged. A small
stop is necessary for depth of focus, so a camera with a ground-glass screen, used on
a tripod, is best, as it allows careful focusing and composition. Here a soft focus lens
(Rodenstock Imagon) was used

Fig. 271—" STILL LIFE "   A. Pastoor

In this outstanding high-key picture the advice given with Fig. 270 has been well applied. The material is only a cup and saucer and a vase with a spray. Two lamps; one on the right and nearly facing the camera, one on the left, near the camera, as " fill-in." A small stop was used for maximum depth of focus

227

Fig. 272—" ON A MISTY MORNING "   L. Vogels

Just a blade of grass, gemmed with mist, yet nothing more was needed for a delightful picture. Only a real nature lover, with a complete technical mastery of photography, could have produced such an original and beautiful picture from so little material

Fig. 273—" BEE'S CAFÉ "   W. Heuveling

A well seen and well photographed subject, requiring considerable skill and patience.
Many exposures must be made to obtain one successful picture of this kind. Such
close-up shots require a supplementary lens or preferably a long-focus lens used with an
extension tube so that the camera will not be so near as to disturb the insects

21 PHOTOGRAPHY BY ARTIFICIAL LIGHT

THE electric lamp has doubled the number of possible subjects. Good artificial-light pictures have their own special charm. At first sight, taking photographs by artificial light seems difficult, but this is chiefly because the technique is unfamiliar to the beginner. We will try to show how easy it really is.

There are five main rules for photography by artificial light:

(1) Use panchromatic films.
(2) Use plenty of light.
(3) See that there is plenty of *reflected* light.
(4) Arrange the lighting well.
(5) Choose a quiet background.

Excellent photographs can be taken with the old-fashioned flash-powder, but it is not very suitable for indoor use, as it may cause a fire, and in any case produces unpleasant smoke. Its place is now taken by the modern flashbulb, in which there is magnesium or aluminium wire fired by an electric current from a battery or charged condenser. One of the reflectors sold for flashbulbs should always be used; reflection is very important in flash.

The stop to use is shown in the exposure table included with the bulb, or obtainable on request from the manufacturer. The farther the subject is from the flash, the less light will reach it and the larger the stop must be. Though the bulb is a source of brilliant light, its diameter is small, so it tends to give very hard lighting. Care must therefore be taken to have light surroundings (rule 3). This is important in all artificial-light work, for plenty of reflected light is essential if dark shadows are to be avoided.

These flashbulbs make snapshots possible after dark, even out of doors where no electric current is available. The time of exposure, which is the duration of the flash, is about $\frac{1}{100}$ second. If the shutter in use is not synchronized for flash (which is the case with box and other simple modern cameras, and old cameras, even of higher grade), then after focusing and setting the stop appropriately, the shutter should be set to Time and opened. The flash is immediately fired, and the shutter at once closed again. With a synchronized camera the process is even simpler: the flash-bulb and battery are connected to the shutter, set to $1/25$ second; as it opens it makes an electric contact which automatically fires the bulb.

Normal Lighting, Indoors and Out

It would be a good preliminary exercise to photograph our own home by its ordinary lighting. First switch on all the lights, particularly any reading lamps. With a fast panchromatic film and with the lens stopped down to $f/11$ to give sufficient depth of focus, the exposure needed will most probably be about a minute. Make one or two trial exposures; the results may well be surprising. As the subject-contrast is high, keep the development time short.

If the success of these indoor pictures makes one want to go further in this work, it is worth while to buy some photoflood lamps. These are overrun lamps, giving a very brilliant light but having only a short life—about 2 hours of actual use. They give much more light per watt of electric power consumed than do ordinary lamps, but in consequence burn out much sooner. The larger studio type of lamp is dearer to buy, but costs less per exposure, as it has a 100-hour life. The ordinary photoflood takes 275 watts, gives an output of some 10,000 lumens, and has a 2-hour running life. The much less overrun lamps of studio type consume 500 watts, burn for 100 hours, and give a light output of 8,500 lumens.

The special advantage of overrun lamps is that they place a great deal of light at our disposal without consuming any very great amount of power. Nevertheless a short time exposure is often needed when using them. A reflector should always be used to direct the light where it is required; a good reflector can increase fourfold the amount of light reaching the subject.

While arranging the lighting there is no need to have the lamps full on. They can be dimmed with the help of a series-parallel switch panel. While getting ready the lamps are connected in series, so that they run on a reduced voltage, and just before the actual exposure they are switched in parallel for full output. Panels of this kind can be bought, or can be made at home; one is shown in Fig. 274.

Lamps and Fuses

There is a simple electrical rule which says that volts $\times$ amperes $=$ watts —or voltage times current equals power. House wiring generally has 5-ampere fuses, so that on 230-volt mains we can safely use $230 \times 5 = 1,150$ watts.

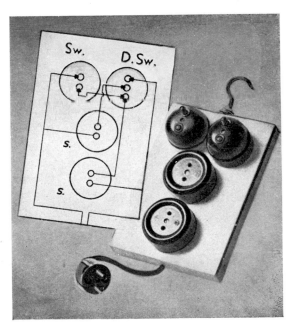

Fig. 274 — Series-parallel switch panel for photo-floods. The wiring runs between the two parts of the double base.

S = socket. Sw = switch. D.Sw. = two-way switch

It is safe to connect four photofloods (4 × 275 = 1,100 watts) or one 500-watt lamp and two photofloods to such a system. With 10-ampere fuses it would be safe to use twice the number of lamps. We recommend using one or two studio (500-watt) lamps for all general work, as their life is such that they will last for years in amateur hands.

One or two photofloods for occasional use as auxiliary lights will complete an excellent amateur outfit.

THE FIVE RULES TO FOLLOW

Rule I: Use Panchromatic Films

Artificial light is not the same colour as daylight, for it contains much more red and much less blue. Therefore it is warmer in colour than daylight. Yellow filters, the purpose of which is to absorb excess blue, are not needed with artificial light; on the contrary, a blue filter to absorb excess red is more likely to be needed, and is to be advised for portraiture.

The curve of colour sensitivity (see Fig. 146) of a film is different in shape by artificial light, and so is the sensitivity curve of the eye, though this is seldom taken into consideration. In Figs. 275 and 276 are shown reproductions

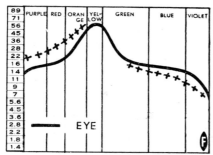

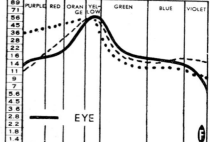

Fig. 275—The curve for the eye in daylight has a different shape from that in artificial light (indicated by crosses), which is more red and less blue

Fig. 276—The film's sensitivity curve closely fits that of the eye. (Dashes indicate panchromatic emulsion, dots ultra-fast pan emulsion)

of curves for the eye and for panchromatic film taken by artificial light. The curve for the eye in artificial light is different from the daylight one, and the curve for the film follows it closely. This refers to " orthopanchromatic " film with normal sensitivity to red; with some ultra-fast panchromatic films the red-sensitivity is far too high, so that red-coloured objects are reproduced too light. For these films the curve is much higher at the left (red) end.

Rule 2: Use Plenty of Light

If too few lamps are used in making a portrait or photographing a group, the result is always disappointing. If the exposure is short, the shadows are black; if a longer exposure is given, there is a good chance that one of the sitters will move and so be blurred. The only remedy is to use enough light, checking its effects with the exposure meter.

A still-life subject, lit by photofloods in reflectors, should be the first subject attempted, as a test. Determine the exposure with the meter in the usual way, and make three exposures, giving the first one only half the indicated time, the second the time shown by the meter, and the third double this time. On development it will be seen which was correct. If, for example, the negative given half the indicated time is correctly exposed, then half the meter time can always be given in future.

Rule 3: Ensure Plenty of *Reflected* Light

Reflected light plays a big part in the success of photographs taken by artificial light. If a single lamp is directed on a sitter surrounded by dark objects, very high contrasts will be produced. But if surrounding objects are light in colour the lighting will be very different, for walls and furniture will be reflecting light on to the sitter from all sides, giving a much more pleasing effect. Excellent lighting can be had in a small room by directing the light towards the wall and placing the sitter between lamp and wall.

Compared with outdoor light, artificial light is often too harsh, giving hard shadows and sharp divisions between light and dark. The reason for the difference is easy to see: in daylight the sun is not the sole source of light, for there is also the whole hemisphere of the sky reflecting light on to the model from every side. To obtain similar softly-lit pictures by artificial light, reflected light from objects surrounding the sitter must take the place of skylight.

Rule 4: Arrange the Lighting Well

Though several lamps may be in use, one must be strong enough to overpower all the rest. This is the main lamp, which gives direction to the lighting. If two lamps of the same power are used, one must be placed farther away than the other. The second lamp should be used simply for throwing light into the shadows. It will be noticed that in some positions the shadows formed by the two lamps will overlap and produce deep furrows on the sitter's face. The second lamp must be so placed that its effect is not noticeable in the finished picture.

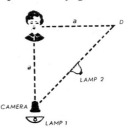

Fig. 277 The triangle rule. A good place for the second lamp is half-way between the camera and the point D

Rule 5: Choose a Quiet Background

In most cases our studio will be the sitting room, and as a background to groups and portraits it is more likely to be intrusive than helpful. Keep a sharp lookout for light-coloured or shining objects, newspapers, picture frames, china, glazed tiles, or anything that can cause reflections. A large sheet of brown paper, hung up as background, will be found very useful. The background should never be distracting, but should be as unnoticeable as possible. Much can be learnt in one evening by trying a portrait with several different backgrounds, light, medium, and dark in tone.

Taking portraits at home by artificial light is one of the most enjoyable of photographic pursuits. The ability to place the lights exactly where we want them makes it possible to arrange the best lighting for each individual portrait.

Fig. 278—" CHRISTMAS CANDLES "   As Bonebakker

Who would have thought, years ago, that pictures of such subjects as this could be
taken ? The miniature camera, with its fast lens and modern high-speed panchromatic
film, has made them possible. These individual and irreplaceable snapshots of home
life are not very difficult to take. For this picture two lamps, carefully placed, were
used to light the intimate little scene

234

Fig. 279—" JOAN "

G. van Eys

A most effective portrait of a child, unposed and without the usual forced smile. The natural expression was caught by a rapid exposure with a miniature camera. The white collar on the dark dress is pleasingly decorative

Success in this calls for good taste and much practice, but the pictures obtainable when skill has been acquired fully repay the time spent in learning.

THE USE OF FLASH

Flashbulbs have now become almost as important to the amateur as studio lamps or photofloods. They consist of a glass bulb, with a metal cap like a lamp, filled with fine wire or shredded foil in an atmosphere of oxygen. There is also a fine filament which, when connected to a battery, becomes white-hot and fires the wire or foil, giving a short and very brilliant flash. Naturally the bulb can only be used once.

Flash pictures can be made with any camera by the open-flash method. For this the shutter is set to Bulb or Time; it is opened, the flash immediately fired, and the shutter at once closed again. Half a second should cover the whole process. The bulb can be fired with an ordinary torch fitted with a suitable adapter (M.E.S.–A.S.C.C.) and a reflector, but a hand-operated flash holder can be obtained quite cheaply. For more than occasional use a proper flashgun that can be fixed to the camera should be bought, especially now that every camera except the cheapest has a synchronized shutter.

Those who are likely to use flash really frequently would do well to consider the possibilities of electronic flash. This involves the use of a " power-pack " that the user slings over his shoulder, and which is electrically connected to a flash-tube filled with xenon, a rare gas. The power-pack, driven by mains or batteries, stores electricity at a high voltage (180 to 500 volts in modern amateur outfits) in a condenser; when the flash is " triggered," this stored electricity is discharged through the tube in about $\frac{1}{1000}$ second, giving a vivid flash. Since nothing in the flash-tube is consumed, it will last for many thousands of flashes.

The outfit is costly to buy, but once bought is very cheap to run; the average cost per flash is well under a penny, as compared with eightpence for the smallest flashbulb. A special advantage is the brevity of the flash, enabling fast-moving objects to be " frozen " in a quite spectacular way (see Fig. 285). The disadvantage is that the average amateur outfit gives hardly half the light of the smallest flashbulb, but this disadvantage only becomes apparent when working with the slower colour-films. For these a flashbulb is usually to be preferred.

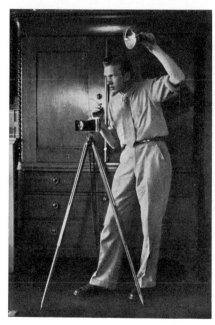

Fig. 280—Open flash. The camera is placed on the tripod, with the shutter set to B. Open the shutter, fire the flash, and close the shutter. The flash should not be too near the camera

Fig. 281—The Johnson capacitor flashgun works from a 22·5-volt battery and uses A.S.C.C. bulbs

Fig. 282—The simple and modestly priced Ilford Junior flashgun for open flash

For successful flash pictures the shutter must be fully open at the instant when the flash is giving its full output of light, which with bulbs is not for an appreciable time after the firing contact is made. This introduces no difficulty in the open-flash method, but becomes vitally important when the shutter is fired at snapshot speeds. Faulty synchronization means that the shutter will be closed, or nearly so, when the flash fires, giving a badly under-exposed negative or even blank film.

At the time of writing there are in effect only two flashbulbs intended for amateur use. The smaller, known as P.F.1 or No. 1 according to make, is " capless "—that is, it has no brass cap but only two leading-in wires to which contact is made. A capless bulb requires either a flash-gun specially made for it, or, if the flashgun is for bulbs with caps, a special adapter is needed. The point of the capless construction is that it saves twopence or so on the cost of each bulb. The larger amateur bulb, giving about three times the light of the smaller, can be had either capless (P.F.5, No. 5) or with the standard A.S.C.C. cap of small flashbulbs; in the latter case it is known as P.F.25. Any of these bulbs can be had with a blue-glass envelope, for use with daylight colour film, instead of clear glass. There are larger bulbs, but they cannot be used in the ordinary amateur's flashgun; we will not concern ourselves with them.

All these flashbulbs take 16 to 20 milliseconds, counting from the instant when the firing contact is made, to reach full brilliance. Electronic flash, on the other hand, fires practically instantaneously—the delay here is only a few millionths of a second. If a shutter is set to $\frac{1}{500}$ second, and if it makes the contact necessary for firing the flash just as the blades reach the full-open position, it will synchronize perfectly with electronic flash; with its instantaneous response and very brief flash, the whole flash will be over and done with before the shutter can even begin to close. With a flashbulb, however, conditions are very different; the shutter will be closed again long before the bulb has emitted any light at all, and the result will be a blank negative.

237

Fig. 284—For electronic flash: the Langham Ministrobe with
its carrying case

There are two possible remedies for this unsatisfactory state of affairs. One, the simplest, is to make the shutter stay open and wait for the light from the bulb; this only means that it must be set to $\frac{1}{30}$ second or a slower speed. One then relies mainly on the briefness of the flash itself to stop subject-movement or camera-shake. The other method, better but more costly, is to have a shutter fitted with an internal clockwork mechanism that makes the firing-contact for the bulb as soon as the shutter-release is pressed, but does not allow the shutter to start opening till about 16 milliseconds later. The shutter then reaches its full-open position just before the bulb is at its brightest. With this arrangement the shutter can again be run at $\frac{1}{500}$ second (or any slower speed) if this is necessary to stop subject-movement but of course the shutter will not catch all the light at high speeds.

Some shutters are described as " synchronized " or " X-synchronized," others as " fully synchronized," and these latter have a little lever that can be set to either of two positions, marked " X " and " M." With the former type of shutter, or the latter set to X, contact is made just as the shutter reaches the full-open position—correct for electronic flash or for bulbs at $\frac{1}{30}$ second or slower. Setting the fully-synchronized shutter to M brings in the delay clockwork described, enabling bulbs to be used with the shutter set to its higher speeds. Note that electronic flash cannot be used at the M setting; the flash would be over long before the shutter could open. To indicate their delay in firing, flashbulbs are often referred to as " M-type "; electronic flash is referred to as an " X-type " flash.

Hints on Using Flash

The stop to use at different distances, and with different shutter speeds, is found from the guide number (or flash factor) given in the data sheets supplied by the manufacturers, whether of flashbulbs or of electronic flash. For a

238

Fig. 285—" PLAYING IN HER BATH "

To get this picture, the girl put her head in the water and then flung it violently back. In the original photograph, taken by electronic flash, her hairs could almost be counted

Fig. 286—A fully synchronized Compur shutter. Note lever 4, by which X or M synchronization can be had at will. Nipple 3 connects to the flashgun

Fig. 287—Miniature reflex with electronic flash attached; a small modern outfit for press and industry. Note the power pack hung on the user's left shoulder

239

P.F. bulb, for example, the guide number for a film of speed 160 Weston is 160. This figure is approximately the product of the stop number to be used and the distance in feet between flash and subject, so that at a distance of 12 ft f/13 will be correct.

As a battery gets old it tends to fire the bulb slowly, which may upset synchronization by delaying the flash. In a battery-capacitor gun a 22½-volt hearing-aid battery (a tiny thing) is used to charge a condenser, the stored energy in which is used to fire the bulb. When the battery gets old it takes a second or two longer to charge the condenser, but so long as the flash is not

Fig. 288—Flash with two coupled bulbs. The first bulb is on the camera, and the second, which is the main light source, is held by an assistant. The resulting picture is shown opposite

fired for five or six seconds after the bulb is put in its socket, the discharge is hardly weaker. This type of gun is now almost universal.

There is quite a difference between firing a bulb out of doors, where surroundings reflect no light, and in a white-walled bathroom. The guide number is calculated for an ordinary room; therefore, use one or two stops wider out of doors, and one stop smaller in the bathroom.

The slit of a focal-plane shutter takes some time to travel over the film, so that for even exposure by flash the bulb must burn for some time. Special long-burning focal-plane bulbs are made; examples are the P.F.24 and the P.F.45. These can be used, with suitable synchronization, even at quite high shutter speeds.

The alternative is to use a short sharp flash and to time it to fire at a moment when the shutter has uncovered the whole film at once—which it does for an

Fig. 289—" TUNING UP FOR THE SCHOOL CONCERT "
Coupled flash. General fill-in light from bulb above camera, modelling
flash to the right

Fig. 290—Back-lit, without flash. The face is too dark, and a " fill-in " is needed

Fig. 291—Back-lit, with flash. The result is much more pleasing. But too much flash will swamp the sunlight and give a most unnatural effect

instant at the slower speeds. All types of flash (including electronic) *except* the special focal-plane bulbs can be used this way.

In a picture taken out of doors against the light, it can be very useful to throw some light into the shadowed side that faces the camera. A flash, on the camera itself, does this, and press photographers use the method every day. Too strong a flash should not be used, or the effect of the daylight is lost; the picture should not suggest that an auxiliary light was used.

To balance sunlight and flash correctly against one another calls for some care, although it is not difficult. There is a practical example in the comparison pictures in Figs. 290 and 291. The distance of the girl from the camera was 10 feet, the camera was loaded with a pan film of speed 26° B.S., and the flashbulb used to give better details in the shadows was a P.F.1. From the instructions with the flashbulb we find a guide-number, or flash-factor as it is sometimes called, of 80 for a film of speed 26° B.S. This number is found by multiplying together the distance of the subject from the flash, in feet, and the f-number of the stop required to give correct exposure. As the girl is 10 feet away, the stop to use is $80 \div 10$, or f/8. If the stop number found in this way is not marked, the next bigger stop can be used. The next step is to use the exposure-meter in the normal way, and read off from the scale the shutter-speed that is correct for the stop found necessary for the flash. If this speed is faster than $\frac{1}{30}$ second, it will be necessary to use the M synchronizing setting of the shutter.

242

If a picture of this kind is being taken in colour, use of an ordinary clear bulb will give a reddish tinge to the shadows illuminated by the bulb—to avoid this, a blue-tinted bulb must be used, or alternatively electronic flash, which is quite satisfactory with daylight colour film. But when electronic flash is the *sole* source of light, a very pale yellow correcting filter should be used for the most perfect colour-rendering.

It is not a bad plan to use your first colour film for indoor work with blue flashbulbs; results are nearly always excellent and it is a great advantage to have a light-source constant both in brightness and in colour. The guide-number correct for the colour film you use can be found from the instructions with the bulb, but it is wise to try numbers a little higher and a little lower, as experiments, with the first film. There are two reasons for this; first, the reflector on the particular flashgun used may be more or less efficient in throwing light on to the subject than the average reflector for which the guide-number is given, and secondly, the walls and furniture of the room may reflect more or less than the average amount of light. In a room with dark walls and ceiling, it is wise to take a stop larger than the guide-number suggests.

For single figures, and especially for close-ups, the P.F.1 or No. 1 bulb gives enough light even for colour film, but for groups of people the larger bulb still (in blue, of course) is more suitable, especially as a small stop may be needed for depth of focus. Take advantage of opportunities for such pictures, particularly on birthdays and special occasions. Often the best hours are those spent indoors.

The blue filter on the bulb absorbs a good deal of light, and one has to pay extra for it. Some colour-films are available with an emulsion specially balanced for clear flashbulbs; use of these is an evident economy where much flash work is to be done in colour.

T HE first rule for the traveller is to take a camera he knows well, *not* an exciting new one, which is still unfamiliar and possibly even faulty. But if the journey is so important as to demand a new and better camera, buy it a month or two in advance and get to know it thoroughly.

The same rule applies to films; if there seems little chance of being able to buy a familiar brand *en route*, take a supply from home rather than trust to a strange film of unknown characteristics and uncertain speed. Under-exposure might lose you all your pictures. Subjects encountered away from home offer only one opportunity for a picture, so you cannot afford to lose any chances.

Most people see far more subjects when travelling than when at home. Not all are really worth a film; concentrate on those that are. Even in new surroundings watch for good lighting and interesting effects of light.

A photographer should have more pictorial self-respect than to stand a member of his party, staring at the camera, in front of every object of interest that he photographs. Yet it is often done. But if he insists on being included, or if a foreground figure is really needed, work your companion into the composition. Make him look at the cathedral or fountain you are taking, not at the camera. Use, instead of forgetting, the experience gained in landscape and genre pictures already made at home. The pocket " tripod " shown in Fig. 292 has been found invaluable when travelling. Clamped to the back of

Fig. 292—The pocket "tripod" is a useful accessory, particularly for the traveller. It is shown here in use with a Leica

Fig. 293—On the right spot at the right moment. (Photograph by H. Frank)

a church pew it makes a long time exposure possible; with a delayed-action release, the photographer himself can act as his own foreground figure when one is needed.

A yellow filter, and a lens hood that can be used with it as well as alone, are as essential when travelling as at any other time, and are doubly so on a sea voyage.

A photo-electric exposure meter is very desirable, but, like the camera, it should be one the user knows well. Even so, the first film exposed in unfamiliar surroundings should be developed on the spot to check that all is well.

When abroad, do not forget to photograph the people. But be careful never to cause offence, or it may make things difficult for other photographers who come later, as well as for yourself. And if a print is promised, be sure to send it. The word of thanks sent in return will presently go in the album. The writer has such notes from all sorts of people, including the Archbishop of Canterbury and simple country folk.

And, finally, a set of lantern slides from the best negatives of your travels will give pleasure to others as well as yourself.

In most cases there is just one instant when the subject is at its best; if the exposure is made a moment sooner or a moment later the chance is lost. Especially is this true of facial expressions. Some photographers can catch that fleeting moment, others are always too late.

As rapid snapshotting is nowadays the ambition of so many, here is the secret of seizing the right moment: *observation.* Watch the subject closely and seize your chance. In child photography, for example, every scrap of your attention must be focused on the child. For this to be possible, complete

Fig. 294—" O SOLE MIO "   D. van Volen

A first-class travel picture, with well-chosen models, and crosslighting that makes them stand out from the dark background. The low evening lighting, with its long shadows, is an important factor in the success of this picture

Fig. 294a—CAMOGLI   A. P. W. van Dalsum

In this photograph, the small boats make an admirable foreground, and the arches of
the bridge in the background with the local people on it are especially pleasing. The
scene was lit softly from the right and this lighting would also have been ideal for a
colour picture

familiarity with the camera is essential. Hesitation, or tinkering with the focusing and the adjustments, will result in missing all the best pictures. A camera that is quick in use is an advantage, but knowing the camera so well that its use is automatic is even more important. Close observation and unhesitating action are needed. Seize a good chance at once; do not wait for something still better.

It is not always realized, but most of the really good snapshot pictures are waited for. The possibilities are seen in advance. That archway, the photographer thinks, will mean a good picture when the horse and cart down the road appear in that patch of sunlight. The camera is opened, the shutter set, the distance measured, and the picture is awaited, the photographer watching closely all the time. Eventually the cart comes along; just as it reaches the perfect spot the exposure is made. It would be quite impossible to see the picture first and then photograph it; by the time the camera was opened and ready, or even just aimed, the right moment would be gone and the picture lost. In all such cases the possibilities of the subject must be seen in advance; the viewpoint is then chosen, the lighting considered, and the camera made ready. Then when the correct moment arrives, and the subject is perfect for just an instant, the exposure can be made.

Of course, the subject can be arranged. One might tip the carter and get him to walk his horse just where he is wanted for pictorial effect. Why not? A tactful request, and a promise of a print, will often work wonders in improving a composition.

Fig. 295—" ARCHES " M. A. I. Kluit

An excellent travel memento, with beautiful lines and a sunny atmosphere. Careful control of exposure, taking both highlights and shadows into account, has given a negative with a full range of tones, yielding a perfect enlargement. This print is by the bromoil process, which accounts for the grainy appearance

23 ANIMAL PICTURES

THE photography of animals is interesting, but difficult, work. It is not as easy as a certain lawyer supposed when he asked the writer to supply him with a camera which needed no adjusting, and with which he could just snap from his car any interesting bird he might see at the side of the road as he passed! On the contrary, it is a subject for specialists with plenty of patience. The first step is to learn to know the animal by studying its habits. This is an essential for success.

There are several main methods in use by nature photographers:

(1) The hide, a camouflaged tent or hut, in which the photographer conceals himself, with his camera, to wait his opportunity to expose.

(2) The camera, camouflaged or not, is set up at a good spot and operated from a distance by the photographer, who watches the bird's nest or rabbit burrow through glasses.

(3) The trip wire, by which the bird or animal itself operates the camera and fires a flashbulb.

All these three methods are quite fully described in books on nature photography.

But there is no need for the amateur to begin with wild creatures; first efforts can be made at home with a dog or cat (dogs are easier). When some skill has been acquired, visit a modern zoo, where there are no bars or wire netting to obscure the view at all. With a miniature camera, it is usually convenient to use a long-focus lens of 9 cm or 13·5 cm focal length. Then finally try a real wild creature, bird or beast.

For nature photography a miniature with long-focus lens is excellent, as also is a quarter-plate camera with a telephoto lens. The 6 × 6 cm reflex gives rather a small picture, unless one can get very near or is using a single-lens camera (Reflex-Korelle, Agiflex, Exakta) to which a long-focus lens can be fitted.

A strong tripod, or a support screwed to a tree, is needed, and then, with the camera fixed in position, wait and watch. An electrically-operated remote release is ideal for this work. Watching through a good pair of glasses, the right instant is seen and the exposure made. A device for completing the electrical circuit can be placed where the bird or animal will operate it and so take its own portrait, but one then has no means of choosing the pose.

Small creatures, particularly butterflies and other insects, are best photographed with the aid of supplementary close-up lenses or extension tubes, which make close approach possible. All work of this type demands time, patience, and study, but the field is a very rich one for the amateur who takes it up seriously.

Fig. 296—" THE CAPTIVE "   E. G. H. Haighton

An unusually good animal portrait, this picture of the tragic head of a caged animal could be called by no other name. The technique is faultless, the rendering of the tones of the skin is excellent, and the definition is very sharp with slight softening towards the background. The expression in the eyes is very cleverly caught, and the wire netting shutting off the picture is symbolic of captivity

Fig. 297—" AN AVOCET AMONG THE REEDS "   D. van Sijn

This is one of the best bird pictures ever taken. The sparkling backlighting has thrown
the feathers, and the unusual beak, into strong relief. Careful focusing and choice of
stop have put the background just sufficiently out of focus to make the bird stand well
          away from it. Note that the picture is throughout in a high key

24 PHOTOGRAPHY AS AN ART

A CAMERA can give pictures worthy to rank with those made by artists in other media—but only if an artist is using it. In whatever he may do, an artist will always produce art. The instrument he uses as a means of artistic expression—whether piano, paint brush, or camera—is not of great importance; it is the man behind the instrument who matters. Even in using a piano once owned by Beethoven, Beethoven himself, or someone of equal musical stature, is needed to bring forth from it music such as it once gave.

There are two aspects of photography. First, it is a recording, documentary process, and the camera only reproduces what it sees. Second, guided by the eye of an artist, the camera can become a means of conveying beauty the artist himself has seen. In this way photography can become a very personal means of expression, and in the hands of an artist the camera can give pictures of real artistic value. But that does not mean that the beginner's first back-lit snapshot will be a picture, however greatly the subject may have delighted him. Conveying that delight to others through the medium of the print needs long practice and much skill, both pictorial and technical.

There is a wide gulf between documentary, or applied, photography and true pictorial work. The first tells one impersonally what was before the camera. The second shows one how the artist saw it. Anybody can learn the first, but success in the second needs both natural gifts and training, and is not reached without effort. One must continue to photograph a single subject, a single still-life, until one is satisfied that no better result is possible.

Nearly all photographs are mementos, snapshots or records, but certainly not works of art. When you next see a good subject, ask yourself why you want to photograph it. Search for your reasons and, when you have found them, keep them in the forefront of your mind as you work out your picture. Photograph few subjects and make the very most of each. Go to exhibitions of pictures and to picture galleries, and learn from what you see. By degrees such study will make you see both the limitations and the possibilities of the camera as a picture maker.

If you should find that, though a capable photographer, you cannot aspire to real artistry, then be glad you have found the line of work that you should make your own. Not everyone can be an artist, and it is far better to be a distinguished producer of documentary photographs than a maker of second-rate pictorial ones. Specialize in technically perfect reproductions of land-scapes, architecture, and records of any subjects in which you are interested, and your photographs will give pleasure to many besides yourself.

Photographic Societies

Every amateur should join a camera club if there is one in his neighbourhood. The beginner in particular will learn much by meeting more advanced workers, seeing their prints, and listening to discussions. Sometimes a travelling collection of pictures will be on view, and usually one of the advanced members will give a commentary on it, pointing out both bad and good points of composition and design, and perhaps of technique too. Demonstrations of various processes give practical knowledge that the beginner might take years to discover if he were working alone, and there will be a lecture or discussion at almost every meeting. Every photographer, beginner, advanced worker, or professional, will gain by joining a photographic society. A letter to the Editor of *Amateur Photographer*, at the address of the publishers of this book, will bring to any enquirer the names and addresses of the secretaries of the societies nearest his home.

CONCLUSION

If, by careful study of this book, the reader has progressed far enough to have a real mastery of the principles of photography, then my purpose has been achieved. But even the finest mastery of principles is only a beginning, a stage from which advances can be made. Photography offers many opportunities for such advances, for it is more than just a pleasant hobby that awakens ingenuity and artistic taste; it performs important work in almost every department of life, and is becoming more and more fully recognized as an independent form of art.

The way to further advance lies through constant practice and further reading, both of books and photographic periodicals.

f/8, two-times filter, 1/100 second

EXPOSURE GUIDE
FOR THE FOUR SEASONS

Average exposures are given for a number of typical subjects, allowing for a filter if one is needed. Valid for films of speed 27° Sch, with normal development

Spring

f/4, no filter, 1/100 second

f/5·6, two-times filter, 1/50 second

f/5·6, two-times filter, 1/50 second

f/11, two-times filter, 1 second.   Tripod used

f/8, two-times filter, 1/200 second

f/8, two-times filter, 1/50 second

Summer

f/8, two-times
filter, 1/100 second

f/11, two-times filter, 1/5 second

f/8, two-times filter, 1/50 second

f/8, no filter, 1/50 second

f/5·6, no filter, 1/200 second

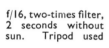

f/16, two-times filter, 2 seconds without sun. Tripod used

Autumn

f/5·6, no filter, 1/25 second

f/3·5, no filter, 1/50 second

f/5·6, no filter, 1/25 second.   No sun   f/4, no filter, 1/25 second.   No sun

Winter

f/8, two-times filter
1/25 second

f/8, no filter, 1 second.   By twilight plus   f/11, no filter, 2 minutes.   Artificial
     artificial light.   Tripod used   light alone.   Tripod used

Tables for Reference

1 SPEED NUMBERS
of plates and films

Relative Speed	B.S. (or Scheiner)	A.S.A. Weston	Weston (Old)*	D.I.N.
	degrees			degrees
1	20	8	6	10
1·26	21	10	8	11
1·58	22	12	10	12
2	23	16	12	13
2·5	24	20	16	14
3·16	25	25	20	15
4	26	32	25	16
5	27	40	32	17
6·3	28	50	40	18
8	29	64	50	19
10	30	80	64	20
12·5	31	100	80	21
16	32	125	100	22
20	33	160	125	23
25	34	200	160	24
32	35	250	200	25
40	36	320	250	26
50	37	400	320	27
64	38	500	400	28
80	39	650	500	29
100	40	800	650	30

* For use with Weston meters earlier than the Master III

DEPTH OF FOCUS TABLES

2 Table for depth reaching to infinity
$f = 5$ cm (2 in). Circle of confusion $\frac{1}{30}$ mm

For sharpness from:	Focus on:	And use stop:
60 ft to ∞	120 ft	f/2
44 ft to ∞	88 ft	f/2·8
34 ft to ∞	68 ft	f/3·5
27 ft to ∞	54 ft	f/4·5
19 ft to ∞	38 ft	f/6·3
13 ft to ∞	26 ft	f/9
10 ft to ∞	20 ft	f/12·5
7 ft to ∞	14 ft	f/18

3 Table for depth reaching to infinity

f = 7·5 cm (3 in). Circle of confusion $\frac{1}{20}$ mm

For sharpness from:	*Focus on:*	*And use stop:*
50 ft to ∞	100 ft	f/3·5
45 ft to ∞	90 ft	f/4
40 ft to ∞	80 ft	f/4·5
32 ft to ∞	64 ft	f/5·6
23 ft to ∞	45 ft	f/8
16 ft to ∞	32 ft	f/11
11 ft to ∞	22 ft	f/16
8 ft to ∞	16 ft	f/22

4 SUPPLEMENTARY LENSES

for photographing small objects close to the camera
The camera lens is throughout to be set to infinity (symbol ∞)

Dioptres	*Distance of object (equal to focal length of supplementary) (inches)*	*Approximate size of object included*	
		*6 × 6 cm reflex** *(inches square)*	*Miniature* *(inches)*
+ 1	$39\frac{1}{2}$	$29\frac{1}{2}$	$16\frac{1}{2} \times 25$
+ $1\frac{1}{4}$	$31\frac{1}{2}$	$23\frac{1}{2}$	$13\frac{1}{4} \times 20$
+ $1\frac{1}{2}$	$26\frac{1}{4}$	$19\frac{1}{2}$	$11\frac{3}{4} \times 17\frac{3}{4}$
+ $1\frac{3}{4}$	$22\frac{1}{2}$	$16\frac{3}{4}$	10×15
+ 2	$19\frac{3}{4}$	$14\frac{3}{4}$	$8\frac{1}{4} \times 12\frac{1}{2}$
+ $2\frac{1}{2}$	$15\frac{3}{4}$	$11\frac{3}{4}$	$5\frac{7}{8} \times 9$
+ 3	$13\frac{1}{8}$	$9\frac{7}{8}$	$4\frac{1}{4} \times 6\frac{1}{4}$
+ 4	$9\frac{7}{8}$	$7\frac{1}{4}$	4×6
+ 5	$7\frac{7}{8}$	$5\frac{7}{8}$	$3\frac{1}{2} \times 5\frac{1}{2}$
+ 10	4	3	2×3

* In focusing a twin-lens reflex, put the supplementary on the viewing lens and focus. Then transfer the supplementary to the taking lens, and expose. Remember to allow for parallax.

The power of a lens in dioptres is found by dividing 100 by its focal length in centimetres ($2\frac{1}{2}$ cm = 1 in nearly). Thus a 50 cm (20 in) lens has a power of 2 dioptres. The focal length, in inches, corresponding to various powers in dioptres is shown in Column 2 of the above table.

5 PROJECTING COLOUR TRANSPARENCIES

When projecting transparencies, the size of the picture on the screen depends on the focal length of the projector lens and on the distance of the projector from the screen. The table below gives in feet and inches sizes of projected pictures from 24 × 36 mm transparencies.

Distance (ft)	FOCAL LENGTH OF LENS				
	5 cm 2 in	7·5 cm 3 in	9 cm 3½ in	13·5 cm 5¼ in	20 cm 8 in
5	2 ft 4 in × 3 ft 6 in	1 ft 6 in × 2 ft 3 in	1 ft 4 in × 1 ft 11 in	0 ft 10 in × 1 ft 3 in	0 ft 6 in × 0 ft 9 in
6	2 ft 9 in × 4 ft 2 in	1 ft 10 in × 2 ft 9 in	1 ft 6 in × 2 ft 3 in	1 ft 0 in × 1 ft 6 in	0 ft 8 in × 1 ft 0 in
8	3 ft 9 in × 5 ft 8 in	2 ft 6 in × 3 ft 9 in	2 ft 1 in × 3 ft 1 in	1 ft 4 in × 2 ft 0 in	0 ft 10 in × 1 ft 3 in
10	4 ft 9 in × 7 ft 1 in	3 ft 1 in × 4 ft 8 in	2 ft 7 in × 3 ft 11 in	1 ft 8 in × 2 ft 6 in	1 ft 1 in × 1 ft 8 in
12	5 ft 8 in × 8 ft 6 in	3 ft 9 in × 5 ft 8 in	3 ft 1 in × 4 ft 8 in	2 ft 0 in × 3 ft 1 in	1 ft 4 in × 2 ft 0 in
15	7 ft 0 in × 10 ft 6 in	4 ft 8 in × 7 ft 0 in	4 ft 0 in × 6 ft 0 in	2 ft 7 in × 3 ft 11 in	1 ft 8 in × 2 ft 6 in
20	9 ft 6 in × 14 ft 3 in	6 ft 4 in × 9 ft 6 in	5 ft 3 in × 7 ft 11 in	3 ft 6 in × 5 ft 3 in	2 ft 3 in × 3 ft 5 in
30	14 ft 4 in × 21 ft 6 in	9 ft 6 in × 14 ft 3 in	7 ft 11 in × 11 ft 11 in	5 ft 3 in × 7 ft 10 in	3 ft 6 in × 5 ft 3 in
40	19 ft 3 in × 28 ft 8 in	12 ft 8 in × 19 ft 1 in	10 ft 7 in × 15 ft 11 in	7 ft 0 in × 10 ft 6 in	4 ft 8 in × 7 ft 0 in

6 DEPTH TABLE FOR 24 × 24 mm CAMERAS   f = 3.5 cm   Circle of confusion $\frac{1}{30}$ mm

Stop	∞	50	25	15	Focused on (feet) 10	7	5	3 ft 6 in
2	60 ft to ∞	27 ft to 300 ft	17 ft 9 in to 43 ft	12 ft to 20 ft	8 ft 6 in to 12 ft	6 ft 3 in to 8 ft	4 ft 8 in to 5 ft 4 in	3 ft 4 in to 3 ft 7½ in
2·8	43 ft to ∞	23 ft to ∞	15 ft 9 in to 60 ft	11 ft 2 in to 23 ft	8 ft 1 in to 13 ft	6 ft 1 in to 8 ft 4 in	4 ft 5 in to 5 ft 7 in	3 ft 3 in to 3 ft 9 in
3·5	34 ft to ∞	19 ft 6 in to ∞	14 ft 6 in to 95 ft	10 ft 5 in to 27 ft	7 ft 10 in to 14 ft	5 ft 10 in to 9 ft	4 ft 4 in to 5 ft 9 in	3 ft 3 in to 3 ft 10 in
4	30 ft to ∞	18 ft to ∞	13 ft 7 in to 150 ft	10 ft to 29 ft	7 ft 7 in to 14 ft	5 ft 9 in to 9 ft	4 ft 1 in to 6 ft 4 in	3 ft 2 in to 3 ft 11 in
5·6	21 ft 6 in to ∞	14 ft to ∞	11 ft 3 in to ∞	8 ft 9 in to 50 ft	6 ft 10 in to 18 ft	5 ft 4 in to 10 ft	3 ft 10 in to 7 ft 1 in	3 ft 1 in to 4 ft 2 in
8	15 ft to ∞	11 ft to ∞	9 ft 5 in to ∞	7 ft 6 in to ∞	6 ft 1 in to 28 ft	4 ft 10 in to 12 ft 9 in	3 ft 5 in to 7 ft 10 in	2 ft 10 in to 4 ft 5 in
11	10 ft 6 in to ∞	8 ft to ∞	7 ft 3 in to ∞	6 ft to ∞	5 ft 1 in to 49 ft	4 ft 2 in to 21 ft 6 in	3 ft 1 in to 9 ft 6 in	2 ft 8 in to 5 ft 2 in
16	7 ft 6 in to ∞	6 ft to ∞	5 ft 10 in to ∞	5 ft to ∞	4 ft 4 in to ∞	3 ft 8 in to 106 ft	2 ft 9 in to 15 ft	2 ft 5 in to 6 ft 6 in

7 UNIVERSAL DEPTH OF FOCUS TABLE

Negatives 24 × 36 mm or 3 × 4 cm f = 5 cm, 4½ × 6, 4 × 6½ or 6 × 6 cm f = 7·5 cm (3 in), 2¼ × 3¼ in f = 10·5 cm (4⅛ in).

Circle of confusion $\frac{1}{1500}$ of focal length of lens

The table on the opposite page is calculated for a circle of confusion of diameter equal to $\frac{1}{1500}$ of the focal length of the lens, thus giving equal sharpness at the limit of depth in enlargements of equal size irrespective of the size of camera used. Note, however, that the larger the negative size the smaller the stop that has to be used to obtain any pre-determined depth of focus.

Example

Suppose an interior is being photographed; the wall of the room is 18 ft away, and there is a chair in the foreground only 7 ft from the camera. The correct focusing point to get both sharp (nearer than half-way) will evidently be 10 or 12 ft;

last column but one. The focusing scale is therefore set to 10 ft, and the lens stopped down to f/11 if the camera in use is a miniature with 5 cm lens, to f/16 in the case of a 6 × 6 cm or V.P. camera with 7·5 cm lens, or to f/22 if the camera is a 2¼ × 3¼ in one with 10·5 cm lens. In the negative the chair will be sharp; the wall, only 4 in beyond the limit of depth in the table, will be only imperceptibly less so, and everything between will be sharper than either wall or table.

Lens 5 cm	1·5	2	2·8	4	5·6	8	11	16
7·5 cm	—	2·8	4	5·6	8	11	16	22
10·5 cm	3·5	4·5	5·6	8	11	16	22	32
Focused on				STOP				
∞	160 ft to ∞	125 ft to ∞	93 ft to ∞	65 ft to ∞	46 ft to ∞	32 ft to ∞	23 ft to ∞	16 ft to ∞
100 ft	62 ft to 266 ft	56 ft to 500 ft	48 ft to ∞	40 ft to ∞	32 ft to ∞	24 ft to ∞	19 ft to ∞	14 ft to ∞
50 ft	38 ft to 72 ft	36 ft to 84 ft	33 ft to 108 ft	28 ft to 216 ft	24 ft to ∞	19 ft to 480 ft	15 ft to ∞	12 ft to ∞
30 ft	25 ft to 37 ft	24 ft 3 in to 39 ft 6 in	22 ft 9 in to 44 ft 3 in	20 ft to 56 ft	18 ft to 86 ft	15 ft to 115 ft	13 ft to ∞	10 ft to ∞
25 ft	21 ft 6 in to 29 ft 6 in	20 ft 10 in to 31 ft 2 in	19 ft 9 in to 34 ft	18 ft to 40 ft	16 ft 2 in to 55 ft	14 ft to 53 ft	12 ft to 150 ft	9 ft to ∞
20 ft	17 ft 10 in to 22 ft	17 ft 3 in to 23 ft 10 in	16 ft 6 in to 25 ft 6 in	15 ft to 29 ft	14 ft to 35 ft	12 ft 4 in to 53 ft	10 ft 9 in to 43 ft	8 ft to ∞
15 ft	13 ft 8 in to 16 ft	13 ft to 17 ft	12 ft 11 in to 17 ft 10 in	12 ft to 19 ft	11 ft to 22 ft	10 ft 3 in to 28 ft	9 ft to 25 ft	7 ft 9 in to 240 ft
12 ft	11 ft 2 in to 13 ft	11 ft to 13 ft	10 ft 8 in to 14 ft	10 ft to 14 ft	9 ft to 16 ft	8 ft 9 in to 19 ft 8 in	7 ft to 17 ft	6 ft to 48 ft
10 ft	9 ft to 10 ft	9 ft 3 in to 10 ft 10 in	8 ft 9 in to 11 ft	8 ft to 14 ft	8 ft to 12 ft	7 ft 8 in to 14 ft 6 in	6 ft to 12 ft	6 ft to 26 ft
8 ft	7 ft 8 in to 8 ft 5 in	7 ft 6 in to 8 ft 6 in	7 ft 5 in to 8 ft 6 in	7 ft 2 in to 9 ft	6 ft 10 in to 10 in	6 ft 5 in to 10 ft 8 in	5 ft 11 in to 12 ft	5 ft to 16 ft
7 ft	6 ft 8 in to 7 ft 5 in	6 ft 8 in to 7 ft 5 in	6 ft 6 in to 7 ft 7 in	6 ft 4 in to 7 ft 10 in	6 ft to 9 ft	5 ft 8 in to 9 ft 9 in	5 ft 5 in to 10 ft	4 ft 11 in to 12 ft
6 ft	5 ft 9½ in to 6 ft 3 in	5 ft 9 in to 6 ft 3½ in	5 ft 8 in to 6 ft 5 in	5 ft 5 in to 6 ft 7 in	5 ft 4 in to 7 ft	5 ft 1 in to 8 ft	4 ft 9 in to 8 ft	4 ft 4 in to 9 ft
5 ft	4 ft 10½ in to 5 ft 2 in	4 ft 10 in to 5 ft 2½ in	4 ft 9½ in to 5 ft 3½ in	4 ft 8 in to 5 ft 5 in	4 ft 6 in to 5 ft 7 in	4 ft 4½ in to 6 ft ½ in	4 ft 3 in to 6 ft	3 ft 10 in to 7 ft
4 ft	3 ft 11 in to 4 ft 1 in	3 ft 10½ in to 4 ft 1½ in	3 ft 10 in to 4 ft 2 in	3 ft 9½ in to 4 ft 3 in	3 ft 8 in to 4 ft 3 in	3 ft 7 in to 4 ft 6 in	3 ft 5 in to 4 ft 8 in	3 ft to 5 in
3 ft 6 in	3 ft 5 in to 3 ft 7 in	3 ft 5 in to 3 ft 7 in	3 ft 4½ in to 3 ft 7½ in	3 ft 4 in to 3 ft 8 in	3 ft 3 in to 3 ft 9 in	3 ft to 3 ft 11 in	3 ft to 4 ft 1½ in	2 ft to 5 in

263

8 SOLUBILITY OF CHEMICALS

100 parts of water at about 65° F will dissolve the quantity of chemical shown in the table

Chemical						Parts
Ammonium persulphate	..	..	..	..	..	58
Boric acid ..	..	..	..	..	..	3
Borax ..	..	..	..	..	..	3·5
Chrome alum	..	..	..	..	..	12·5
Potassium bichromate	..	..	..	..	..	10
,, bromide ..	..	..	..	..	..	66
,, ferricyanide	..	..	..	..	..	45
,, hydroxide	..	..	..	..	..	111
,, carbonate	..	..	..	..	..	105
,, metabisulphite	..	..	..	..	..	30
,, permanganate	..	..	..	..	..	6·3
Sodium hydroxide ..	..	..	..	..	..	108
,, carbonate (cryst.) ..	..	..	..	..	60
,, carbonate (anhydr.)	..	..	..	..	20
,, sulphite (cryst.)	..	..	..	..	50
,, sulphite (anhydr.) ..	..	..	..	..	25
,, thiosulphate (cryst.) (Hypo.)	..	..	..	45

Index

Developers—*Cont.*
  Ilford ID. 11, 145–146
    ID. 36, 145
    Pan F, 146
  Kodak D76, 145
    Panatomic X, 146
  Leitz two-bath, 132, 146–147
  M.Q. ordinary, 132
    borax, 132, 146–147
  Microdol (Kodak), 145
  Microphen, 145
  mixing, 133
  Promicrol, 145
  superspeed, 149–150
Development
  darkroom arrangements, 127
  dishes, 131
  enlargement (bromide paper), 172
  equipment for, 131
  fine grain, 113
  plates, 133–138
  tank development (films), 138–144
  times, 148–149
  ultra-fine-grain, 147
D.I.N. speed ratings, 259
Drying
  films, 142
  plates, 138
  prints, 167
  racks, 137–138

Electronic flash, 236–237, 243
  power-pack, 236
Emulsions, 5
  grain in, 113
Enlargers, 170–171
Enlarging, 169–176
  accessories, 171
  Callier effect, 171
  developers for, 172
  diffusing light, 171
  illumination, 170
  lens, 170
  papers for, 172
  pilot print, 175
Exposure
  correct choice of, 120–124
  factors controlling, 120
  guide to, 255–258
  latitude in, 98, 120
  record of, 124
  time of day and year, 121
  type of subject, 121
  weather, 121
Exposure meters, 122–124
  calibration of, 124
  choice of, 123
  indoors, 230

F numbers, 75
Farmer's reducer, 153

Film
  for copying, 183
  cut, 90
  double coated, 103
  gradation, 92, 104
  keeping qualities, 119
  for landscapes, 203
  orthochromatic, 105
  panchromatic, 105
  roll, 89
  sensitivity to colour, 104
  speed ratings—
    A.S.A., 92, 259
    D.I.N., 259
    H and D, 92
    Scheiner, 92, 259
    Weston, 92, 259
Filters, 106–111
  blue, 106, 243
  copying, 184
  factor, 108
  graduated, 110
  infra-red, 111
  for landscape, 203
  mounts, 109
  polarizing, 110
  quality of, 109
  red and orange, 109
  ultra-violet, 110
  yellow, 106–109
  yellow-green, 109
Fine grain, 111–114, 132
  developers, 132
Fixing
  formulae, 137
  lantern slides, 179
  plates and films, 136
  prints, 167
Flash, use of, 236–243
Flashbulbs, 237, 240
  P.F.1, 237
  P.F.5, 237
  P.F.24, 240
  P.F.25, 240
Focal length, 63–64
Focal plane shutters, 51–53
Focus, depth of, 78
Focusing, 5, 72–75
  circle of confusion, 72–75
  close-ups, 79
  general subjects, 79

Gamma, 97–98
General outline
  the camera, 3–10
  subject, 11–26
  technique, 27–44
Genre, 204
Glazing prints, 167
Gossen exposure meter, 197
Gradation, negative materials, 92–104

266

Baldamatic 35 mm. I

with

COUPLED RANGEFINDER
and
Shutter and Exposure Meter AUTOMATICALLY COUPLED TOGETHER

★ XENAR f 2·8/45 mm. Four Element Lens
★ 10–speed SYNCHRO COMPUR shutter speeded up to 1/500th sec. with unique automatic depth of focus indicators

and *THE SENSATIONAL*

LUMINOUS MOVING RANGE/VIEWFINDER

with AUTOMATIC PARALLAX CORRECTION

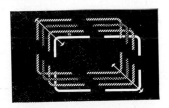

As you focus the frame moves, constantly keeping the subject exactly centred.

i

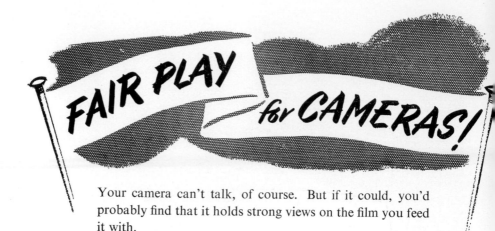

FAIR PLAY for CAMERAS!

Your camera can't talk, of course. But if it could, you'd probably find that it holds strong views on the film you feed it with.

'It's not only the man behind the camera that counts,' it might say. 'The film inside can make a world of difference. Upon my lens, I feel twice the camera when I'm working with 'Kodak' film!'

It's only fair to your camera (and to yourself) to use the finest film you can get—'Kodak' film. And though your camera may not talk, the results speak for themselves!

For your every need —
black-and-white and colour

'Verichrome' Pan Film
fast, with high acutance — ideal general-purpose film.

'Plus-X' Film
the miniaturist's favourite.

'Panatomic-X' Film
for the perfectionist. Micro-fine grain, needle-sharp definition.

'Tri-X' Film
the lightning-fast 'quality' film.

'Royal-X' Pan Film
World's fastest film—by far!

'Kodachrome' Film
for brilliant colour transparencies.

'Ektachrome' Film
the fast colour film for home processing.

'Kodacolor' Film
for wonderful colour prints.

They come out best on

Kodak FILM

Kodak Limited, London

'Kodak' is a registered trade-mar

iv

'he RIGHT film is just as important as

e RIGHT subject
e RIGHT lens
e RIGHT focus
e RIGHT aperture
e RIGHT shutter speed
e RIGHT developer

Choose ILFORD to be sure!

ILFORD films

SELOCHROME PAN (roll film only) for general outdoor photography in normal daylight.

FP3 (roll and 35mm) for perfect rendering of delicate tone and texture at high degrees of enlargement.

HP3 (roll and 35mm) for action shots and for exposures in all lighting conditions where high film speed is essential.

COLOUR FILM 'D' (35mm only) for making colour transparencies by daylight or with electronic flash.

COLOUR FILM 'F' (35mm only) for use with clear flashbulbs or (with filter) for photoflood exposures.

FORD LIMITED . ILFORD . ESSEX

eighteenth edition

Dictionary of Photography

edited by A. L. M. SOWERBY, BA, M SC., FRPS

A comprehensive reference book, alphabetically arranged, covering every aspect of photography. It contains the essence of a dozen ordinary textbooks and provides the answer to every photographic problem. The articles are in no sense advanced or difficult to read, but in nearly every case they do go a little more deeply into their subject than does the average textbook. This edition has been meticulously revised throughout, with particular attention to the sections on flash and colour photography. It provides readily accessible information for the beginner and includes a mass of material that will be of great help and value to the advanced worker.

21s net by post 22s 5d

obtainable from leading booksellers and photographic dealers
published for AMATEUR PHOTOGRAPHER by
ILIFFE & SONS LIMITED
Dorset House, Stamford Street, SE1